Crises of Memory and the Second World War

CRISES OF MEMORY AND THE SECOND WORLD WAR

Susan Rubin Suleiman

HARVARD UNIVERSITY PRESS

Cambridge, Massachusetts
London, England   2006

Library of Congress Cataloging-in-Publication Data
Suleiman, Susan Rubin, 1939–
    Crises of memory and the Second World War / Suleiman, Susan Rubin
Suleiman.
       p. cm.
    Includes bibliographical references and index.
    ISBN 0–674–02206–8 (alk. paper)
      1. World War, 1939–1945—Historiography. 2. Memory—Social
aspects. 3. Memory—Psychological aspects. 4. Narration (Rhetoric) I. Title.

    D743.42.S85 2006
    940.5301'9—dc22   2005049540

For Michael and Daniel
once again, always

Contents

Acknowledgments

As always, this book could not have been written without the help of others. I am grateful to the Center for Advanced Judaic Studies at the University of Pennsylvania and to the Florence Gould Foundation for the fellowship and the research grant they accorded me in the spring and summer of 2001. The Leverhulme Trust of Great Britain made possible the research professorships I held at the Institute of Romance Studies of the University of London in the summers of 2002 and 2003. Colleagues at numerous conferences and public lectures in the United States, England, France, Germany, and Holland offered precious suggestions when I presented portions of the work-in-progress. A Radcliffe Institute Fellowship for 2005–06 has allowed me to put the finishing touches on the manuscript.

Individual chapters have benefited from close reading and criticism by friends and colleagues, as well as from extensive discussions during the writing. Chapter 1 received expert commentary from Dorothy Kaufmann; Chapter 2, from Claire Andrieu, Nicole Racine, Henry Rousso, Anne Simonin, and Margaret Collins Weitz; Chapter 5, from Éva Forgács, Eric Rentschler, and Brooks Robards; Chapter 7, from Alan Rosen and Meir Sternhell. The help of Julie Buck, Steffen Pierce, David Rodowick, and the Harvard Film Archive was essential in preparing the film stills for Chapters 4 and 5.

My ongoing conversations with a number of scholars and writers working in the fields of Holocaust studies and studies of individual and collective memory have been crucial to my thinking. Sidra Ezrahi, Richard J. Golsan, Marianne Hirsch, Andreas Huyssen, Irene Kacandes, Philippe Mesnard, Henri Raczymow, Régine Robin, Gisèle Sapiro, Michael Sheringham, Diana Sorensen, Leo Spitzer, Annette Wieviorka, Froma Zeitlin—I am grateful for their intellectual generosity as well as their friendship. For the kind of support that only dear friends can offer, I thank Wini Breines, Marcia Folsom, Christie McDonald, and Ruth Perry.

My research assistant of the past two years, Sara Kippur, has done indispensable work in the preparation of the manuscript and the bibliography, for which I am especially grateful. Tali Zechory helped to track down sources for the copyedited manuscript; in earlier stages, I appreciated the research assistance of Lia Brozgal and Yumi Kim.

Finally, but not least in importance, I wish to express my thanks to my family, whose love has been—and will continue to be—a beacon.

Earlier, often quite different versions of some chapters appeared in previous publications: Chapter 1, in *La Naissance du 'phénomène Sartre'*, ed. Ingrid Galster (Paris: Seuil, 2001); Chapter 2, in *South Central Review* 21:1 (2004); Chapter 3, in *Revue André Malraux Review* 30:1/2 (2001); Chapter 4, in *Critical Inquiry* 28:2 (2002); Chapter 5, in *Yale Journal of Criticism* 14:1 (2001); Chapter 6, in *Journal of Romance Studies* 4:2 (2004); Chapter 7, in *Poetics Today* 21:2 (2000).

Introduction

CRISES OF MEMORY

$\mathcal{U}$NDER "CRISIS," *Roget's Thesaurus* lists the following nouns, among others: key moment, turning point, pressure, predicament. "Crisis" and "criticism" have the same Greek root: *krinein*, to discriminate, to separate, to choose. A crisis of memory, as I use that term, is a moment of choice, and sometimes of predicament or conflict, about remembrance of the past, whether by individuals or by groups. At issue in a crisis of memory is the question of self-representation: How we view ourselves, and how we represent ourselves to others, is indissociable from the stories we tell about our past. In the crises of memory I examine in this book, individual self-representation overlaps with—and sometimes becomes the crux of —collective self-representation; put another way, individual remembrance takes on collective significance, occasionally becoming a conflicted "affair of memory." An affair of memory differs from other public "affairs" or scandals in that what is at stake is not the outcome of an event that is still unfolding—as, for example, in the Dreyfus Affair, where the conflict involved the fate of Captain Dreyfus and, according to some, of the French Republic itself. Rather, the object of conflict in an affair of memory is the interpretation and public understanding of an event firmly situated in the past, but whose aftereffects are still deeply felt. In Chapter 2 I explore one such affair in detail, relating to French national memory of the Resistance. Not

1

all crises of memory become full-blown public "affairs," but they all involve an intersection between personal memory and collective memory, between what matters to an individual and what matters to a larger group.

This book examines crises of memory related to World War II, chiefly in France and Central Europe, but my contention is that the memory of World War II, while nationally specific, transcends national boundaries. This is due not only to the global nature of the war but also to the increasingly global presence of the Holocaust as a site of memory. "Whoever says memory, says Shoah"—Jay Winter, one of the foremost historians engaged in the study of public memory, attributes this statement to Pierre Nora, whose massive group project on sites of memory in France, *Les lieux de mémoire* (published between 1984 and 1992) is often credited with initiating the "memory boom" in contemporary historiography and cultural studies.[1] Nora's reported statement may have been a rhetorical exaggeration, but other commentators too have noted the degree to which the Holocaust has become a template for collective memory in areas of the world that had nothing to do with those events but that have known other collective traumas. Andreas Huyssen calls the Holocaust "a powerful prism through which we may look at other instances of genocide."[2] Daniel Levy and Natan Sznaider see it as "a central political-cultural symbol facilitating the emergence of cosmopolitan memories." Alongside the "nationally bounded memories" we associate with collective memory, Levy and Sznaider posit the emergence of a new, global, cosmopolitan memory in which "issues of global concern are able to become part and parcel of everyday local experiences and moral life worlds of an increasing number of people."[3] The question of "who should remember the Holocaust," or, even more pointedly, "who owns the Holocaust?" is a vexed one, and I treat it in some detail in Chapter 4 of this book. Insofar as the Holocaust revealed (in Zygmunt Bauman's words) "the hidden possibilities of modern society," its memory clearly transcends national or religious frontiers.[4] At the same time, any study of Holocaust memory must take account of local or even individual specificities if it is to avoid the banality of pious generalizations.

Should memory of the Holocaust be considered as part of the memory of World War II? Or is it perhaps the other way around: Is memory of World War II part of the memory of the Holocaust? Geographically and strategically, World War II was "larger" than the Holocaust, but if it is true that memory of the Holocaust has become global, the same cannot be said of the war. Every country involved in it has its own crises of memory, not necessarily applicable to others. For France, the issue after the war was how to remember and recount the years of German occupation, when the country was technically an ally of the occupant and was the only country in Western Europe to have formally collaborated with the Germans after being invaded. For postwar Germany, the issues were even more critical. In their collective volume on *War and Remembrance in the Twentieth Century*, Jay Winter and Emmanuel Sivan exclude discussion of "Germany and the Holocaust" from consideration, on the grounds that so enormous a subject deserves a whole separate volume. Furthermore, they reason, to include that subject among a set of essays on a whole range of twentieth-century wars would run the risk of "historicizing" the Holocaust by making it just "one more chapter in the history of warfare."[5] While this position is justifiable, it carries, as the editors recognize, its own risks. And certainly it would be difficult to exclude Germany and the Holocaust from a collective volume devoted to World War II. Although the Holocaust was unique in all the ways we know— notably, in its industrialization of mass murder—it was part of the war and would not have been possible without it. If World War II was arguably the central event of the twentieth century, whose aftereffects and afterimages are still firmly lodged in public consciousness, it is in large part because the Holocaust was part of it. If history is what took place in the past, and the writing of history is the attempt to record and interpret "what once was," in Paul Ricoeur's succinct formulation, then memory is what remains of history in the present, for an individual or a group.[6] Neither September 11, 2001, nor the arrival of a new millennium has effaced the collective archive of memories associated with that war. The massive exhibit organized in 2005 by the German Historical Museum in Berlin, devoted to international perspectives on memories of World War II, offers ample confirmation of this fact.[7]

Somewhat provocatively, Susan Sontag affirmed in her last book, "Strictly speaking, there is no such thing as collective memory." She then explained, "All memory is individual, unreproducible—it dies with each person. What is called collective memory is not a remembering but a stipulating: that *this* is important, and this is the story about how it happened, with the pictures that lock the story in our minds."[8] Indeed, no one else can have and *feel* exactly the same memories as I do. Still, memories are communicable; they can be recorded and transmitted, as any member of a family knows. Maurice Halbwachs, the pioneering theorist of collective memory, located the first level of transmission in the family, where children inherit the remembrances of others even about their own past.[9] As Gertrude Stein whimsically put it, "To begin with I was born. That I do not remember but I was told about it quite often."[10]

If enough people consider a given set of individual memories significant, then those memories contribute to the formation of collective memory precisely as the stipulation of what is important to a group at a given time. World War II remains part of our collective memory because it has been stipulated as important—and vice versa, one could say. But the circle here is not a vicious one—rather, it is like the hermeneutic circle, which constructs the interpretation of a text progressively, modifying it as one's reading unfolds. The point is that there is an interplay between certain individual memories and group memory, so that the expression of one is in a symbiotic relation with the other. The set of individual, personal memories that relate to World War II is extremely varied, both locally and globally; before long, it will disappear with those who were alive during the war. But recorded personal memories, whether in the form of written documents, filmed interviews, audio archives, or literary and artistic figurations, will remain, alongside historical investigations and official commemorations, what Winter and Sivan call "public acts of remembrance."[11] Collective memory is shaped by all these ways of recollecting the past, and as long as a past event continues to be stipulated as important for the present, collective memory of it will persist and evolve the way all memory evolves. Psychologists as well as historians have shown that the memory of past events is not fixed but changing, influenced by the individual's or the collective's present situation and projections for the future. Similarly, history itself is, in István Rév's suggestive formulation, a "perpetually remade past."[12]

World War II and the Holocaust are clearly still with us. In this book, I study specific instances where individual memories of the war, presented in the form of literary memoirs, complex autobiographical fictions, historical epic film, or personal documentary, intersect with collective or public memory. Individual memories may become an object of public debate or conflict; they may help to establish a consensus or an "official memory" about the collective past; they may figure as representative of the experience of a particular group; and, finally, they may crystallize the difficulties of remembrance itself, self-reflexively. Focusing in detail on specific cases, I aim at the same time to formulate theoretical concepts that are applicable generally. Crises of memory are moments that highlight the relations between individual memory and group memory, concerning a past event that is stipulated as important by the group at a given time. Such stipulations are not eternal, nor universal, but, after all, one writes for the present. What the next century will consider important is not my concern.

One can, however, ask whether memory itself is still of interest, be that interest historical or theoretical. As we know, the study of memory—with its attendant concepts of trauma, testimony, monuments, specters, nostalgia, forgetting, forgiveness, and repression, among others—has proliferated across the disciplines in the past two decades, only to come under increasing criticism almost as soon as it got started. Has the "memory boom" run its course? Writing in the 1950s in Germany, Theodor Adorno could advocate, like George Santayana before him, the necessity of not forgetting the past in order not to repeat it.[13] Forty years later, the warnings were not against an excess of forgetting but rather against a "surfeit of memory." Charles Maier, whose essay by that title has often been quoted, argued in 1992 that the current obsession with memory, especially with the memory of World War II and the Holocaust, in Germany and elsewhere, "is a sign not of historical confidence but of a retreat from transformative politics." For Maier, the fascination with memory, which today often takes the form of group memories vying with each other for recognition of the groups' suffering, "reflects a new focus on narrow ethnicity" and acts as an obstacle to democracy. No wonder that Maier concludes his essay with the flippant but serious wish: "I hope that the future of memory is not too bright."[14] For Adorno, by contrast, democracy required a self-critical working through of the past.

As a historian, Maier is, of course, not in favor of forgetting. But he pits history against memory: the historian, even the postmodern historian who has rejected "naive positivism," seeks causal explanations for events. The "retriever of memory" has no such imperative. The historian seeks understanding, whereas the rememberer seeks emotion—specifically, according to Maier, the emotion of melancholy. Practical democrat that he is, Maier distrusts such emotion as a "collective self-indulgence," (137), seeing in it an "addiction to memory" that is potentially "neurasthenic and disabling" (141).

Although Maier's critique is open to debate in its details and its choice of metaphors (Is melancholy the only emotion associated with memory? Is addiction the right analogy?), its general argument seems to be a shared one; the past decade has brought extended critiques of the focus on memory, especially on collective memories of World War II and the Holocaust, by other historians as well. In another often-cited article, the Israeli historians Noa Gedi and Yigal Elam argue that " 'collective memory' has become the predominant notion which replaces real (factual) history, on the one hand, and real (personal) memory, on the other hand." They conclude that "collective memory is a myth."[15] In the United States, Peter Novick's 1999 book, *The Holocaust in American Life*, develops the charge that the emphasis on both public and private memory of that event has acted as a block against perceiving—and attempting to act on—more current problems, whether concerning human rights or other urgent issues.[16] In France, Henry Rousso, who gained international acclaim for his 1987 book *The Vichy Syndrome*, tracing the history of the memory of the Occupation years in postwar France, has deplored in his more recent works the "obsession with memory" and the "judaeo-centrism" of current memories of Vichy.[17] This judaeo-centrism, according to him, not only splinters national memory into rival group memories; it is also an anachronistic distortion of history, for the "Jewish question" was not central to Vichy as Vichy saw itself.[18] Rousso has insisted on the rights and responsibilities of the historian as opposed to the historical agent or witness, in terms that recall Maier's insistence on the necessary primacy of history over memory, of understanding over emotion. A similar reservation about emotion is found in Kerwin Lee Klein's richly nuanced critique of the "memory industry" in historical studies.[19] Klein worries, in particular, about the "vague theological concepts as well as vague connotations of spirituality and authenticity" that often creep into both academic and popular discourses about memory, despite the avowedly postmodern (and therefore presumably anti-essentialist and antitheological) cast of much contemporary theorizing about the subject.[20] Régine Robin, who is both a historian and a writer and theorist of autobiographical fiction, has similarly called for a "critical memory" to counteract what she sees as the unfortunate "saturation" of memory in contemporary culture.[21]

Personally, I find these critiques of the emphasis on memory, together with the foregrounding of the need for continued historical research, on the whole salutary. They are a corrective to the "sacralization" of memory, the "duty to remember" that can all too quickly degenerate into kitsch, the very opposite of critical self-reflection. Claude Lanzmann, explicating his masterpiece *Shoah* (1985), has insisted on the "obscenity" of any attempt to "understand" the Holocaust, that is, to find causal, historical explanations for it. Lanzmann seeks, instead, to relive the most unfathomable aspects of the Holocaust—the organization and industrialization of mass murder on an unprecedented scale—by an active process of witnessing, a joint enterprise of survivors and those who receive, in reverence and awe, the survivors' testimony.[22] Lanzmann's idea about the "obscenity of understanding" appeared attractive to many people (at least, among literary scholars) when it was first formulated, and Lanzmann's film is a brilliant enactment of it. But the idea, and even the film insofar as it is its enactment, have come under criticism in recent years: The refusal to understand, as Dominick LaCapra has argued in an extended critique, has its limits, both ethical and aesthetic.[23] (Lanzmann, in turn, has protested that those who criticize him on this score are deforming his ideas).[24]

Finally, the emphasis on memory has been justly criticized because it can lead not only to dogmatism and kitsch but to political instrumentalization of every kind, including some very bad kinds. As has often been pointed out about the bloody ethnic wars in the former Yugoslavia, collective memory of ethnic humiliation or of religious conflict can be put to cynical political uses. In a different register, the bitter debates throughout the 1990s over the Holocaust memorial in Berlin can be considered as examples of the political instrumentalization of memory, in addition to being (in some instances) critiques of it.[25]

As salutary as the recent critiques of memory may be, however, there is also a sense in which they miss the point. For the "obsession with memory," by the very fact that it is an obsession, is not something that can be made to go away. Whether in the purely private realm, as manifested by the increasing practice of writing diaries and memoirs, most of which will never reach publication, or in the public realm, as manifested by the unabated interest in (and production of) memorials, anniversaries, documentaries, public commemorations, truth commissions, artistic representations, and literary memoirs—including especially the historical memoir that recounts an individual's experiences in a time of collective crisis or trauma—memory and memorialization continue to be central preoccupations not only in Europe and the United States but in Latin America, Asia, and Africa. What the historian Annette Wieviorka has called the "era of the witness," the era we are living in, is also, more generally, the era of memory.[26]

The question we might salutarily ask, therefore, is not (or not only), "Why the obsession with memory?" or, "When will it fade?" but rather, "*How* is memory enacted or put to public use?": a poetics of memory, rather than a history or a politics. And, I would add, an ethics too—not only "how," but to what good end? The question then becomes: How is memory *best* enacted or put to public use? But since all poetics and ethics are situated (in the Sartrean sense, located and given meaning in a specific time and place), history and politics come back another way: How is memory best served at a given moment, in a specific place? And who does the judging, to what end?

Memory is a form of self-representation, and under the best circumstances, as Adorno clearly saw, it is also a form of critical self-reflection. This idea, which seems to me crucial for any discussion of memory, whether public or private, is especially so for discussion of the ethics of memory, which is often indissociable from politics. The most intense political conflicts involve areas of contested memory, where opposing groups confront each other with narratives that seem to allow for no negotiation and no commonality. At a conference at Harvard in February 2004 on the subject of "cultural citizenship," one of the recurring themes was that of conflicting narratives opposing Israelis and Palestinians. The Israeli philosopher Avishai Margalit and the Palestinian philosopher Sari Nusseibeh spoke persuasively about the need to arrive at a political settlement before trying to negotiate mutual recognition for both groups' narratives of suffering. But the literary scholar Homi Bhabha argued equally persuasively for the importance of narratives, independent of (or concurrent with) political negotiations. If political settlements cannot exist without mutual recognition by the parties involved, then the recognition of each others' memories—which involves the acknowledgment that one's own memories are not the only ones that matter—must somehow be part of that process.[27]

Let me not stray too far, however, from the subject of this book. Being neither a historian nor a philosopher, although I have more than a passing interest in both fields, my approach to questions of memory is primarily textual; and my deepest interest goes toward texts that are self-consciously literary—in other words, that manifest a difficult engagement with language and meaning.

In this sense, texts are not limited to written works; film too can be "literary," and I discuss two such films in Chapters 4 and 5. If I am right about the broader implications of a poetics of memory, then a textual approach that pays close attention to individual works should prove illuminating about more than individual works. Understanding the intricacies of a single text can open up large perspectives, especially if that understanding is informed by historical, philosophical, and psychoanalytic concerns.

Some books resemble a train journey, moving steadily on the rails of an argument from A to Z. Others are more like a hitchhiking trip across a country or a continent: there is an end point, but the journey itself is unpredictable, open to chance, with unexpected side trips and discoveries along the way. This book fits into neither of those categories. If I had to find an ambulatory metaphor for it, I would describe it as a series of extended walks in the mountains. Some years ago, I spent a few days in the Swiss Alps with my sister. Every morning, we would set out on a different excursion, some quite arduous; it was late June, the weather was superb, and the fields were covered with wildflowers. No matter where we walked, we had the same mountains around us in the distance, reappearing in different perspectives. In the late afternoon, when we returned, tired, to our hotel, we would look up and see the Matterhorn, with its unmistakable spire. The mountain became increasingly familiar, yet inexhaustible.

So it is with the subject of memory. This book makes excursions into an inexhaustible landscape dominated by memory, with its surrounding peaks: history, testimony, imagination.

History, because despite the irreversibility of time, the past as "what once was" must not be lost sight of; testimony, because however fallible human memory is, the authority of the witness who recounts, in good faith, what he or she has personally experienced must not be denied; and imagination, because the human faculty to create and invent, to give form and shape to memory and experience, endows the vicissitudes of individual lives with collective meaning. It allows them to endure.

The first three chapters focus most specifically on the relations between history and memory, examining French memories of the Occupation and of the Resistance, from the period immediately after the liberation of France to our own day. As we know, every country in Europe had to contend, after the war, with its own "myths and memories" (as Tony Judt has put it) about World War II.[28] Given France's particular situation between 1940 and 1944, with its official collaborationist government in Vichy and its "resisting" government in London as well as its internal Resistance movements, its crises of memory highlight in an especially acute way general problems about the evolution of public memory and about the relation of individual testimonies to historical investigation.

Chapters 4 and 5 move to collective memories of the Holocaust in Europe and the United States, with a nod to Latin America, where many Nazi war criminals like Klaus Barbie found refuge. They also introduce the question of imagination, by examining the self-conscious artistry of two major European filmmakers, Marcel Ophuls and István Szabó. Chapters 6 and 7 deal specifically with the role of artistic imagination in literary testimony. While I make a strong case for the freedom of aesthetic shaping in memoir, I draw a firm line between artistry and fraud or delusion. Jorge Semprun, a survivor of Buchenwald, is a self-conscious memoirist, who deliberately eschews "straight" referential testimony and claims the rights of artifice in order to arrive at deeper truths about the camp experience. Elie Wiesel, rereading his own work after many years, revises a detail in his celebrated memoir *Night*, and learns something in the process about the role of imagination and fantasy in testimony. Benjamin Wilkomirski, however, is either a charlatan or a deluded soul, imagining himself to be a child survivor of the Holocaust.

In Chapter 8, I discuss the imaginative work of two genuine child survivors, Georges Perec and Raymond Federman, who write from "the edge of memory" and who make the absence of memory into a crucial element of their work. Finally, Chapter 9 turns to the ultimate edge of memory, forgetting. Historical as well as individual forgetting is inevitable, but under what circumstances is it delayed, and what is the role of forgiving (or not forgiving) in that process?

Even the Matterhorn fades from the mind, after many years. The photographs we took there, traces of the event, survive.

✌ 1

"Choosing Our Past"

JEAN-PAUL SARTRE AS MEMOIRIST OF OCCUPIED FRANCE

> History, and in particular national history, has always been written
> from the perspective of the future.
> —*Pierre Nora*, "Comment écrire l'histoire de France?"

> Thus we choose our past in light of a certain end, but after that it
> imposes itself and devours us.
> —*Sartre*, Being and Nothingness

$\mathcal{T}$HE MUCH-PUBLICIZED trial in 1997 of Maurice Papon, a high French functionary accused of crimes against humanity for his role in the deportation of Jews from Bordeaux in 1942 and 1943, demonstrated that France had not yet finished with its histories of World War II more than fifty years after the event. Papon's trial, like the others in the series of French trials beginning with that of Klaus Barbie in 1987, confirmed once again that the notion of *a* national history is problematic, or downright untenable. Even if certain facts are proven and accepted by all, their meaning varies according to the particular groups and moments that recall them. This understanding lies at the basis of the ambitious historical project directed by Pierre Nora, *Les lieux de mémoire*, and incidentally explains its huge success. If, as Nora affirms, the existence of " 'one France' has become purely problematic," then the only way to write the history of France is "to the second degree," focusing less on events themselves than on the multiple ways in which they have been interpreted and passed on in public memory.[1] Similar volumes by historians specializing in the history of memory are under way in Germany and other European countries.

13

Intellectuals, with their acknowledged role as interpreters of public events, contribute significantly to the shaping of collective memories. Jean-Paul Sartre, arguably the foremost French intellectual of the twentieth century, played an important role in interpreting France's experience during World War II for the immediate postwar public, both in France and abroad. As historians have often pointed out, the problem that faced France after the Liberation was unique among European nations: how to account for four years of collaboration with the German occupant and at the same time claim a rightful place at the negotiating table as one of the conquerors of Germany. Furthermore, how could France reclaim a Republican heritage after four years of authoritarian rule under Vichy?

The Gaullist solution to this problem, which worked extremely well for many years, has been brilliantly analyzed by Henry Rousso in his book *The Vichy Syndrome*. General de Gaulle offered the French a "unitary and unifying mirror" of their immediate past, papering over internal differences and implying that all but a very small handful of "traitors" (who would be duly tried and punished) had unanimously resisted the enemy. De Gaulle's rhetoric was extremely powerful, as shown by his very first speech in liberated Paris on August 25, 1944. Accompanying his words with grand gestures, de Gaulle proclaimed to the assembled crowd in front of the Hôtel de Ville, Paris's immense city hall: "Paris liberated! Liberated by itself, liberated by its people, . . . with the support and help of all of France, of fighting France, the only France, the true France, eternal France!"[2] Rousso remarks that with these few sentences "General de Gaulle laid the groundwork for the founding myth of the post-Vichy period." From then on, he "sought tirelessly to write and rewrite the history of the war years," always with the aim of showing a France united in its opposition to the occupant. This came to be known as the "resistancialist myth."[3]

Of course, de Gaulle was not alone in needing to "write and rewrite" the history of the war years. All those who had lived through the defeat of 1940 and the years of occupation that followed felt the need for a narrative that would explain their immediate past and in a sense justify it, both to themselves and to others. Who better to give them such a narrative than a talented writer—one, furthermore, who was young enough to represent the new postwar generation but old enough and accomplished enough to speak with authority?

Sartre's three essays about the Occupation, "La République du silence" ["The republic of silence"], "Paris sous l'occupation" ["Paris under the Occupation"] and "Qu'est-ce qu'un collaborateur?" ["What Is a Collaborator?"], were written and published between the Liberation of Paris and the end of the war (August 1944–August 1945), when the "founding myth" of post-Vichy France was being elaborated. Interestingly, this was also the period that saw the emergence of Sartre himself as the major intellectual presence not only in postwar France, but the world. I will suggest that Sartre's role as memoirist of occupied France and his role as intellectual leader of a generation were in fact linked and that this link can be demonstrated by tracing the arguments as well as the publishing history of his three essays. These essays— which, although well known, have received surprisingly little critical attention until now—were crucial both in the construction of their author's career and in the construction of a certain "image of France" that was propagated, in France and abroad, after the war.

Celebrating Liberation: "Un promeneur dans Paris insurgé"

Before his essays on the Occupation, Sartre helped to celebrate the liberation of Paris. Under the paradoxical title of "A Stroller in Insurrectionary Paris," he published seven euphoric articles from August 28 to September 4, 1944 in the newly liberated daily *Combat*, which, along with a number of others, had been a clandestine paper during the Occupation. The Liberation of Paris, involving street battles between members of the Resistance and the remaining Germans, with the enthusiastic support of much of the local population, had occurred over a period of six days from August 19 to August 25, when the French Second Armored Division led by General Leclerc entered Paris and received the German capitulation.[4] Sartre's articles (which were actually written by Simone de Beauvoir, according to her biographer, although Sartre signed them) recount a moment of heroic history in the making, which may explain the tone of lyrical exaltation, quite uncharacteristic of both Sartre and Beauvoir, that dominates these texts.[5] The second article, "Naissance d'une insurrection" ["Birth of an insurrection"], for example, describes a crowd that reassembles after having been dispersed by German soldiers: "They are not yet combatants, since they have neither arms nor orders, but they are not altogether civilians either. They have chosen their side. They remain at their windows, in the street, a little pale, hard, watchful. The war is there, beneath the sun."[6]

The next article is titled "La colère d'une ville" ["The anger of a city"] and evokes "the memory of Oradour," the town and its inhabitants brutally destroyed by the Germans just a few months earlier, before its ringing conclusion:

> Toute la matinée, c'est la colère qui souffle sur la ville. Cette foule a enfin décidé de prendre son destin dans ses propres mains. Vers 11 heures, on voit apparaître les premières barricades. Le chemin qui mène de la docilité douloureuse à l'insurrection est enfin parcouru. A partir de ce moment, il n'y aura plus que des combattants.[7]

> All morning long, anger pervades the city. This crowd has finally decided to take fate into its own hands. Around 11 A.M., the first barricades appear. The road that leads from painful docility to insurrection has finally been run. From this moment on, there will be only combatants.

Passage like these could come straight out of a novel by Malraux or Nizan, engaged novelists of the 1930s, celebrating "virile fraternity" or revolutionary fervor. But they also have a ring similar to de Gaulle's speech praising a free, heroic, and united France. A passage from the article that describes the entry of Leclerc's troops into Paris attains heights of unanimist fervor:

> Ils regardent, ils rient, ils sourient, ils nous saluent de leurs deux doigts écartés en forme de V et nous sentons que leur coeur bat au même rythme que le nôtre. Des femmes, des gamins ont envahi les camions et les autos, des voitures de FFI défilent derrière les tanks, civils et militaires sont d'une seule race: des Français libres.[8]

> They look, they laugh, they smile, they salute us with their fingers shaping V and we feel that their hearts beat in unison with ours. Some women and children have invaded the trucks and cars; cars full of FFI [Forces Françaises de l'Intérieur, Resistance fighters]

follow the tanks, civilians and military are of one race: free French.

The call for unity among all French people to face the hard tasks ahead resounded in the columns of all the newspapers during the days following the Liberation. Writers as diverse as the Catholic philosopher Maritain and the atheist philosopher Camus agreed that unity was essential; but de Gaulle not only called for unity in his speeches, he rhetorically *presupposed* it. When he spoke of "true France, eternal France," unanimous in its resistance to the occupant, he was expressing a wish, not describing an actual state of affairs. In rhetoric, presupposition is a means of persuading your interlocutor that something exists, without empirical verification.

Did Sartre, in those first days of September 1944, presuppose the unity of all French people? He didn't speak about "la France éternelle," but he shared with de Gaulle, as well as with the majority of the French and many Americans and English people, the wish that France had been unanimous in its rejection of the occupant. The desire to believe that all of France had resisted the Germans, even if few had actually fought them in the Resistance, corresponds to what Pierre Nora defines as writing history from the point of view of the future. The future of France, after the Liberation, was that of a strong nation among those that had conquered the Germans. Therefore, all of France had to have resisted the occupant. In this perspective, the future perfect is the historical tense par excellence.

"No One Failed It": Three Essays on the Occupation

Sartre's short text, "La république du silence," made a dramatic first appearance less than two weeks after the Liberation. It was published on September 9, 1944, in the first free issue of *Les Lettres françaises*, a journal run by the writers' Resistance group, the Comité National des Ecrivains, which had appeared clandestinely for two years.

The front page of *Les Lettres Françaises*, where this piece appeared, was itself testimony to a desire for unity among a wide range of voices. An essay celebrating France's "soul," by the well-known Catholic author François Mauriac, appeared above Sartre's text. (Mauriac had published a book with the clandestine publisher Editions de Minuit in

1943, a sign of strong commitment to the Resistance.) Next to Mauriac's essay was a harsher and more partisan piece by the paper's Communist editor-in-chief, Claude Morgan. Featured centrally was the
"Manifesto of French Writers," signed by all the members of the
Comité National des Ecrivains, a group that had been meeting secretly
since 1941 and that included some of the best-known names of the
intellectual Resistance: Vercors (pseudonym of Jean Bruller), Paul
Eluard, Jean Paulhan, Mauriac, Louis Aragon, André Malraux, Albert
Camus, and Edith Thomas, as well as Sartre.[9] "Let us remain united
in victory and freedom as we were in sorrow and oppression," proclaimed the Manifesto. It is worth noting that among its signers, Sartre
was not the most famous—he would become so within a year—but
he was known in intellectual circles as both a novelist (*La nausée* was
published in 1938) and a philosopher (*Being and Nothingness* appeared
in 1943), as well as the author of some brilliant articles of literary
criticism. Also, he had gained considerable notoriety in the spring of
1944 with his play *Huis clos* [*No Exit*], which elicited a lively debate in
the Occupation press.[10] He had participated in the meetings of the
Comité National des Ecrivains since 1943 and had contributed three
articles to the clandestine *Les Lettres Françaises*, but he was not known
as a major *résistant*. He had never published with the Editions de
Minuit, unlike Aragon, Eluard, Paulhan, Vercors, and many others.[11]
Having had two plays produced under German censorship was not in
itself reprehensible at the time, but it was not a sign of resistance
either. Thus, Sartre's central presence on the front page of *Les Lettres
Françaises*, while not unjustified, did not go without saying. In a sense,
his authority as a *résistant* was created, rather than confirmed, by this
event.

Here, then, is Sartre affirming in the famous opening sentence of
"La république du silence": "Never have we been freer than under the
German occupation." Who exactly are "we"? This pronoun occurs no
less than twenty-three times (twice as the possessive "notre") in the
first twenty lines of text, confirming what can be called its unanimist
rhetoric; however, the extension of the pronoun (Who is included in
"nous"? Is anyone excluded?) does not remain stable. At times it seems
that "nous" includes all those in France, or virtually all, who lived
through the Occupation; at other times, it refers only to some French
people and not others.

What is most interesting is that this semantic slippage, or what might be called the "wavering *we*," turns out to be not a weakness in the text but its strength, not an inadvertence but a rhetorical strategy.

The opening lines seem to refer to everybody. Sartre even includes a mention of the Jews, the only mention he will make in these three essays: "We were deported en masse, as workers [forced laborers sent as part of the "Service du Travail Obligatoire" to work in Germany], as Jews, as political prisoners [presumably members of the Resistance]." A few lines later, the unanimous "we" is qualified by an exclusion: "Et je ne parle pas ici de cette élite que furent les vrais Résistants, mais de tous les Français qui, à toute heure du jour et de la nuit, pendant quatre ans, ont dit *non*." ["And I do not speak here of that elite who were the true Resisters, but of all Frenchmen who, at every hour of the day or night, during four years, said *no*."] Here Sartre puts the "true Resisters" into a separate category: his words of praise refer not to that elite minority (presumably, they do not need praise), but to all those "ordinary" French who said *no* to the occupant.

Does that mean everybody? Allowing for the linguistic sexism that includes women under "Frenchmen," it does seem to include everybody. But this is where the wavering *we* comes into play. Grammatically, Sartre's sentence does not say that all Frenchmen said *no*. He is speaking of "*all Frenchmen who* said no," not of "*all Frenchmen, who* said no." The absence of a comma before the relative pronoun is crucial, for it restricts the antecedent: Some Frenchmen did not say *no*, and Sartre is referring only to those who did. This is grammatically unambiguous (the commaless relative clause is called a "determinative relative" by grammarians), but rhetorically less so. One has to deduce the absence of unanimity—it is grammatically implied, but not stated. In "What Is a Collaborator?" Sartre will actually state that "the nation had said *no*" to the occupant: the nation, that is, all the French. Here, he does not go that far, but the rhetoric of his text, based on the hammering repetition of "we" and on indirection rather than direct statement, leans strongly toward that meaning.

From here on, semantic slippage in this text becomes more and more pronounced. For example:

Mais la cruauté même de l'ennemi nous poussait jusqu'aux extrémités de cette condition en nous contraignant à nous poser de ces questions que l'on néglige dans la paix: tous ceux d'entre nous—et quel Français ne fut une fois ou l'autre dans ce cas?— qui connaissaient quelques détails intéressant la Résistance se demandaient avec angoisse: "Si on me torture, tiendrai-je le coup?"[12]

But the very cruelty of the enemy pushed us to the limit of this condition [of saying *no*] by forcing us to ask ourselves questions that we neglect in peace time: all those among us—and what Frenchman was not at one time or other in that position ?—who knew some details concerning the Resistance asked themselves in anguish: "If they torture me, will I hold up?"

After excluding the "elite of true Resisters" in the previous sentence, Sartre here extends the anguish about torture that may have been felt by members of the Resistance to the whole population, by way of a rhetorical question, "[A]nd what Frenchman was not one time or other in that position?" One might think that he was exaggerating, that few Frenchmen actually ran the risk of being tortured by the Gestapo, but the interest of this text is not factual. Its power is rhetorical, even at the expense of facts.

A few lines after these reflections on the generalized fear of torture, the text slips from "we" to "they," "nous" to "ils":

A ceux qui eurent une activité clandestine, les conditions de leur lutte apportaient une expérience nouvelle: ils ne combattaient pas au grand jour, comme des soldats; en toute circonstance ils étaient seuls, ils étaient traqués dans la solitude, arrêtés dans la solitude.

To those engaged in clandestine activity, the conditions of their struggle brought a new experience: they did not fight in broad daylight, like soldiers; in every instance they were alone, they were hunted in solitude, arrested in solitude.

Here begins the development on the "republic of silence," for this phrase refers first of all to the members of organized Resistance movements. A *résistant* who was arrested and tortured felt responsible for all the others in the group, regardless of rank; that is why the Resistance was a "genuine democracy," "the strongest of Republics."

On the way to this conclusion, which concerns only the organized Resistance (thus, "them" rather than "us"), the text slips into a "we" that is almost imperceptible: "Cette responsabilité totale dans la solitude totale, n'est-ce pas le dévoilement même de notre liberté?" ["This total responsibility in total solitude, is this not the very discovery of our freedom?"] One can well ask what this collective "we" is doing in the midst of all the "ils" referring to tortured Resistance heroes. The answer is furnished at the very end of the text, where we find the most daring—and glaring—semantic slippage:

> Cette république sans institutions, sans armée, sans police, il fallait que chaque Français la conquière et l'affirme à chaque instant contre le nazisme. Personne n'y a manqué et nous voilà à présent au bord d'une autre République.

> This republic without institutions, without an army, without a police, every Frenchman had to possess and affirm it, at every moment, against Nazism. No one failed it, and we are now on the verge of another Republic.

In the space of a single sentence, the "republic of silence" moves from the Resistance to every Frenchman, and the fight against Nazism becomes a fight in which the whole French population participated at every instant, unanimously: *No one failed it.* Sartre himself seems to have realized, with the passage of time, that the rhetorical exaggeration here was too strong, too flagrantly "resistancialist." He omitted that sentence from the version of the essay that appeared five years later in his book *Situations, III.*[13] But the sentence remained in all the other versions of the essay, French or English, that had been reprinted until then.

What shall we say today about this beautifully high-flown piece of oratory? A hostile critic like Gilbert Joseph (in his book *Une si douce Occupation*) treats it as a "fantasy of heroism," part of a calculated strategy on Sartre's part to gain a dominant place in the postwar literary sun.[14] But the reality seems to me more complicated, and more interesting than that. If there is a fantasy of heroism at work here, and one can easily admit that there is, then we should think about it not primarily as a careerist move, nor even as a matter of individual psychology, but as a collective phenomenon. The cultural and political work accomplished by this text in September 1944 was considerable: By his talent as a writer, Sartre succeeded in constructing a version of the immediate past in which not only his French readers but all those Francophiles abroad who needed reassurance would recognize an image of France that they could accept, even love, at a time when the war was not yet over and French forces were fighting alongside the Allies.

Anna Boschetti, in her influential book *Sartre et les Temps Modernes*, argues that Sartre's true public, the public that made him famous, consisted of intellecuals who were drawn to his triple prestige (or, in the vocabulary of Boschetti's mentor Pierre Bourdieu, to his "accumulated cultural capital") as novelist-philosopher-essayist. According to Boschetti, Sartre's short programmatic texts, "Presentation of *Les Temps Modernes*" and "Existentialism Is a Humanism," which both appeared in the fall of 1945, furnished a "seductive mythology" to this intellectual public—a mythology that accorded pride of place to intellectuals, "those tormented, unfailingly lucid and solitary heroes."[15] Although I think that on the whole Boschetti is right, I would say that in the fall of 1944, Sartre succeeded in furnishing a seductive mythology to a much broader public. The heroism he imagines in "The Republic of Silence" is not restricted to intellectuals, nor even to the "elite of true Resisters"; it is a democratic heroism, shared by "every Frenchman." Indeed, this wider public may have been responsible for the astonishing worldwide celebrity that Sartre gained during the year following the Liberation.

Contributing to this celebrity were the other two essays Sartre wrote about occupied France. "Paris sous l'Occupation" ["Paris under the Occupation"] appeared in December 1944 in London, in the Gaullist journal *La France Libre* edited by Sartre's old friend Raymond Aron. "Qu'est-ce qu'un collaborateur?" ["What Is a Collaborator?"] appeared in New York, in August and September 1945 in the monthly *La République Française*, a journal founded during the war by a group of exiles including Jacques Maritain, Paul Rivet, Georges Wildenstein, and other notables who would soon be returning to France. These two essays are addressed to Francophiles in England and America, as well as to French exiles who had not experienced the Occupation. Sartre is again constructing a version of the immediate past, but this time for readers outside France. Just as in "La République du silence," he is writing here for people who *wish* to hear a story of collective heroism and suffering—and he gives it to them, even if it involves leaving certain things unsaid. One must therefore read these texts with an eye to their silences as well as to their affirmations if one wants to understand the cultural work they accomplished at that time. It will also be enlightening to look at some of the changes he made when he reprinted these essays in *Situations, III*, for he revised them more extensively than "La République du silence."

In "Paris sous l'Occupation," Sartre undertakes to explain and in a sense provide the apology for the attitude adopted by the large majority of French people during the Occupation. He begins by correcting a misapprehension: "Many Englishmen and Americans," arriving in Paris at the Liberation and seeing that people were "less skinny than they had thought," may have concluded that Parisians had not suffered much during the Occupation. "I would like to explain to them that they are wrong, that the Occupation was a terrible thing," Sartre writes in his opening paragraph.[16] At the end of the essay, he repeats this idea and addresses himself directly to his English readers:

> Mais nous vous demandons d'abord de comprendre que l'occupation fut souvent plus terrible que la guerre. Car, en guerre, chacun peut faire son métier d'homme, au lieu que, dans cette situation ambiguë, nous ne pouvions vraiment ni *agir*, ni même *penser*." (F18; S42).

> But we ask you first to understand that the Occupation was often more terrible than the war. For in a war, everyone can do his duty as a man, whereas in this ambiguous situation, we could not really *act*, nor even *think*.

This statement may appear odd, coming from a man who had written two full-length plays and all the hundreds of pages of *Being and Nothingness* during those years! Sartre, in any case, was not among those who could not think under the Occupation. But apart from such rhetorical exaggerations, his description of what it felt like to live as an "ordinary" Parisian during that time has the ring of truth as well as of sincerity.

As Sartre indicates, this experience was essentially one of ambiguity.

There was first the ambiguity of living next to German soldiers who were "well-mannered" and "polite" and whom one could not bring oneself completely to hate; "the concept of 'enemy' is totally firm and clear only if the enemy is separated from us by a barrier of fire," he notes (*F* 11; *S* 21). Then there is the ambiguity of one's feelings at seeing Allied planes bomb French cities: "Not the least of our troubles was that temptation to hate you" (*F* 15; *S* 33). Further was the ambiguity of a Resistance whose value was merely symbolic: "Without [the Resistance], the English would have won the war; with it, they would have lost it if they were due to lose it. Its chief value, in our eyes, was that of a symbol" (*F* 14; *S* 30). Finally was the ambiguity of living in a situation where, whatever one did, it was impossible not to be "in complicity with the occupant," because every activity that was needed to maintain a minimum of social and economic organization benefited not only the French population but also the enemy "which lived in symbiosis with us" (*F* 16; *S* 36). Thus, says Sartre, even the armed resisters hiding in the woods, the *maquisards*, "our pride," depended on farmers who, in order to supply them with food, had to raise livestock, "half of which was shipped to Germany" (F16, S37). Even the courageous railroad workers [*cheminots*], who shipped food to the French and "most of whom were in the Resistance," could not help being compromised: "Their zeal in protecting our material also served the German cause" because their trains could be used to transport enemy troops. Whence Sartre's striking conclusion that the situation of the country was one of "total resistance and total collaboration" ("tout entier résistant et tout entier collaborateur") (F16; S36).

Sartre's logic is somewhat troubling, for he seems to place all French people into the same basket, or rather the same paradox: If even the *résistants* were forced to be collaborators in a certain sense, how could one distinguish the two? Sartre does separate a certain class of "collabos" from the rest of the population: "Certainly, there were among us some genuine traitors: we are not ashamed of them; every nation has its dregs, that marginal group of failures and embittered men who profit from times of disaster" (*F* 16; *S* 36). His conclusion does not apply to these "dregs" but to the rest of the population, at once "wholly resisting and wholly collaborating." This conclusion was meant to be, I think, a kind of apology for ordinary French people, who had neither collaborated actively nor resisted actively. If no one could avoid a certain "complicity with the enemy," than the distinctions among different choices made by individuals became irrelevant.

This conclusion, seeing all French people (with the exception of the "dregs") as one, is of a piece with that of "La République du silence." There, he had implied that all the French had resisted; here, he repeats that idea, but adds that they were also forced to collaborate by their very situation as an occupied people. Interestingly, Sartre omitted the words "tout entier résistant" in the version published in *Situations, III*, so the sentence there states that the whole country collaborated. That may appear like a radical change, but obviously it was a rhetorical overstatement that was not meant to be taken literally. The sense of the statement remains that of an apology for ordinary French people, who did nothing other than simply survive under the Occupation. Sartre already suggested as much at the very beginning of the essay:

Quelqu'un à qui on demandait ce qu'il avait fait sous la Terreur répondit: "J'ai vécu . . ." C'est une réponse que nous pourrions tous faire aujourd'hui. Pendant quatre ans, nous avons vécu, et les Allemands vivaient aussi, au milieu de nous, submergés, noyés, par la vie unanime de la grande ville. (F10; S18)

Someone who was asked what he had done under the Terror replied: "I lived . . ." That is a reply we could all give today. During four years, we lived, and the Germans lived too, in our midst, submerged, swallowed up in the unanimous life of the big city.

The historian Philippe Burrin, in his book on France under the Occupation, divides the French population of the period into three categories that fall into a bell curve: active collaborators and active *résistants* at the two ends, and "accommodators"—who simply "lived" as best they could—in the middle.[17] In terms of Burrin's categories, Sartre in this essay functions as the apologist of accommodation. In fact, he himself uses that word: "Will I be understood if I say that it [the horror of the Occupation] was intolerable and that we accommodated ourselves to it quite well?" (*F*12; *S*24). At the same time, however—and this is the brilliant rhetorical move of his essay—he suggests that the "accommodators" resisted in their hearts, and that even the "true Resisters" were forced to participate in accommodation as long as they lived in France. This was a comforting message for the majority, one that had the added advantage of glossing over the very real political and ideological divisions that had existed in France virtually since the French Revolution and certainly throughout the interwar period and beyond. The Vichy government, as Robert Paxton has shown, capitalized on these divisions, blaming France's defeat in 1940 on the "decadent" tendencies of the 1930s, dominated by the Left.[18] Sartre does mention some "old quarrels" that were revived under the Occupation, but the ones he enumerates—Paris *vs.* the provices, peasants *vs.* city dwellers, workers *vs.* bourgeois, fathers *vs.* sons—appear strangely ahistorical and even anodyne, when one considers the bitter "Franco-French wars" (as contemporary historians call them) that had divided the country in the decades since the Dreyfus Affair. The only pair in his enumeration that alludes to this is "workers *vs.* bourgeois," but Sartre does not say "unions *vs.* bosses," which would have had a sharper tone and greater historical specificity.

The other silence, which appears flagrant now (though I am ready to admit it did not appear so in 1944) concerns the fate of Jews. Sartre uses the unanimous "we" to speak about the life of Parisians under the Occupation, as if all Parisians had had the same experience. He forgets that Jews were different precisely because they could not "simply live" like other French people, in the midst of German soldiers. Designated after the spring of 1942 by their yellow stars, rounded up (by French police, not by the Gestapo—Sartre is silent about the French police as well), "concentrated" on the outskirts of Paris, and finally deported, the Jews of Paris could not blend into the great unanimous mass of accommodators. Sartre's silence about this is all the more striking when one considers that at this very time (fall 1944) he was writing his *Réflexions sur la question juive* [*Anti-Semite and Jew*], where the difference between the situation of Jews and "aryans" (the term he uses) is analyzed in great detail.[19] In "Paris under the Occupation," it is as if the Jews did not exist. Their difference would certainly have perturbed the homogeneous picture of French suffering that Sartre sought to paint for his English-speaking readers.

Similar silences exist in "Qu'est-ce qu'un collaborateur?" [What Is a Collaborator?"], where Sartre analyzes the social and psychological aspects of collaboration. The title of this two-part essay has an interesting antecedent. In 1945, the January 7–8 issue of the Parisian daily *Combat* ran a front-page article headlining a recent statement by an American businessman: "An American Industrialist declares: French workers would have accommodated themselves to the German occupation if the war had continued." According to the article, Frederick C. Crawford, returning from an official visit to Europe, gave a talk at the New York Chamber of Commerce in which he asked the question, "What is a collaborator?" and answered, "Here it is: If you ran your business for the Germans, but without enlarging it, you were a patriotic citizen. If you ran your business for the Germans and enlarged it with some profits, you were a collaborator." After this explanation, Mr. Crawford declared that a good friend of his in France had told him that "if things had continued for another year and a half, he believed all French workers would have accommodated themselves to the situation."[20]

Sartre must have read that article, because in the same issue of *Combat* he published a piece titled "Une grande revue française à Londres," profiling the journal *La France libre*, which had published his "Paris sous l'Occupation" essay the previous month. He was getting ready to leave on his first trip to New York, where he would meet many people, both American and French, who wanted to know how things had been in France during the war. It is therefore quite possible that Sartre took up the question posed by the unsympathetic American businessman in order to give his own answer to it. "All the workers, and almost all the farmers [*paysans*] were *résistants*," he affirms peremptorily in "Qu'est-ce qu'un collaborateur?"[21] In reality, according to statistics cited by Philippe Burrin, workers constituted 8.8 percent of active collaboratonists and farmers 12.2 percent.[22] These percentages were lower than the percentage of these groups in the French population, so Sartre was at least partially right: though it is unlikely that most workers and farmers were in the Resistance, relatively few were in active collaboration.

What is the gist of Sartre's argument about collaboration? He divides it into two "aspects," the social and the psychological. Concerning the former, Sartre argues that collaboration was not a class phenomenon (despite his statement about workers and farmers), but rather the choice of "unintegrated" individuals who belonged to no particular class—the dregs of society, in sum:

> Le déchet social, pratiquement négligeable en temps de paix, devient important dans le cas d'une défaite suivie d'occupation. *Précisément parce qu'une nation dit non et parce qu'il est hors de cette nation, il veut servir contre elle la politique de l'ennemi. Sous la protection des autorités étrangères, il demeure une minorité marginale et désintégrée comme auparavant.*[23]

> The dregs of society, practically negligible in peace time, become significant in the case of a defeat followed by occupation. *Precisely because a nation says no and because they are outside that nation, they want to serve against her the politics of the enemy. Under the protection of the foreign authorities, they remain a marginal and unintegrated minority, as before.*

This is an emphatic restatement of what Sartre had already stated in his two earlier essays about the Occupation: Collaborators were not "real Frenchmen," but a marginalized fringe excluded from the nation. Their existence did not contradict the thesis of French unanimity, but rather affirmed it. The collaborator worked for the enemy, he was not part of France.

Somewhat surprisingly, Sartre omitted the sentences italicized above from the version published in *Situations, III.* Too categorical? Too hyperbolic in its insistence on unanimity, for a reader in 1949? Probably both. But the deletion does not significantly change his argument, for the major silence remains; Sartre does not mention that the most notorious collaborators (including the very ones whose names he will cite) were not at all marginal, but were members of powerful groups and institutions—politicians, journalists, members of the French Academy, and graduates of France's top schools. Thus he mentions Robert Brasillach, a writer and journalist who was an enthusiastic supporter of Hitler and was condemned to death and executed after the Liberation, but he fails to note that Brasillach (whose name he spells as "Brazillade," or "Brazillach," reinforcing the suggestion that he was "non-French" and close to the Nazis) was a graduate of the most prestigious institution of higher education in France, the École Normale Supérieure—like Sartre himself.[24] Nor does Sartre mention, among collaborators, the high civil servants (like Maurice Papon, or the Paris Police Chief René Bousquet) who were perfectly able to reconcile their socioprofessional status with a routinized collaboration that would later be qualified as crimes against humanity.

In the second part of his essay, Sartre extends the notion of social marginality to the realm of individual psychology; in his view, collaboration was a kind of pathology. Collaborators suffered from "that intellectual malady we may call historicism," which consists in "accepting a fait accompli simply because it exists."[25] Even more pathologically, the collaborator is a "feminized" man, or an outright homosexual. "The Parisian homosexual milieux" were rife with collaborators, Sartre claims, and he again mentions the name of "Brazillade"; in fact, not much is known about Brasillach's sex life. If they were not homosexuals, Sartre adds, collaborators were certainly neurotics, like Pierre Drieu La Rochelle, the fascist writer who had committed suicide a few months after the Liberation and who was full of self-loathing. Sartre had devoted one of his clandestine articles in *Les lettres françaises* to an analysis of Drieu as a self-hating intellectual.[26]

And here we have another major silence: Sartre never mentions that many collaborators—and certainly the well-known ones he mentions— were not merely "neurotic" but had explicitly *ideological* motives for collaboration, including rejection of parliamentary democracy and virulent anti-Semitism. Not all anti-Semites were collaborators, nor can one say that all collaborators were anti-Semites, but many collaborators certainly were. Brasillach wrote anti-Semitic articles during the war that amounted to calls for murder; so did Céline, and Drieu was not far behind. Furthermore, these men did not consider themselves as "servants" of Germany. Brasillach proclaimed himself a *French* fascist; and, as Alice Kaplan notes, he cited the tradition of French anti-Semitism as part of his defense at his trial.[27]

One wonders why Sartre kept so quiet about collaborationist ideology and anti-Semitism, especially as he would soon publish the magnificent "portrait of the anti-Semite" that opens his *Réflexions sur la question juive*. Perhaps he did not want to speak about French anti-Semitism in a New York journal, for he too was aware that anti-Semitism in France was not limited to collaborators but had a long tradition. Mainly, however, I would say that Sartre's silence was the result of his drive toward unanimity. According to him, the "marginal" collaborator hated himself, his country, and humanity in general, like Drieu La Rochelle. The specific hatred that some Frenchmen (whether "ordinary" or collaborators) directed against Jews, including their fellow citizens, would have undermined Sartre's argument.

Finally, these three texts on the Occupation share a single purpose: to persuade a broad public, whether at home or abroad, that France had been united, that France had suffered, and that France was ready to take its place among the deserving victors over Germany. Whatever did not fit into that demonstration got left out.

"Fearless and Active": Sartre in America

It is fascinating to consider the extraordinary success that one of these essays, "La république du silence," enjoyed in the immediate postwar years and the fame that it brought to its author, especially in the United States. Less than three months after its first publication, in December 1944, "La république du silence" was reprinted in the first free issue of a poetry review edited clandestinely during the Occupation, *L'éternelle Revue*. The journal was close to the Communist Party, which incidentally shared the "resistancialist" rhetoric of de Gaulle at the time. The journal's motto, printed under a drawing by Picasso on the cover, was "A Review that is of its time as one is of a party/A Review that is French as one is universal." Sartre's text heads the Table of Contents, followed by contributions by virtually every major figure of the literary Resistance and of the postwar literary scene: Michel Leiris, Louis Aragon, René Char, Francis Ponge, Jean Paulhan, Paul Eluard, Raymond Queneau, Jacques Prévert, Tristan Tzara, Guillevic, Elsa Triolet, and others. The eminent classicist and historian Pierre Vidal-Naquet, who was sixteen years old at the time, recalls that "La république du silence" in that publication was the first text he ever read by Sartre, and it earned his undying admiration.[28] Sartre also recorded the text for the radio, and many years later that recording was featured in the documentary film by Alexandre Astruc and Michel Contat, *Sartre par lui-même*.

In short, a monumentalization of this text took place almost immediately after it first appeared, and continued in the United States, where it received a new twist; not only did the text become a monument to the heroic French resistance, but Sartre himself became a living monument, an incarnation of the Resistance. In December 1944, just before Sartre's first trip to New York, "La république du silence" appeared in *The Atlantic Monthly* under the title "Paris Alive: The Republic of Silence," translated by the Harvard-educated New York esthete and intellectual Lincoln Kirstein. (A young soldier at the time, Kirstein would go on after the war to found, with George Balanchine, the New York City Ballet). In the *Atlantic* too, Sartre's was the lead article, accompanied by the following blurb about the author: "Jean-Paul Sartre is a French dramatist and poet who distinguished himself as one of the military leaders of the FFI [French Forces of the Interior, the armed Resistance] during the long years of German domination."[29]

The misunderstanding is downright comical. Whereas to the French public of 1944 Sartre's text offered the image of ordinary Frenchmen who had resisted in their hearts (this is the resistancialist myth), to Americans Sartre himself appeared as an incarnation of the "true Resister," a military hero—precisely the elite that he claimed to exclude in his essay.

Does Sartre's rhetoric encourage this kind of misunderstanding? Undoubtedly.[30] But circumstances contributed as well, starting with the desire of francophile Americans to find a hero. Sartre was aware of the misunderstanding and felt somewhat embarrassed by it, as one can see in the first article he sent to the French daily *Le Figaro* in January 1945, while he was visiting New York as part of an official delegation of French journalists. He and seven others were the guests of the Office of War Information (OWI), and were received everywhere as representatives of newly liberated France. Sartre had the added prestige of being a philosopher and writer as well as a journalist, and his eloquent essay had just appeared in the *Atlantic*. In his first dispatch to the *Le Figaro*, dated January 25, 1945, and titled "Victoire du Gaullisme," he writes:

Il ne faut pas demeurer longtemps à New York pour comprendre ce qu'ils attendent de nous. Ce qui est sûr, en tout cas, c'est que l'accueil émouvant qui nous est réservé partout vise à honorer à travers nous la Résistance Française. Je me suis senti d'abord très

gêné, parce que nous n'avions pas été envoyés comme représen-
tants de la Résistance et que, si les journaux avaient pressenti le
sens de l'invitation qui leur était faite, ils n'auraient pas eu de
peine à choisir de plus digne que moi. Mais, en fait, c'est encore
se donner trop d'importance que d'avoir de ces délicatesses. Nos
personnes ne sont pas en cause; à travers elles, et simplement
parce que nous sommes Français, ces manifestations d'amitié, si
délicates et touchantes, s'adressent aux Résistants de France, c'est-
à-dire à une démocratie de combat.[31]

One need not be in New York for long to understand what they
expect from us. What is certain, in any case, is that the moving
welcome we are receiving everywhere aims to honor, through us,
the French Resistance. At first I felt very uneasy, because we had
not been sent as representatives of the Resistance, and if the
newspapers had realized the meaning of the invitation, they would
have had no trouble choosing someone more worthy than I. But,
in fact, such scruples are too self-centered. Our individual personalities are not at stake: Through us, and simply because we
are French, these effusions of friendship, so considerate and
touching, are addressed to the Resisters of France, that is, to a
fighting democracy.

This paragraph, which figures only peripherally in the article (Sartre
goes on to discuss American attitudes and policies toward de Gaulle),
sums up a reasoning, one might even say an existential choice, that
would have important consequences. Since the American public wants
him to have participated heroically in the Resistance, Sartre will fulfill
their desire—not out of self-centeredness, for he knows, and knows
that his French readers know, that he does not deserve that role (others
would have been "more worthy" than he). If he accepts the role, it is
due more to a certain patriotism: by allowing Americans to clothe him
in the mantle of a Resistance hero, Sartre is affirming his solidarity
with his country, democratic and at war. Paradoxally, he becomes depersonalized ("Our individual personalities are not at stake") at the
very moment when he is being feted as a hero.

   He may have been depersonalized, but his public image gained a
great deal, both in the United States and in France. Could we not say

that the postwar years inaugurate the time when, in order to be world famous even in one's own country, one must be famous in America?

A few months after the *Figaro* article, just before Sartre became a truly big media star in France, *Vogue* magazine published its July issue, with a special section on "People and Ideas . . . Summer Reader." Between an article by Virgil Thomson on contemporary music and an article by Senator William Fulbright on "the price of peace" (a very eloquent essay, arguing that the United States must renounce its prewar isolationaist policy) is an article by Sartre, titled "New Writing in France." Above his name, as a running head, is a quote from the article: "The Resistance 'taught that literature is no fancy activity independent of politics.' "[32] Indeed, Sartre's essay, very passionate and eloquent, states that the new writing in France was born of the Resistance, "four years of struggle, of hope and despair, humiliation and pride." The word "Resistance" occurs eight times in the two pages. The word "man" in its universal, humanistic sense (or else the abstract word "humanity") appears more than six times; "the powers and limits of man," "the reign of man," "the grandeur of humanity" are the themes that preoccupy the writers who came out of the Resistance. And the best representative of those writers, according to Sartre, is Albert Camus.

According to the editors of *Vogue*, however, Sartre himself is such a representative. His article is followed by an unusually long Editor's Note, which is worth quoting in full:

> Jean-Paul Sartre looks like the men on the barricades in pictures of the Paris Insurrection. Just forty, he is small, intent. On his O.W.I.-sponsored travels here in the spring, his worn trench coat, his pipe, his heavy-rimmed glasses marked him as definitely as any uniform. He was, indeed, a man of the Resistance. . . . He is certainly the most admired of the younger men shaping the direction of French writing today. As a philosopher and a novelist Sartre was the centre of a cult among young French intellectuals before the war: his part in the Resistance seems to have made his work broader, more human, greater. Two of his plays, now running, "Les Mouches" and "Huis Clos," pointed arguments for resisting the oppressors, were presented in Paris under the Germans.[33]

The Resistance halo with which Sartre surrounds Camus is given here (with *Vogue*-like attention to clothing and external appearance!) to Sartre himself. But the note also sketches a portrait of Sartre as the most influential writer and philosopher of his generation—which he will indeed become, in Paris and then everywhere, a few months later.

Finally, the last avatar of "La République du silence" in postwar America was a starring role in a widely used college textbook published in 1946 by Harcourt, Brace: *La République du Silence: The Story of the French Resistance.* Edited by the noted journalist and war correspondent A. J. Liebling, with Columbia University professor Eugene Sheffer to provide pedagogic aids (explanatory notes, vocabulary, and grammar exercises based on the texts), this anthology presented an excellent selection of writings published in French journals between 1940 and the Liberation. In 1947, an English translation for the general public appeared under Liebling's name alone. In both versions, the book carried as an epigraph the last sentence from "La république du silence": "May this republic about to be set up in broad daylight preserve the austere virtues of that other Republic of Silence and of Night." And in both versions, Sartre is identified (in 1946 with Camus, in 1947 all by himself) as one who "was fearless and active in the underground and continues so in French politics."[34]

What conclusions may we draw from all this, both concerning Sartre's role as a public intellectual and concerning collective memory in postwar France? I believe that Sartre's existential decision to allow himself to be transformed into a Resistance hero affected the rest of his life, not unlike the process he describes in the sentence I quoted as an epigraph: "One chooses one's past in light of a certain end . . ." Having chosen, for himself and for France, a past in the Resistance, Sartre lived his life after the war trying to rise to that choice. "From 1945 on, Sartre did more than any other intellectual in the world to denounce injustice and to support the wretched of the earth," writes John Gerassi at the end of his very filial biography, in a chapter titled, not by chance, "The Resistant."[35] But as I have tried to show, the version that Sartre constructs of French life under the Occupation was possible only at the price of many things passed over in silence. At the time, those silences were not perceived as such; perhaps they were not even perceivable as such. Today, they are glaring.

Is Sartre diminished as a result? Is France diminished as a result?

Not necessarily—at least not in the eyes of those who are suspicious of mythic aggrandizements. If, over the past decade or so, "the past has resurfaced, heterogeneous, problematic" (in Philippe Burrin's words)[36]—and if we are now aware of contradictions and shortcomings, as well as successes, concerning both Sartre and the France of the Occupation, that is not such a bad thing. For if we really want to see the past become past, not remain caught in our throats, a "past that will not pass,"[37] we will do well to confront it in all of its complexities and even its failures. Heroes are not always what (or who) one may think.

✺ 2

Narrative Desire

THE "AUBRAC AFFAIR" AND NATIONAL MEMORY OF THE FRENCH RESISTANCE

CONTRARY TO WHAT ONE still occasionally reads or hears, the French have not, in recent years, refused to remember the so-called "dark years" of the Vichy regime under German occupation (1940–44). While the more shameful aspects of Vichy—notably, its collaboration with the Germans in rounding up and deporting 75,000 Jews from French soil—was for many years a taboo subject in public discourse as well as in the academy, that is no longer the case. Indeed, some historians have lately deplored the French "obsession" with memory of the Vichy years. Henry Rousso, in his acclaimed 1987 book *The Vichy Syndrome*, showed that after the mid-1970s, Vichy and its turpitudes increasingly became a focus of public attention.[1] This was aided by a series of highly publicized trials for crimes against humanity, starting with the 1987 trial of Klaus Barbie, a Nazi functionary notorious for his role in the persecution of *résistants* and Jews in Lyon and ending with the 1997 trial of Maurice Papon, a highly placed French bureaucrat in charge of the roundup of Jews in Bordeaux.[2]

Just a few months before the opening of the Papon trial, in February 1997, the so-called "Aubrac Affair" burst into the French press, where it occupied considerable attention for over six months. Raymond and Lucie Aubrac, who enjoyed national and international fame as heroes of the Resistance, were suddenly placed under suspicion of having

36

betrayed their comrades, and in particular the Resistance hero Jean Moulin, fifty-four years earlier. The "Aubrac Affair" raises fascinating issues about the history and memory of the Resistance in France. It also raises important issues about narrative, in particular about what I call narrative desire: on the one hand the desire for heroic aggrandizement (or for its opposite, the toppling of heroes), and on the other hand the desire for narrative coherence and plausibility, or what in fiction is called verisimilitude.

An Affair of Memory

Modern French history is rife with "affairs." One interesting feature of the Aubrac Affair of 1997 is that, while arousing passions and involving high stakes, it seemed to be concerned exclusively with past history. In the Dreyfus Affair, the immediate fate of the accused was at stake, and the historical event that was the crux of the affair (somebody had transmitted military secrets to Germany) was almost exactly contemporary to the debates about it. In the Aubrac Affair, the historical event (somebody had tipped off Klaus Barbie to the secret meeting at which the Resistance leader Jean Moulin and others were arrested in 1943) had occurred more than half a century earlier, and nobody's immediate fate was at stake. But can a public "affair" arouse passions without being in some way about the present? The passions aroused by the Aubrac Affair suggest that the Resistance, and certain events of the Resistance like the arrest of Jean Moulin, continue to be "present" in France, even while being historical.

What happened in the Aubrac Affair, exactly, and why is it of interest? In order to answer that question, we must take a leap back to the trial of Klaus Barbie, which constituted a watershed in French memories of the Vichy period. This was especially true regarding the memory of Vichy's role in the persecution of Jews. It was largely because of the efforts of those acting on behalf of Jewish victims—notably, Beate and Serge Klarsfeld, who had made it their mission to bring to justice perpetrators of crimes against humanity in France—that Barbie was tracked down in South America and extradited to France.[3] However, given Barbie's role in the arrest and death of Jean Moulin, his trial also reactivated, in a troubling and complicated way, the memory of the Resistance.

The trial itself lasted only a few weeks, in the spring and early summer of 1987, but its preparation took more than four years. Barbie, first identified under his false identity (as the shady businessman Klaus Altmann) in 1972, had been extradited from Bolivia in February 1983 and jailed in Lyon. From that moment on, until his trial, Barbie and his flamboyant defense lawyer Jacques Vergès were constantly in the public eye. Vergès's strategy was to try and turn attention away from Barbie's actions against Jews (which clearly fell under the rubric of crimes against humanity) and to emphasize, instead, his actions against the Resistance, which came under the heading of war crimes. War crimes have a statute of limitations, which by 1983 had run out for crimes committed during World War II. Vergès was using Barbie's crimes against the Resistance as a diversion.[4]

Vergès's focus on the Resistance revived painful memories. He emphasized, in his numerous media appearances and in his book *Pour en finir avec Ponce Pilate* (1983) that the Resistance was not the unified entity of legend but consisted of groups with differing, sometimes hostile agendas. Thus, he recalled, Barbie's arrest of Jean Moulin and other Resistance leaders at a meeting in the Lyon suburb of Caluire in June 1943 was the result of a betrayal. Moulin, a former Préfet who had been dismissed from his post by the Vichy regime because of his left-wing sympathies (he had been involved with the Popular Front and also showed a clear animus against the German occupants in 1940), joined de Gaulle in London in 1941 and was parachuted into France as de Gaulle's representative in January 1942. He worked for more than a year to bring the diverse groups of the interior Resistance together into a single organization and finally succeeded with the formation of the Conseil National de la Résistance in May 1943.[5] Despite this show of unity, however, his leadership was not unchallenged. His arrest by Barbie, Vergès insisted, was due chiefly to internal dissension and jealousies among Resistance leaders, particularly between those who were close to the Communist Party and those who came from right-wing backgrounds. In Vergès's version, both left-wing and right-wing Resistance groups had reason to want Moulin out of the way.[6] After being tortured by Barbie, Moulin was sent to Paris, half-dead, and deported; he died in the train on the way to Germany.

At least two factors made Vergès's revival of the Moulin story particularly sensational in the early 1980s. First, Moulin had become, over the years, the national symbol of the Resistance: In 1964, de Gaulle had enshrined him in the Pantheon, France's repository of "great men," an occasion on which André Malraux pronounced what is perhaps his most famous speech, the funeral oration in praise of Moulin as heroic martyr of the Resistance.[7] This was at the height of what Rousso calls the period of "repressed memory" in French collective remembrance of the Vichy years: no memories of collaboration, only of glorious Resistance. After May 1968 and de Gaulle's departure from the political scene, however, other memories began to surface that put to rest the Gaullist myth of "la France résistante," according to which all of France (not just a small minority) had actively resisted the enemy. In the process, Moulin himself became a target of accusations and insinuations: A former *résistant*, Henri Frenay, leader of the anticommunist group *Combat*, accused Moulin of having been a "cryptocommunist."[8] By launching his own accusations not against Moulin but against those who had allegedly betrayed Moulin, Vergès was recalling the political divisions and fault lines within the Resistance, which had been forgotten during the period of "repressed memory" and were still not a subject of open discussion even in the 1980s. Vergès could claim to be seeking historical truth, but his role as Barbie's defender made that claim dubious. To most observers, and in particular to former *résistants*, his emphasis on betrayal was an attempt to discredit the Resistance as a whole, as well as to divert attention from Barbie's crimes—whence the public outrage provoked by his media appearances.

Another factor of sensationalism was that no one had ever been condemned in court as Moulin's betrayer. René Hardy, a member of *Combat*, was tried twice after the war (in 1947 and 1950), and is generally considered to be the culprit. Like Raymond Aubrac and five other Resistance leaders who were arrested and imprisoned with Moulin, Hardy was present at the meeting at Caluire—unlike the others, however, he had not been invited. The arrests at Caluire occurred during a period of increased pressure on the Resistance, when the Germans were stepping up their manhunts. In fact, the meeting of June 21, 1943, was called in order to find a replacement for the head of the Secret Army (the newly formed armed branch of the interior Resistance), Général Delestraint, who had been arrested in Paris a few weeks earlier. Present at the meeting, besides Moulin, were representatives of the left-wing Libération group (including Raymond Aubrac), of the more conservative Combat group (including René Hardy), and three other men invited by Moulin. All were arrested by Barbie and his lieutenant, but Hardy, the only one not to be hand-cuffed, escaped, thus drawing the others' suspicion.[9]

Raymond Aubrac, as well as his wife Lucie, testified against Hardy at his postwar trials. But Hardy denied the charge to his dying day, and despite conclusive evidence furnished at his second trial, he was acquitted. The fact that both of Hardy's trials became highly politi-cized in the context of the Cold War (he staunchly proclaimed his anticommunism) undoubtedly contributed to his acquittal. Klaus Barbie himself had confirmed, in testimony taken from him in Ger-many at the time of Hardy's second trial, that the latter had been the one who led him to Moulin.[10] In 1972, shortly after he was identified in Bolivia, Barbie gave an interview to a Brazilian journalist in which he named Hardy again. The interview was reproduced and much com-mented upon in France, but Hardy continued to deny the charge. In 1984, just before he died, Hardy published a long and rambling book of self-justification, *Derniers mots,* in which he repeated his claim of innocence and accused others, notably his former "boss" at *Combat* Pierre de Bénouville and Raymond Aubrac. Aubrac, who was close to the communists and had been accusing Hardy for years, thus became an ally of Bénouville, a staunch anticommunist who had supported Hardy in his postwar trials. Meanwhile, Jacques Vergès was making the same accusations in the media; both Vergès and Hardy preferred insinuation to explicit statement, but their meaning was unmistakable. In the spring of 1984, both men repeated their accusations in a doc-umentary film that never attained distribution, but that was shown at least once at a public screening.[11]

Once again, the outcry in the press was enormous.[12] It appeared clear that the Resistance itself was being attacked, its memory tainted. The Aubracs and Bénouville sued Vergès and Hardy for libel (and won, though it took a long time).[13] Henri Noguères, a lawyer who had written a multivolume history of the Resistance, published *La vérité aura le dernier mot* [*Truth Will Have the Last Word*], refuting Hardy point by point. And Lucie Aubrac, ever an outspoken woman, with an advanced degree in history and years of experience as a *lycée* history teacher, wrote a bestselling memoir about her and Raymond's adventures in Lyon during the dramatic months between March 1943 and February 1944. In her book, *Ils partiront dans l'ivresse*, she recalled that they had been among the founders of the Resistance group *Libération* and that Raymond was one of its leaders. She recounted his arrests in March and June 1943 (by French police the first time and then by Barbie at Caluire) and her foolhardy but courageous schemes to free him. The first time, she threatened a French magistrate with reprisals if he did not free Raymond; the second time, she pretended to be Raymond's pregnant girlfriend, enrolling the Gestapo's help in making "an honest woman" out of her, and then organized an armed commando to hold up the truck returning Raymond and other prisoners from Gestapo headquarters to prison. She told of their hiding in the countryside after his dramatic escape in October and of their airlift to London in February 1944, where she gave birth to their second child upon arrival.

It is a tale of risk and romance, almost too beautiful to be true. But true it is, writes the author in her Preface: "I have tried to give an account as exact as possible in time and in the facts. I have been helped in this by my own memories, by my husband's, and by the testimonies of our comrades."[14] As corroboration of the latter, the book contained an Appendix consisting of two brief testimonies by comrades involved in the story. A note preceding these testimonies stated that they had been "established so as to be presentable in court"—not mere narrative recollections, but testimonies in a legal sense.[15] This book too, then, was a response to the accusations coming from Hardy and Vergès; the quasi-legal language of the Appendix alluded to Barbie's trial, which was then being prepared.

Narratives of heroism are deeply satisfying, like fantasies of wish-fulfillment. They are also, generally speaking, morally unambiguous, the characters drawn in broad brushstrokes and the plots linear and schematic: confrontation, apparent defeat, ultimate triumph. The story told by Lucie Aubrac in her memoir conforms to this pattern, with the added twist that she frames it in the nine months of her second pregnancy: the heroine who organizes her husband's spectacular escape from the Nazi prison is a loving wife and mother, five months pregnant. The book's plot is best summed up by its English title, *Outwitting the Gestapo*. The French title, more poetic, emphasizes the elated, larger-than-life aspect of the heroic experience: *Ils partiront dans l'ivresse*, "They Will Depart in Ecstasy." The author explains in her preface that this was the coded message transmitted by the BBC in February 1944, to signal the couple's airlift to London.

Ils partiront dans l'ivresse, published in the fall of 1984, became a bestseller, translated into many languages; and Lucie and Raymond Aubrac, in their seventies, became media stars. Featured on radio and television programs, in newspaper and magazine articles, in classrooms and learned conferences, the Aubracs were, throughout the 1980s and well into the 1990s, the country's favorite Resistance heroes. Lucie, tireless, went into schools to talk about her book and to inspire young people with the "spirit of resistance," past and future. Raymond, more reserved, recollected his interrogation sessions with Klaus Barbie when called upon by journalists or filmmakers; and he, too, wrote a memoir, *Où la mémoire s'attarde*, in fact a full-scale autobiography, which was published in 1996. Raymond Aubrac, an engineer and graduate of an elite *grande école*, had an important career after the war; he was named by de Gaulle as a Commissaire de la République in Marseille in 1945 and then occupied a series of influential positions as an engineer or consultant in France and abroad. Raymond spends relatively little space, in his book, on the episode with Barbie, but his version does not contradict Lucie's.[16]

Jean-Pierre Rioux, a well-known historian and specialist in the wartime period, reviewed Raymond Aubrac's autobiography glowingly in *Le Monde*, noting that the book would "play an important role in the history of Resistance testimonies." And he ended his review with a heartfelt homage: "There remains Raymond, sparkling with wicked wit, courageous in the extreme, likable as all hell. On his feet, always. With Lucie. And that alone matters. God, how we love those two!"[17] Rioux's exclamation reflects both the historian's appreciation and the 'ordinary' Frenchman's admiration of these two elderly figures (by now, they were well into their eighties). It also reflects what I am calling the desire for heroic aggrandizement in narrative—specifically, in narratives that possess collective significance. In collective terms, Lucie and Raymond Aubrac represented not only an ideal couple, still united after so many years, but also an ideal image of the French Resistance. The Resistance, in turn, represented what was best and most noble about France during the Vichy years—it embodied what de Gaulle called "la France éternelle."

The popular, collective appeal of the Aubracs' story is confirmed by the fact that it inspired not one but two film adaptations, both of them based on Lucie Aubrac's memoir and focusing on the woman-in-love-who-is-also-a-heroine. The 1992 film, *Boulevard des Hirondelles*, directed by Josée Yann, met with little reaction or success, perhaps because neither the actors nor the director were well known. Five years later, the version by the popular director Claude Berri, known for his large-scale adaptations of French classics like *Germinal*, elicited huge public commentary. Starring two famous actors, Carole Bouquet and Daniel Auteuil, as the heroic couple, Berri's *Lucie Aubrac* was panned almost universally by critics at its release in February 1997: too stereotypical, too focused on the love story, not accurate enough about the Resistance, altogether too "Hollywood," was the critical verdict.[18] Yet the film did well at the box office; in fact, in terms of tickets sold, it has been the most popular film about the Occupation in the past thirty-five years in France, outdoing Truffaut's *The Last Metro*, Malle's *Lacombe Lucien*, and even his *Au revoir les enfants*. It received the blessing of the French Ministry of Education, which featured it in publications intended for teachers, who took schoolchildren in droves.[19]

As if to prove that reality is rarely simple, it was during the very week that Berri released his hero-worshiping film that the Aubracs' name became attached to an "affair." They were accused, by a journalist who was about to release a book on the subject, of having falsified certain crucial aspects of their story. The long-forgotten insinuations of Barbie's lawyer, concerning Raymond Aubrac's role in Moulin's arrest, were suddenly revived. Just as France was getting ready for the Papon trial, which would once again point to the ignominies of Vichy toward the Jews, the Aubrac Affair churned up troubled memories of the Resistance.

The distinguished classicist Jean-Pierre Vernant (himself an active member of the Resistance) has spoken about possible conflicts or tensions among three kinds of memory as far as the Resistance is concerned: personal memory, social memory, and the memory of historians.[20] In fact, these categories are applicable to all events of collective significance, including most recently the American catastrophe of September 11. Personal memory is the memory of actual participants or witnesses of the event. Social or collective memory refers to the way the event is recalled and interpreted in a given society at a given time, as indicated by a wide range of public discourses, from official statements to works of art and literature. Historical memory, finally, refers to the specialized work accomplished by those who, trained in the historian's discipline, seek to distinguish public mythologies and illusions from documented facts. Vernant points out that all three kinds of memory are dynamic and contextual, continually reworked in light of present needs and interests; they are to be understood as part of an ongoing negotiation between past and present.

The mutual influences among these three kinds of memory have interested theorists for a long time, and continue to do so. Maurice Halbwachs, in his pioneering work on collective memory, showed that individual memory always takes place within—and is influenced by—a social framework, beginning with the family and moving out to larger groups and the community.[21] Historians rely on documents rather than on social memory. Yet, to the extent that historians are themselves individuals living in a specific setting, their work is inevitably influenced by collective categories; furthermore, as Hayden White has shown, the writing of history relies on patterns of narrative that shape the raw documentary material, thus establishing at least formal similarities between historical narratives and fictional ones.[22]

The overlappings as well as the potential conflicts among these three kinds of memory become especially evident concerning historical events with strong affective resonance, such as the Vichy regime and the Resistance in France. Where such events are concerned, the relations among historical research, collective representations, and personal testimony become increasingly tense. What makes the Aubrac Affair so interesting, aside from its specific content, is that it offers a complex illustration of such tensions.

Social Memory vs. Historical Memory: The Power of Legends

It is highly significant that the accusations against the Aubracs were timed to coincide with the release of Berri's film, *Lucie Aubrac*. Gérard Chauvy, whose book *Aubrac: Lyon, 1943* was to be released in early April, jumped the gun by publishing an article that listed the major accusations the week before the film's release.[23] The first time the words "Affaire Aubrac" appeared in print was in an article in the conservative daily *Le Figaro*, which criticized the film for "magnifying the legend of the Aubrac couple," and then went on to give a brief summary of Chauvy's forthcoming book; the latter thus appeared to be the historically accurate corrective to the "official legend" propagated by the film.[24] That was exactly the way Chauvy himself presented his book; in addition, he enlisted a former *résistant* to write a Preface, which also insisted on the priority of history over legend.[25]

As part of his painstaking investigation, Chauvy had combed through the *dossier d'instruction* (the criminal investigation file, assembled by an investigating magistrate, the *juge d'instruction*, in every criminal case) of the 1987 Barbie trial, as well as through the dossier of a second trial that never took place because of Barbie's death in 1991. Among some hitherto-unpublished documents, Chauvy found various depositions made by Raymond Aubrac between 1944 and 1990 concerning his two arrests in Lyon in 1943 and his time in prison from June 1943 until his escape in October. Some of these depositions, which Chauvy published in an appendix, contradict (or appear to contradict) each other about certain details and also contradict what Raymond and Lucie had written in their memoirs. In addition, the appendix included a notorious document that Barbie had placed into the dossier shortly before his death: the so-called "testament de Barbie," written in impeccable French and thoroughly researched, looking more like a legal brief than a personal narrative. In this fifty-page text, Barbie claimed—for the first time in all the years since 1944, during which he had made numerous depositions and given numerous published interviews—that Raymond Aubrac, aided by his wife Lucie, had been the betrayer of Jean Moulin.[26] The existence of this "testament" had been known since 1991, when it had occasioned a media flurry and a vigorous reaction by Raymond Aubrac.[27] But it had never been published before Chauvy's book. As any reading makes clear, the "testament," although signed by Barbie, was not written by him. Most likely, it was the work of Jacques Vergès, stating baldly what Vergès had only insinuated in his accusations against Aubrac seven years earlier.

Although Chauvy claims the status of dispassionate historian, his obvious animus against the Aubracs and his attempt to discredit every major aspect of their story place him squarely in the role of accuser.

Thus, even while recognizing that Barbie's "testament" is not to be trusted, he implies in the end that the document tells the truth. Through his minute examination of certain details deprived of larger context, and through his uncritical use of some documents combined with a "hypercritical" approach to others, Chauvy succeeds in creating—by insinuation and innuendo, not outright statement—an abject counternarrative to Lucie Aubrac's (and Claude Berri's) heroic one. Of course, one can ask: Is there absolutely nothing valid in Chauvy's demonstrations? What about the real inconsistencies in the Aubracs' statements? I will get to them shortly. For now, I want to emphasize the role that Chauvy's book played in the construction of social memory; in fact, it fostered a confusion between social memory and historical memory, even while claiming to "correct" the former by the latter.

Chauvy, as we have seen, defined his book as history opposed to legend, fact opposed to fantasy. Yet, he too offers a powerful fantasy and satisfies a narrative desire, one that is perhaps even stronger, in our time, than the other: It is the desire to unmask, to demystify—in a word, to dethrone what was previously extolled. True, the myth of "la France résistante" had been destroyed decades earlier; but individual *résistants*, and even the Resistance itself, reduced to a small but heroic minority, continued to be revered. Vergès's attempt in the early 1980s to discredit the Resistance had been successfully countered; the Aubracs had played a major role in that success, due to the popularity of Lucie Aubrac's memoir and their frequent appearances on radio and television, in classrooms, and at public conferences, as well as to their charismatic personalities (especially Lucie's, by all accounts). Now, Chauvy's book insinuated a different story, a story of abjection: Raymond Aubrac betraying his comrades as early as his first arrest in March 1943, followed by the betrayal of Moulin in June. Chauvy offers no documentary proof for this story, as all the historians who have weighed in on his book agree.[28] Indeed, he does not even tell the story, contenting himself with suggesting it by means of conjectures and innuendos. The Aubracs sued him and his publisher for libel, and won.[29] But a court judgment is no protection against popular fantasy.

The problem is that the abject scenario is appealing: It not only reverses the heroic plot, but also complicates the character of the protagonists. The Aubracs suddenly become people with secrets to hide, people who may have been living a lie for fifty years, so much more interesting than a straightforward hero to a postmodern sensibility! It is not an accident, I think, that Jean-Luc Godard, in his 2001 film *Éloge de l'amour [In Praise of Love]*, features an old couple of *résistants* of whom we are told that the husband betrayed his own wife and caused her to be deported during the war—Godard, the antithesis of a popular filmmaker, would obviously prefer the abject scenario to Berri's heroic one. Somewhat shockingly, he goes so far as to report (via the character of the granddaughter) that the couple's real name is Samuel, different from the name they have been using since the war.[30] Raymond Aubrac's given name was Raymond Samuel (he is Jewish); Aubrac is his Resistance pseudonym, which he legally adopted for his family after the war. In Godard's film, the couple's current name is Bayard, as if to underline their fictional status (they are "not the Aubracs"). But the insertion of Raymond Aubrac's real given name into a fictional representation in the abject mode (Bayard betrayed his wife during the war) creates a troubling amalgam, reminiscent of the innuendos in Chauvy's book. Indeed, one could suggest that Godard's amalgam reflects a change in collective representation or social memory, rendered possible by those very innuendos. What was purportedly history as a "corrective" to the heroic legend of social memory has become the vehicle for another kind of social memory, another kind of legend.

The desire to replace heroism with abjection is not limited to modern (or postmodern) times. Pierre Vidal-Naquet has shown that the social tendency to "deheroize" even the greatest heroes has existed since antiquity.[31] Nevertheless, I think a strong case can be made that this tendency has become increasingly dominant. In literature as in life, we tend to be suspicious of heroes. Chauvy's book capitalized on that suspicion, as have a number of other recent books by journalist-historians who have taken Jean Moulin himself as their target; there have been numerous "affaires Jean Moulin" since Frenay published his accusations of "crypto-communism." According to one recent book, Moulin, immortalized as de Gaulle's martyred representative, contacted an American agent in a maneuver against de Gaulle before his arrest! The historian Annette Wieviorka, reviewing the book in *Le Monde*, deplored the public's taste for "affairs" and "secrets," which risked reducing the Resistance to no more than "a series of detective stories."[32]

Chauvy's book provoked a huge polemic in the press. Many journalists and historians rushed to the Aubracs' defense; others, even while condemning Chauvy's methods, were troubled by some of the contradictions he had unearthed and asked the Aubracs for explanation.[33] Furthermore, as in all "affairs" concerning collective events, the stakes not only involved a search for historical truth, but were also political. The Aubracs had never hidden the fact that they had lifelong left-wing sympathies; it is clear from Raymond Aubrac's autobiography that they were for a long time very close to the Communist Party, even if they never formally joined. In 1997, the intellectual mood in France was largely anticommunist; fierce debates were being waged, even among politically liberal intellectuals, over whether communism had been as great an evil of the twentieth century as fascism and Nazism, or even a worse one. The way people lined up, in defense of the Aubracs or in suspicion of them, was at least partly influenced by their position in the debates over communism.[34] Another political factor was the imminence of the Papon trial. Since official French collaboration with the Nazis in the persecution of Jews would be the focus of that trial, any suggestion of abject behavior during the war by a Jewish *résistant*—whose parents, moreover, were deported and murdered in Auschwitz, as Raymond Aubrac's were—necessarily had a political resonance.

What may we conclude from all this about the relation between historical memory and social memory? First, that it becomes increasingly difficult to draw the dividing line when works of history become immediately transformed into vehicles of public scandal, and even more difficult when works claiming to seek "historical truth" become themselves purveyors of legend—albeit a different kind of legend. Second, that the writing of history is deeply implicated in shaping social memory, as well as being shaped by it. The fact that Gérard Chauvy's book is not "responsible" history merely emphasizes this point, which even historians who have greater respect for historical objectivity and responsibility can take to heart.

But what about the contradictions unearthed by Chauvy? This question brings us to the next item of interest in the Aubrac affair: the confrontation between historians and memoirists, and the relation between historical and personal memory.

Historical Memory vs. Personal Memory:
The Power of the Plausible

Historians of the World War II and the Occupation have tremendous popular prestige in France today and are constantly solicited as "experts" by the media. They were also called as expert witnesses in the highly publicized trials for crimes against humanity, notably in the Papon trial. It was no doubt because of this prestige that Raymond Aubrac requested, soon after Chauvy's book appeared, that a group of distinguished historians meet with him and his wife to discuss the accusations. Aubrac fully expected to be "exonerated" at such a meeting of all suspicion that he had been involved in the betrayal of Jean Moulin: "I have been calumnied, and I want to respond to the calumny."[35] In 1991, at the time the "testament de Barbie" first surfaced, he had requested a similar meeting at the Institut d'Histoire du Temps Présent, a research institute with which a number of distinguished historians of World War II and the Occupation have been affiliated. But that meeting never took place.[36]

This time, a day-long meeting took place in the offices of the daily *Libération* on May 17, 1997. Participating in the discussion were five well-known historians affiliated with the IHTP, specialists in World War II and the Occupation: Henry Rousso, Jean-Pierre Azéma, François Bédarida, Laurent Douzou, and Dominique Veillon; the former *résistant* and admired biographer of Jean Moulin, Daniel Cordier; and two other distinguished scholars who were there as personal friends of the Aubracs, Maurice Agulhon and J.-P. Vernant. All of the participants knew the Aubracs personally. Also present, though not taking part in the discussion, were two journalists from the paper, Béatrice Vallaeys and Antoine de Gaudemar.

From almost every point of view, the meeting was a failure. The historians, even while castigating Chauvy's animosity and lack of adequate historical method, and even while affirming that his allegations of betrayal were not supported by any documentary evidence, declared at the end of the day that "areas of shadow" existed in the Aubracs' version of the story. Instead of an exoneration, the *Libération* roundtable thus produced only further suspicion and increasing animosity among the participants. The discussion was taped, and a slightly edited version was published in July.[37] Impassioned commentaries on the event followed over a period of several weeks, published in *Libération*, *Le Monde*, and other papers—first by all the participants, including the Aubracs, then by other historians who responded to the published transcript, often extremely critically. A large number of ordinary readers also gave their opinion. Three years later, the *Libération* roundtable was still the subject of heated discussions: In summer 2000 the legal journal *Justice* published two lengthy critical analyses of the proceedings by a jurist and a sociologist, followed by responses from the participating historians.[38]

What was the crux of the criticisms of the roundtable? First, critics deplored the use of a daily newspaper for an attempt to arrive at historical truth; a roundtable that lasts a whole day is neither an interview nor a scholarly inquiry and can only lead to confusion, in addition to the pressure and negative effects of "mediatization." This confusion between journalism and scholarship would be another version, then, of a negative overlap between historical memory and social memory. The second criticism concerned the historians' mode of questioning the Aubracs, which gradually turned into an interrogation. The historians, according to this view, had breached the ethics as well as the methodology of historical research. The noted historian François Prost wrote in a much-cited article in *Le Monde*, "The historian must examine all hypotheses and there are no taboos for him . . . But he does not have the right to formulate hypotheses without foundation."[39] Prost was referring to a particularly painful moment in the discussion, toward the end of the afternoon (p. XXI), when Daniel Cordier, soon followed by François Bédarida, voiced the "hypothesis" that Lucie Aubrac had been followed by Barbie's men after her visits to the Gestapo pretending to be Raymond's pregnant girlfriend, and that that may have lead to the arrest of Raymond's parents a month later (they were deported and died in Auschwitz). In formulating their hypothesis, according to Prost, the historians had "crossed the yellow line." Or, in our terms, they had transgressed a line between historical memory and personal memory.

With that in mind, I want now to look closely at the published transcript of the roundtable, reading it as a dramatic text; it even has the structure of a classical drama, with five chapters/acts and an introduction and epilogue.[40] What were the interpretive twists and the interpersonal dynamics that led to the negative dénouement? And how can that question illuminate the role of narrative desire, both in the writing of history and in the writing of personal memory or testimony?

Testimony, Fiction, History

Paul Ricoeur has noted, in his book *La mémoire, l'histoire, l'oubli*, that the activity of testifying, whether orally or in writing, is linked to both narrating and promising.[41] The witness narrates what he or she has experienced, and promises that the account is true to the best of her or his knowledge. Ricoeur also notes that a historian who manifests suspicion toward a given testimony (and by implication, toward a witness) does not betray the historian's vocation—on the contrary, a certain kind of suspicion is necessary to historical research: "We must rely on testimony and on the critique of testimony to accredit the historian's representation of the past" (364). By "historian's representation" [*représentation historienne*], Ricoeur means an account as faithful as possible of something that "once was" but is no longer (367). The ontological status of something that "once was" distinguishes the historical past from an imagined or fictional past. Even though we can never recapture the historical past in its absolute "truth," the fact that it *once was* confers a special status on the historian's representation of a past event. It follows that for the historian, the value of a written or recorded testimony—a first-person narrative that purports to tell what the narrator actually lived through—is determined above all, and essentially, by its veracity. How can one determine the veracity of a testimony? Through the confirmation of the account by other documents in the best case, through the coherence and explicative power of the narrative, and/or through the personal reliability of the witness. Reliability is confirmed both by the "character" of the witness and by the fact that his or her account does not vary over time. Ricoeur and other theorists of testimony (whom he cites) call this invariance the principle of reiteration: "The reliable witness is one who can maintain his testimony over time" (206).

What did the historians do at the *Libération* roundtable? Chauvy had supplied them with documents they had not seen until then—not the fraudulent "testament de Barbie," but genuine transcripts of depositions made by Raymond Aubrac between 1944 and 1972, usually in the context of judicial proceedings (trials of René Hardy and Klaus Barbie). The historians compared these various depositions, and also compared them to the memoirs published by the Aubracs in 1984 (Lucie) and 1996 (Raymond). They noted some contradictions, and they charged ahead. Critics blamed them for acting like judges, and that did in fact become a problem, but it is worth noting that judges— especially the *juges d'instruction* of French legal proceedings, who gather evidence and question witnesses in preparation for a trial—and historians have some traits in common, as well as differences. Ricoeur points out similarities between the search for judicial proof and the search for historical proof: "Both accord priority to questioning, to the play of the imagination with possibilities; both make an effort to detect contradictions, inconsistencies, implausibilities . . . In that regard, the judge and the historian are . . . equally masters in the art of suspicion" (417).

Of course, the judge and the historian work with different time frames and different aims. The confusion between these two roles in the roundtable became flagrant (as the critics noted) because the historians were confronting not only documents but persons. The Aubracs were counting on the fact that they were known *in any case*, personally and publicly, to be honorable people, from which it followed that they were reliable witnesses. The problem occurred because the historians, even while repeatedly affirming the witnesses' honorability (sincerely, it must be assumed), allowed their professional "suspicion" to prevail. In the process of confronting not the written texts but the witnesses themselves, they moved into the role of judge and even of prosecutor, and ended up putting the witnesses' reliability as a whole into question. Thus, quite late in the day, in the fourth "act" of the drama (the chapter titled "Le rapport du commissaire Porte"), they began to express doubt about a key episode of the story told by Lucie Aubrac in her book. How, they asked, could she enter several times, without being stopped, into the headquarters of the Gestapo (to arrange the fake marriage with Raymond)? "Can one really say that one could enter the Gestapo like a windmill?" asked Jean-Pierre Azéma. "It is hard to believe that in Lyon one could come and go freely, without being checked, in the headquarters of the Gestapo," added François Bédarida. And Henry Rousso: "During all those visits . . . , they never at any time had knowledge of who you were?" (p. XV).

Lucie Aubrac could only repeat that indeed, that is how it was, that no one ever asked her for proof of identity, just as later she would repeat that she had not been followed after her visits. But it seems clear that the historians were not convinced.

Raymond Aubrac was conscious of that fact, for at that point he intervened: "When the 'testament de Barbie' was composed, the author took advantage of all those aspects of our adventure that are hard to believe in order to construct the accusation of betrayal. At this moment we are treading on the terrain of Gérard Chauvy" (p. XVI). This exasperated comment, which sounds like an accusation ("You are like Chauvy!") may have been somewhat unjust, but it was not wholly unjustified. For, paradoxically, the historians would embark, *in the name of historical truth*, on the quest for counternarratives that appeared to them more plausible and logical than the narrative told by Lucie. The hypothesis that Lucie was followed, leading to the arrest of Raymond's parents, was the culminating example (in the last act, Chapter 5); but already in the morning, well before Raymond's exasperated comment, we can see three of the questioners trying to find a more "plausible" version of an episode told by Lucie in her book, describing her visit to the prosecutor Ducasse in May 1943 to obtain Raymond's release from prison after his first arrest by French police. The historians all agree that it was a foolhardy act, and so does she; but in her version, the foolhardy act was effective: she threatened Ducasse with reprisals by the Resistance, whereupon he ordered Raymond's release. The historians find this explanation implausible and offer various alternatives. Henri Rousso proposes "a simpler hypothesis. Prosecutor Ducasse . . . did not really take you seriously. Luckily for you and especially for Raymond Aubrac, he believed neither that he was holding 'an envoy of General de Gaulle' nor that he might be personally threatened." To which Lucie Aubrac replies: "I think he got scared." But her old friend Vernant intervenes: "Not I. Things are more complicated," and he launches into an explanation of the motives of the French police in 1943! (p. X).

It is a curious, one could almost say a charmingly comic moment, as the historians and the witness spar over the meaning of the event and even over what actually happened. One can see here an instance of the "play with the imagination of possibilities" that Ricoeur referred to as part of the historian's activity. And one can also see the witness defending her own account, with some irritation at being challenged, but without animosity. No position definitively prevails, and the mood remains cordial.

Later, however, the mood worsens. Noticing the obvious (and increasing) skepticism of the historians, Raymond Aubrac exclaims that they are treading on the terrain of Gérard Chauvy. And Lucie makes an unexpected admission that radically alters the debate; furious at the historians' questioning, she says to François Bédarida, "I am not a researcher at the IHTP. I am a woman who wrote her book because people were starting, with Vergès, to attack the Resistance. . . . I did not write a history book with a capital H, but a book in which I told the story of a pregnancy and a life" (p. XVI). At this, the historians jump. Henry Rousso: "Ever since I started to work on this period, I have always heard *résistants*, and you in particular, repeating constantly: 'Listen to our testimonies.' . . . Now how are we to react when you tell us that we cannot do that because you 'arranged' some details?" Lucie Aubrac replies: "You are right."

Next, it's Daniel Cordier's turn: "You wrote an exciting adventure novel that you rashly presented as your memories. I consider that slippage shocking." Cordier explains why: Famous *résistants* speak for "all the unknown members of the Resistance," and they have the duty to tell the truth. "You have a duty to remember that is the duty of a historian" (p. XVI).

It is a fascinating moment. Does a memoir that "arranges" some details become, by virtue of that fact, a novel? And if so, is it a matter of *some* details only, or do all details have the same importance? If details do not all have the same importance—if some can be "arranged" without transgressing the genre of the memoir—how is one to decide at which point the balance shifts and the memoir becomes a novel? Lucie Aubrac does not consider her memoir a novel. And yet it is certain that some of the details she recounts, including some nontrivial ones, are false, and that she knew them to be so when she wrote her book—which does not mean that she consciously intended to deceive the reader.[42] She states right at the beginning of the round-table: "I am now accused of having made some errors in dates in a book that I dictated in four months and that students in middle school and high school read and study. It must be recalled why I wrote that little book. It was because Jacques Vergès was starting to attack us. Of course, my book is not the work of a historian, but of a teacher, a pedagogue. My life as a teacher is that of an activist, it's not a life that insists on searching for exact times, names, or dates" (p. VII). Personally, I have some problem with the notion implied by this statement: that the work of a teacher or pedagogue—which consists, according to Lucie Aubrac, of "making things come to life"—requires that one should overlook the difference, in a historical narrative, between factual elements and invented ones. But I understand that for Lucie Aubrac, what matters are the values associated with the Resistance, values that she feels she transmitted in her book.

Still, the question must be asked: Under what circumstances and for what reasons does the author of a historical testimony (for it is as a historical testimony that Lucie Aubrac's book is presented and read and studied in schools) feel authorized to recount things that she knows (and I am willing to accord all the necessary ambiguity to that verb) to be inaccurate? A somewhat different version of this question will come up again in Chapter 5, relative to the Buchenwald memoirs of Jorge Semprun. Without anticipating too much on that discussion, I will remark that one major difference between Lucie Aubrac's memoir and Semprun's works is that he makes self-conscious literary use of the failures—and even of the artistic falsifications—of memory, often making them the very subject of his writing, whereas in her case the lapses and inaccuracies showed up only through examination from the outside. Another, perhaps even more important difference, resides not in the works themselves but in the interpretive and genre context in which they are being discussed.

Narrative Desire

We arrive here at the most problematic aspect of the *Libération* roundtable, and more generally of the "Aubrac Affair." For independently of the procedure, which was rightfully criticized, the historians at the meeting pointed to genuine inconsistencies in the various accounts of the Aubracs' adventure given by them since 1944. I believe that one must be able to say this, without being accused of wanting to besmirch the Resistance; but one must also be able to say it without wishing to put into doubt the courage and honorability of two aged *résistants*.

The need to balance respect for the witness with the pursuit of historical truth is, as Henry Rousso pointed out in a book published not long after the roundtable, the difficult task of any historian whose subject is the "history of the present."[43] In the case of the roundtable, this led him to a suspension of judgment: "In the absence of other elements, and considering the replies of the witness [Raymond Aubrac] who declared that he could not explain [the contradictions], I forbade myself to draw any conclusion."[44] Jean-Pierre Azéma was somewhat harsher: he maintained, in an article published even before the transcript of the roundtable, that the Aubracs' story contained "zones of shadow" that "for reasons known only to him, Raymond Aubrac does not intend to clear up."[45] As for Daniel Cordier, he concluded in good positivist fashion that "new discoveries will have to be made in the archives in order to know the replies" to the unresolved questions concerning Raymond Aubrac.[46]

Personally, I am interested in the psychological as well as the literary and historical implications of these inconsistencies—and of one in particular, to which the historians returned again and again during the roundtable. It concerns the question of what Klaus Barbie knew about Raymond Aubrac's identity after his arrest at Caluire. Comparing Aubrac's numerous statements between 1944 and 1996, the historians noted that he gave varying answers to that question. We must recall that "Aubrac" was a pseudonym, designating a highly placed member of the Secret Army, the newly formed military wing of the interior Resistance. The Germans knew the name and the role, since they had captured an organigram of the Secret Army in an earlier operation. Like all members of the Resistance, Raymond, whose real name was Raymond Samuel, carried false papers with other names—Vallet when he was arrested in March, Ermelin in June. Soon after his arrest in June, Barbie recognized "Ermelin" as Vallet, the man he had questioned months earlier.[47] But did Barbie also know that Ermelin/Vallet was Aubrac, a leader of the Secret Army?

By all indications, the answer is yes. Raymond stated it clearly in his first "debriefing" in London in February 1944 ("I was obliged to admit that I was Aubrac when they identified me as Vallet . . ."),[48] and he reconfirmed it during the *Libération* roundtable (p. XIV). (It is thought that one of the other men arrested at Caluire, Henry Aubry, revealed both Moulin's identity and Aubrac's under torture). But according to the documents published by Chauvy, Raymond did not always say the same thing, and in particular, he did not say it in his 1996 autobiography. On the contrary, he affirmed in the book (at least, that is what one concludes on a first reading) that Barbie had "never gone beyond" his identity as Vallet: "Each time my name was called for a confrontation with Barbie, . . . I feared that my true role had been discovered, my identity exposed. In that case, all would have been lost."[49] After the roundtable, and until the present day, Raymond Aubrac has explained that he did not deny in his book that Barbie knew he was Aubrac. When he wrote that Barbie did not know his "true identity," he was referring to his identity as Raymond Samuel. "When I repeat several times that my identity was not discovered I'm thinking of Samuel," he said in a published interview after the roundtable.[50]

Here we face a question of textual analysis, if ever there was one: When Raymond Aubrac writes that he feared his "true role" and "identity" had been discovered, is he referring to Aubrac or to Samuel? All the historians at the roundtable pointed out that while "identity" could refer to Samuel, "role" designated a role in the Resistance and could therefore only refer to Aubrac. Hence their repeated question: Why did you sometimes say that Barbie knew you were Aubrac, and at other times that he did not? In fact, as Daniel Cordier pointed out after analyzing the documents (most of them furnished by Chauvy), Aubrac's various statements fell into three categories, not two (pp. XVII–XVIII). Below is a summary of Cordier's analysis at the *Libération* round table, to which I have added a few details based on my own subsequent research:

1. *Affirmation*—Raymond states that Barbie recognized him as Vallet and as Aubrac: February 1944 (debriefing in London); April 1948 (*dossier d'instruction* for second trial of René Hardy); 1950 (testimony in court at Hardy's second trial); and 1992 (*dossier d'instruction* for second trial of Klaus Barbie, which never took place).

2. *Omission*, or I would say *ellipsis*—Raymond states that Barbie recognized him as Vallet, without adding anything more (he was not asked): June 1944 (debriefing in Algiers); 1983 (preliminary investigation, Barbie trial); 1987 (testimony in court, Barbie trial—not cited by Cordier);[51] one could also cite here Lucie Aubrac's version in 1984.[52]

3. *Contradiction*, or I would say *denial*—Raymond states that Barbie

did not recognize him as Aubrac: 1996 (*Où la mémoire s'attarde*—
but note that Raymond Aubrac refuses this reading); January
1997, television program, "La marche du siècle," where the
statement is clear and unambiguous—not cited by Cordier. I
will return to it.

Cordier is ready to excuse what he calls the omissions, but he feels
that Raymond Aubrac's autobiography of 1996 contains a "horrendous
contradiction." And he adds: "It intrigued me all the more because
your Memoirs are a carefully thought-out and edited text, specifically
destined for the public, where you weighed every word and phrase,
since it represents the version you are bequeathing to history"
(p. XVIII). Cordier is stunned at what he considers to be dissimulation
on Aubrac's part: "For it is evident to all those who seek the truth that
there is a black hole there" (p. XIX). At that moment, Raymond Aubrac can offer no explanation in reply; he simply acknowledges that
his testimonies over the years have varied. A few weeks later, however,
in his published commentary on the roundtable, he will state that he
has never denied—either in his 1996 autobiography or earlier—that
Barbie knew he was Aubrac.[53]

A curious moment, when the author of a text and his readers disa-
gree over the meaning of a sentence! But why all the fuss, one might
ask? Why parse a text with no claim to literary status as if it were a
page of Proust or a sonnet by Baudelaire? The answer is not as simple
as one might think. To be sure, personal reliability and historical truth
were at stake—matters of importance both for the historians and for
the witness. But there was more. If the historians (not only Cordier,
but Rousso, Bédarida, and Azéma) returned repeatedly to the question
of "what Barbie knew," it was because they were trying to explain what
they considered a mystery: Why, alone of all those arrested with
Moulin, was Raymond Aubrac not transferred to Paris after his first
interrogations? (Besides Moulin, two of the men captured at Caluire
died in deportation). Why was he left to vegetate in his cell for
months, with no further action? According to the historians' criteria
of plausibility and narrative coherence, it was impossible that Barbie
knew he had "Aubrac" *and* that he left him alone, practically forgetting
him, as he did. As François Bédarida put it: "According to whether
it's yes or no, everything changes. For if you are François Vallet, it's

really a very small matter. . . . But the moment you are identified as Aubrac, you become a very big catch" (p. XVIII). In fact, Barbie did know he had Aubrac—and yet, Raymond Aubrac remained in prison for several months (he had been condemned to death, he recounts in his book) without being otherwise disturbed. "Area of shadow." Black hole.

The aim and duty of historians is to search for the truest version of past events—of what "once was," as Ricoeur said. One way to accomplish this is by the construction of coherent narratives that conform to a logic of plausibility and cause and effect, which guarantees that history *makes sense*. The historians' persistent questioning of the witnesses at the roundtable, whether on grounds of plausibility ("Could one really enter the Gestapo without being checked?") or on those of cause and effect ("If Barbie knew, why did he not act differently?") indicates the power of that narrative desire.

And not surprisingly, that desire is shared by the witnesses themselves. Whence the fascinating phenomenon whereby the person who recounts his or her past experience feels obliged to provide the plausible version, even while knowing (or "knowing") that it does not fully correspond to the facts. This is somewhat similar to what psychoanalysts call rationalization (providing plausible motives or explanations for actions whose real motives remain hidden), except that in this case it is the events themselves, not their motives, that become "smoothed over" in the telling. And on some level, the process occurs consciously, although—as I have tried to suggest by the quotation marks around "knowing"—the exact degree of consciousness may be hard to determine. Suppose that the facts appear incomprehensible, or suppose that one is called on to reply to an accusation that provides a more "plausible" version than what actually happened, as far as one knows or recalls. Such circumstances may explain why a historical witness might feel authorized to "arrange" certain facts without consciously intending to deceive. In a context of accusation, the accused person feels obliged to furnish a logical version of past actions if the truth appears too illogical—or if he or she feels that others will consider it so. Lucie Aubrac, seeing her husband (and by extension, herself) accused by Barbie's lawyer in 1984, wrote a book in which she implied that Barbie never knew him as "Aubrac."[54] Raymond Aubrac, who in 1992 told the truth unambiguously in a deposition before the *juge d'instruction* of the second Barbie trial, could have (and, according to a historian's logic, should have) done the same in his autobiography, which he was starting to write at the time. He would thereby have "corrected" the ambiguity of Lucie's account. Instead, he too opted for ambiguity, as the argument over the meaning of some sentences in his book makes clear. And a few months after the publication of his book, just a few weeks before the explosion of the Aubrac Affair, he stated unambiguously, to a public of *lycée* students filmed by television cameras at the Center for the History of the Resistance and Deportation in Lyon: "Neither Vallet nor Ermelin was recognized as Aubrac. Otherwise, all would have been lost." ["Ni Vallet ni Ermelin n'ont été reconnus comme Aubrac. Autrement, tout aurait été perdu"].[55] The occasion was a live program in January 1997, featuring Lucie and Raymond Aubrac and Elie Wiesel, around the theme "transmission of memory to young people." Raymond Aubrac stated the above sentence (or variants) three times, in response to questions by the journalist Ladislas de Hoyos, who had written a book about Barbie in the 1980s.

How can one explain this blatant denial? The simplest explanation would be that Raymond Aubrac has something to hide, because he is guilty—this is the counter-legend of abjection, all too tempting and harmful. A more complex explanation, albeit one that remained quite unsympathetic to the witness, was offered by Daniel Cordier at the *Libération* roundtable: According to this hypothesis, Raymond Aubrac told the truth in situations unknown to the public (*dossiers d'instruction*, which are never published, testimony at the forgotten trial of René Hardy), but wanted to "bequeath to history" a different version (p. XVIII). (Cordier was referring to Raymond's book, not to the January 1997 television program, which never came up in the discussion.) This explanation is plausible, but it implies a conscious decision on Raymond Aubrac's part to deceive the public. And even if it were correct, it would not answer the main question: *Why* was it necessary, according to Raymond Aubrac, to make people think that Barbie did not know he was "Aubrac"?

In my opinion, what Raymond's wavering testimony and outright denial indicate is not that he has something to hide, and even less that he is guilty of betraying Jean Moulin; rather, it indicates that he labors under the same logic of plausibility and cause and effect as the historians: "Otherwise, all would have been lost." Here is a case, furthermore, where personal memory falls victim to the pressure of media celebrity. In the fall of 1996, when Raymond Aubrac published his book, he and his wife were widely known and respected, and had become—with their willing participation, but also by a momentum of its own—quasi-legendary figures. That was even more the case in January 1997, only a few weeks before the release of Claude Berri's "heroic" film. Add to that the pressure of a live television broadcast, in a solemn place (museum of the Resistance and Deportation, once the headquarters of the Gestapo where many had been tortured) on a solemn occasion (the theme of the program was "the duty to remember"): Is it surprising that, in front of a public of admiring adolescents, facing a journalist whose questions were becoming more and more pressing, the octogenerian Raymond Aubrac could not "remember" a story that would include both the fact that Barbie knew he was Aubrac and the fact that he was not deported? "Because if he had, all would have been lost." But what if reality does not follow the logic of plausibility? What if reality is not coherent?

Obviously, one cannot blame historians for seeking to construct, if not coherent stories, at least coherent explanations. Nor can one blame individual witnesses for allowing their desire for coherence to shape their memories. In any case, distributing blame has not been the aim of this analysis. Serge Klarsfeld, who has studied in intense detail all of Barbie's activities in Lyon, offered an explanation, after the publication of the roundtable, for why Raymond Aubrac was allowed to vegetate in Lyon until his escape in October: Barbie was absent from Lyon between mid-July and December 1943, and the Germans in Paris were preoccupied with more important business during that time.[56] Jean-Pierre Azéma, who was present at the roundtable and has written a great deal about the affair, accepted Klarsfeld's explanation about Barbie, but contested his explanation regarding the Germans in Paris.[57] Maybe one day it will all make sense, at least for historians. Meanwhile, from a literary and cultural perspective, the Aubrac Affair continues to fascinate because it points up the problematic relations between public and private memory, and between history and fantasy in the construction of both an individual and a collective past.

✣ 3

Commemorating the Illustrious Dead

JEAN MOULIN AND ANDRÉ MALRAUX

*T*HE NAMES OF Jean Moulin and André Malraux are firmly linked in French public memory, just as they rest literally side by side in Crypt Number VI of the Panthéon at the end of the rue Soufflot in the Latin Quarter of Paris. In this chapter I want to explore the Moulin-Malraux connection in the context of the politics of national memory in France and in the context of personal memory as well, for the figure of Moulin (not the man himself, but what he stood for) plays a significant role in Malraux's important autobiographical work, the *Antimémoires*, published in 1967.

Moulin's remains were transferred to the repository of the nation's illustrious dead in a solemn ceremony on December 19, 1964. It was Malraux who, as de Gaulle's Minister of Culture, delivered the funeral oration on the steps of the Panthéon. Since then, that grand piece of oratory, celebrating the Resistance hero tortured to death by the Gestapo, has been quoted on innumerable occasions when the name of Moulin or the heroism of the Resistance is invoked. Typical in this respect is the thirty-minute documentary film on Moulin's life produced by the Musée Jean Moulin in Paris, *Sur les pas de Jean Moulin [In the Footsteps of Jean Moulin]*. After the opening credits, above which appear a series of photographs of Moulin (including the iconic photo of him in fedora and scarf) the first words we hear are those of Jean Moulin when he was Préfet of the Department of Eure et Loire, in a speech delivered in May 1939 extolling the virtues of loyalty to one's country; the next words on the sound track, above a shot of the Panthéon, are those of André Malraux: "Entre ici, Jean Moulin, avec ton terrible cortège" ["Enter here, Jean Moulin, with your fearsome procession"]. The camera then cuts to Moulin's coffin draped in the flag, in front of which stands Malraux. As he continues with his speech, which is excerpted to its flourishing final sentences, the camera pans over the crowd, stopping on the way on the figures of General de Gaulle and his Prime Minister Georges Pompidou. Only after Malraux has finished and stepped down from the podium does the title of the documentary come on the screen: Malraux's face and Moulin's name succeed each other in the frame.[1]

On November 23, 1996, almost thirty-two years after that solemn ceremony and twenty years after his own death, Malraux himself lay in the casket on the steps of the Panthéon, only the fifth writer to enter there (after Voltaire, Rousseau, Hugo, and Zola). Delivering the eulogies were the former *résistant* and radio voice of Free France Maurice Schumann, and the President of the Republic Jacques Chirac. Both of them recalled in their speeches on that November evening Malraux's link to Moulin. Just as in 1964 all the newspapers had carried stories about the ceremony for Moulin, with long excerpts from Malraux's oration, so in 1996 every paper from the conservative *Le Figaro* to the Communist *L'Humanité*, along with *Libération*, *Le Monde*, the Catholic daily *La Croix*, and the popular *Journal de Dimanche*, carried voluminous dossiers on Malraux.[2] Unfailingly, they mentioned his 1964 funeral oration for Moulin, as well as, of course, all of Malraux's other claims to fame: his novels and works on art, his autobiographical writings, his activism during the 1930s, his courageous participation in the Spanish Civil War, his command of a Free French army brigade (the Brigade Alsace-Lorraine) in 1944, and his years as de Gaulle's Minister of Culture. A cartoon in *Le Figaro* of November 25, appearing above the text of Chirac's speech and the account of the ceremonies, summed it all up. Towering above the Panthéon, the fedora-clad figure of Jean Moulin, his throat wrapped in his eternal scarf, addresses an aging Malraux below, his eternal cigarette dangling from his lips: "Your turn to enter here, André Malraux."

The historian Laurent Douzou has claimed, more than half-seriously, that Malraux's "pantheonization" of 1996 was the direct result of his funeral oration thirty-two years earlier: "In effect, what designated Malraux [for pantheonization] was his discourse of December 19, 1964, at least as much as his battles for freedom and his writings. The ceremony of November 23, 1996 can doubtless be interpreted largely as a commemoration of commemoration. What was being celebrated was Malraux celebrating Moulin."[3] For Douzou, this "commemoration of commemoration" is a sign of the "vigor of the Resistance" in French national memory.

Political Uses of the Illustrious Dead: 1964/1996

As many analysts have noted, public ceremonies of commemoration always involve a certain instrumentalization of memory, an interpretation of the past in light of current political goals.[4] The transfer of Jean Moulin's ashes to the Panthéon in 1964 was a highly political act by the de Gaulle government, designed to promote its particular view of France's wartime past; and also designed to reintegrate a figure who had become an emblem of the anti-Gaullist left into the Gaullist ranks. At the time of his death in 1943, Moulin was closely identified with de Gaulle as leader of the Free French, designated as the General's representative to the Resistance groups inside France. By 1964, however, he had become the icon of the Club Jean Moulin, which had been founded in 1958 specifically in opposition to de Gaulle as President of the Fifth Republic.[5] As Henry Rousso recalls in his analysis of the 1964 ceremony, the original proposal to transfer Moulin's remains to the Panthéon came from a member of the opposition, a Socialist deputy from Moulin's home department of l'Hérault in southwestern France. De Gaulle appropriated this project by issuing a Presidential decree for the transfer, rather than having it discussed and voted on by the National Assembly. The careful choreography of the ceremony, including the final parade by the military honor guard as well as the choice of Malraux to deliver the funeral oration, guaranteed that Moulin's loyalty to de Gaulle would be properly emphasized; the honor guard was positioned in such a way that when it saluted Moulin's casket, it would also be saluting de Gaulle.[6]

As concerns the wartime past, Rousso speaks of a veritable "hijacking of memory" [(détournement de mémoire)] by de Gaulle, who sought to forge an "official memory in keeping with the country's renewed 'grandeur' " (p. 101). As we saw in Chapter 1, from the Liberation on, de Gaulle had advanced a "unanimist" or what is often called a "résistancialiste" view that downplayed ideological divisions in the country (whether within the Resistance itself or, more seriously, between supporters and opponents of the Vichy regime) and claimed that "all of France" had resisted the enemy. Now, under de Gaulle's presidency and France's "renewed grandeur," this view could be reinforced: The early years of the Fifth Republic were the highpoint of what Rousso calls the period of "repression" of the Vichy past.

Jean Moulin, a martyr of the Resistance, had all the necessary qualities of a unifying symbol. Although a devoted loyalist of de Gaulle during the war, he had a left-wing past and could thus represent both sides of the political spectrum: He had been *chef de cabinet* of Pierre Cot, the Minister of Aviation during the Popular Front government, and was dismissed in November 1940 by the Vichy government from his post as Préfet because he refused to cooperate with the Nazis.[7] Furthermore, in his double role as unifier of Resistance groups within France and as de Gaulle's envoy from London, he could represent both the external and the internal Resistance—in Laurent Douzou's pithy formulation, he was both an "homme de Londres" and an "homme de l'ombre," a man representing both "London" (de Gaulle) and "the shadows" (the internal Resistance).[8] Before his arrest by Klaus Barbie on June 21, 1943, Moulin had accomplished the feat of bringing wildly divergent groups together under the umbrella of the Conseil National de la Résistance. But no doubt his greatest virtue, from de Gaulle's point of view, was that he was dead, unable to change his mind or his loyalties. Unlike some former *résistants* who had become de Gaulle's outspoken opponents (both on the right and on the left), Moulin could forever be seen as the General's man.

All of this was beautifully brought out in Malraux's eulogy on the steps of the Panthéon. Moulin the unifier and organizer (Malraux calls him the "Carnot de la Résistance," referring to the French Revolutionary leader Lazare Carnot), Moulin the man who kept silent under torture, Moulin the leader of the "terrible cortège" of heroes and martyrs, undivided, Moulin whose beaten up face was "the face of France"—this emblematic figure was offered by Malraux as a model for the youth of France. Malraux lavished a great deal of attention on his eulogy, reworking it several times, as indicated by the intermediate manuscript he gave to Moulin's sister Laure Moulin, quite different from the published text.[9] In its final form, this eloquent text conformed beautifully to the genre of the secularized funeral oration that had replaced, around the end of the eighteenth century, the model of "sacred eloquence" practiced by clerics such as Cardinal Bossuet. Jean-Claude Bonnet has shown that this new kind of oration, which coincided almost exactly with the creation of the Panthéon as the receptacle of France's "great men," was addressed to a community of citizens rather than a community of the faithful; it was "founded on a social ethic of utility" that replaced the traditional "lamentation on the necessary ruin of all human undertakings."[10]

This new kind of funeral oration thus joined the genre of the public eulogy, or the *éloge de réception à l'Académie*, the speech of praise with which new members were (and still are) received into the Académie Française, and which presented "exemplary destinies" as models to follow. Later still, the *éloge* itself evolved from praising only Academic writers to praising "heroes of humanity." It was this tradition, Bonnet notes, that Malraux renewed with his oration for Moulin: "through his sense for solemn address (to youth and to future generations), through a powerful and visionary mise en scène, André Malraux reinvested the funeral oration with its capacity to create a legend, to found a community" (p. 1850).

By a fascinating coincidence, during the very week when Malraux celebrated the memory of Moulin's heroism on the steps of the Panthéon, the French National Assembly passed two laws that would have long-range consequences on public memory. On December 16, 1964, the Assembly declared that crimes against humanity—which were defined specifically as Nazi crimes—were "imprescriptibles," exempt from the statute of limitations that applied to other crimes, including war crimes; thus, crimes against humanity became persecutable to the end of time.[11] It was this law that made possible, decades later, the trials of Klaus Barbie, Paul Touvier, and Maurice Papon. In the course of those trials, the concept—or rather, the reality—of "crimes against humanity" moved closer and closer to French ground. While Barbie was a Nazi, Papon and Touvier were Frenchmen; and while Touvier could be dismissed as a petty thug, Papon was—both before and after the war—a highly placed *fonctionnaire*, a member of France's elite civil service.

The other law enacted by the National Assembly in the third week of December 1964 was a law of amnesty for crimes committed by Frenchmen in Algeria while opposing the independence movement during the Algerian war. This was one of a whole series of amnesties referring to the Algerian war, the last of them enacted in 1982.[12] What makes the December 1964 actions of the Assembly particularly interesting is that they project eternal remembrance of some crimes committed by Germans next to official forgetting of other crimes committed by Frenchmen. As it turned out, neither of those projects was realized as they may have been originally intended: Crimes against humanity slipped, with the trials of Touvier and Papon, onto French ground, and the major crimes committed by Frenchmen during the Algerian war, those of torture, have kept returning to public memory. Indeed, the trial of Maurice Papon provided the opportunity to revive both kinds of memories, for not only did he serve in Bordeaux in 1942, signing orders for the shipping of Jews to the transit camp of Drancy from where most were deported to Auschwitz; he also served as chief of police in Paris at the time of the police massacre of Algerian demonstrators in October 1961. The press coverage of the trial did not fail to draw the parallel between these two activities occurring almost twenty years apart. Not long after the trial, a general who had served in Algeria, General Aussaresses, published a book in which he confessed to—and defended, provoking a huge outcry—the use of torture in Algeria.[13]

In December 1964, however, the ceremony of national unity behind Moulin served to ward off unpleasant memories, at least for a while.

And what about November 1996? What were the politics of memory behind that official commemoration? Jean-Claude Bonnet mentions, somewhat presciently (since his essay was published well before 1996), that Victor Hugo delivered many a public eulogy before becoming the object of one himself in 1885, when he was buried in the Panthéon in a ceremony of national unity.[14] Conforming to that precedent, in 1996 Malraux the eulogist became himself the object of a eulogy and of a ceremony of national unity, one of the very rare writers to enter the home of France's "grands hommes." (In 2002, Alexandre Dumas became the sixth French writer to be "pantheonized.")

Can we analyze the 1996 ceremony in terms similar to that of 1964?

Certainly, many things had changed, not least among them the way Vichy and the Resistance were evoked in public discourse. Gone were the *unanimisme* and *résistancialisme* of the early 1960s—they did not survive the disappearance of Charles de Gaulle. Gone, too, was the socialist President François Mitterrand, his Resistance image tarnished before his death by the revelations (to which he willingly contributed) about his right-wing youth—"une jeunesse française," typical of a certain French generation, suggested the author of the book.[15] By a striking coincidence, the book was published in exactly the same month, September 1994, that saw the inauguration of the Musée Jean Moulin and the Musée du Général Leclerc, twin museums sharing a single building above the Montparnasse railway station. Général Leclerc, one of de Gaulle's most trusted colleagues, had led Free French troops into liberated Paris in August 1944. Among Mitterrand's first gestures, after being elected President in 1981, had been an official visit to the grave of Moulin in the Panthéon, a visit covered live on television.[16] The belated revelations about the President's past were in a sense counterbalanced by the opening of permanent museums devoted to two World War II heroes.

In November 1996, however, the Papon trial was looming, as were renewed revelations about torture in Algeria. Most importantly, perhaps, France's *grandeur* was being challenged on the stage of globalization, its language threatened by the spread of English as global lingua franca, its "identité républicaine" challenged by group identities and group memories. *La France*, one and indivisible, was turning (had no doubt already turned) into *Les France*, the title given by Pierre Nora to the last three volumes of his monumental *Lieux de mémoire*. And in terms of national politics, de Gaulle's own party, the RPR (Rassemblement pour la République), no longer dominated the political scene.

Given all this, we can see in the solemn ceremonies of Malraux's "pantheonization"—transmitted live in their entirety on two government television stations, TF1 and Antenne 2—an attempt to restore, even if only temporarily and symbolically, elements of grandeur and national unity to public awareness. One could also mention a less-grand design, evident in Chirac's speech at the ceremony: to give a much needed boost to the RPR by evoking Malraux's loyalty to the General. Like Moulin, Malraux was perfect for the role because he, too, could be made to represent heroic action during the war: Even if very late in the war, he did command the Alsace-Lorraine Brigade and take part in the liberation of Strasbourg. Furthermore, like Moulin, he evolved from a leftist past in the 1930s to a personal allegiance to de Gaulle. There exists at least one photo showing Malraux and Moulin on the same public platform in 1936, at a meeting of solidarity in favor of Republican Spain, both of them with their fists raised in the Popular Front salute.[17]

Finally, again like Moulin, Malraux could appear as representative of what was best in France. Maurice Schumann, backed by the authority of his own *résistant* past, drew the parallel between the two great men at the end of his eulogy, in a style almost as sonorous as Malraux's own:

> Jean Moulin l'attend parce qu'il sait comme lui que pour donner corps à l'espoir, le monde ne peut pas se passer de la nation qui lui a offert, non la déclaration des droits du Français mais la Charte des droits de l'homme. Et ces deux vivants nous demandent: que faites-vous ici, ce soir, si vous courez le risque d'oublier qu'on n'aime jamais assez la France pour ce qu'elle a de fragile et qu'on ne l'aime jamais trop pour ce qu'elle a d'éternel?[18]

> Jean Moulin awaits him because he knows, like him, that in order to embody hope, the world cannot do without the nation that gave it, not the declaration of the rights of Frenchmen but the Charter of Human Rights. And these two living men ask us: What are you doing here, this evening, if you run the risk of forgetting that one can never love France enough for its vulnerability, and that one can never love it too much for what it has that is eternal?

Schumann's peroration evokes not only France's glory and grandeur (its contribution to world history by the universal Charter of Human Rights, its claim to eternity) but also its fragility, its vulnerability. It is not insignificant, I think, that Schumann's speech ends with a question mark.

"The Comedy of the Monument": Malraux and Moulin beyond Politics

So far, I have discussed only the public, political meaning of memory and commemoration involving Malraux and Moulin. I would like now to turn to a more private, literary meaning that emerges from Malraux's writing on the subject of public commemoration, including the very ceremony in which he himself participated at the time of Moulin's transfer to the Panthéon. For Malraux was not only a public figure, the hero of a legend created by himself as much as by others. He was also a great writer, even though at least one word from France in 2001, the centenary year of Malraux's birth, claimed the opposite. Antoine de Baecque, a well-known intellectual and film specialist, wrote in the daily *Libération:* "Malraux a great writer? Who would seriously maintain that risky hypothesis?"[19] Baecque's dismissive certainty is surprising, not to say shocking: The author of *Man's Fate, Man's Hope,* and the *Antimémoires* cannot so easily be dismissed. In fact, as his article makes clear, de Baecque was mainly reacting to the official commemorations of the centenary, including the one at the Panthéon a few years earlier; he was also criticizing, from the perspective of 2001, Malraux's politics as de Gaulle's Minister of Culture. All the more reason, then, for us to look beyond the "official" Malraux, whether the Minister or the hero who could be instrumentalized in public ceremonies, to the writer as revealed in his books.

What did Moulin mean to Malraux the writer? We could also ask what Malraux meant to Moulin, for he knew Malraux through his political activities during the 1930s, and being a man of great cultivation he must have known Malraux's novels and other writings. Unfortunately, there is no record of what Malraux's works, or the man himself, meant to Moulin. We do, however, have a record of what Moulin meant to Malraux the writer. Olivier Todd recounts in his biography of Malraux that the latter began thinking of Moulin as a possible subject for a novel very soon after the war; he planned to write a novel about the Resistance, titled *Non,* in which Moulin's arrest at Caluire and its aftermath would play an important role.[20] According to Todd, Malraux intended his fictional alter-ago Vincent Berger (the hero of his previous novel, *Les noyers de l'Altenburg* [*The Walnut Trees of Altenburg*]) to be a kind of successor to the fallen Resistance hero. Although he produced a fragment of several dozen pages, from which Todd quotes, he never went further. In fact, he published no more novels after *Les noyers de l'Altenburg,* first published in 1943. In the 1950s, Malraux devoted all of his writing energies to his volumes on art. Then, in his first years as Minister of Culture (starting in 1958), he wrote mostly occasional speeches, funeral orations, and the like. In 1961, he lost his two sons in an automobile accident, and the few years that followed were among the low points of his life. When he wrote the funeral oration for Moulin in December 1964, he had been "à sec," dried up creatively, for some time. Less than a year later, however, he had started to work on the *Antimémoires*, whose publication in 1967 would inaugurate the series of autobiographical works that crowned his career as a writer.

It would probably be an exaggeration to suggest that Jean Moulin was the "unblocking" agent that led Malraux to his final major works, notably to the *Antimémoires*, a work that ranks as high as his best novels in the Malraux canon. Nevertheless, I believe it is not pure chance that Malraux started this book almost immediately after the eulogy for Moulin. Furthermore, the whole last section of the book, one of its most beautiful segments, is structured around the memory of Jean Moulin. Already, in an earlier chapter, Moulin is evoked without being named, when Malraux recounts his own capture by the Germans in August 1944 and his constant awareness that he might be tortured and killed.[21] He was released unharmed; but the mention of torture as a member of the Resistance necessarily evokes an association to Moulin. The segment that interests me, however, is explicitly linked to Moulin. Comprising the last thirty or so pages of the book (pages 475–510 in the 1976 Pléiade edition), it is a narrative structured around the December 1964 ceremony at the Panthéon, and it ends by putting that ceremony itself into perspective, according to criteria that are not those of politics.

Malraux begins his narrative with the day before the Panthéon ceremony. He recounts how Moulin's remains are transferred from Père Lachaise cemetery to the crypt of the Martyrs of the Deportation (near Notre-Dame Cathedral), where members of the Resistance as well as the public come to pay homage; and how, the next day, the casket makes its way across the Seine to the Panthéon, where he delivers his oration. He quotes almost the whole last part of the oration, where he speaks about Moulin's courage in the face of torture and where he summons Moulin, "poor tortured king of the shadows," to enter into his last resting place with his "terrible cortège." Just before these quotes, Malraux writes: "For most of those who are listening to me in the rue Soufflot, invisible, I am speaking about their own dead.

And about mine."²² In other words, he is mourning here not only a single fallen national hero; he is also mourning individual losses, whether in war or not, including his own. The reader of the *Antimémoires* can fill in the missing he alludes to, even though he does not mention them: his two half-brothers who died in deportation, his companion Josette Clotis who died in an absurd accident in 1945, his two sons who died in a car accident in 1961. Malraux's avoidance of personal "confession" is well known and explains his choice of the work's title; if memoirs insist on the personal and the confessional, then these are "antimemoirs." But that very avoidance makes the occasional, even elliptical, personal statement all the more meaningful. By indicating that he was, in eulogizing Moulin, also speaking of his own dead, Malraux points to a different, more private reading of his most famous public text. It does not mean that he is trying to make his own dead, or himself, the equals of a hero like Moulin; rather, it refers to the loss of any loved one, felt equally for heroes and nonheroes by those who mourn.

The most interesting part, however, comes after this. After recounting the ceremony inside the Panthéon and his brief conversation with Moulin's sister Laure, whom he accompanied inside the crypt, Malraux begins a series of meditations that bring the *Antimémoires* in line with his most permanent preoccupations, traversing his work since the 1920s: death, art, transcendence in a world without God, survival, and being human. First, he remembers a visit to a cave in Périgord in 1944, while he was inspecting hiding places of the Resistance in the backcountry, the *maquis;* the cave turned out to be Lascaux. Emerging from it under the night sky, Malraux remembers asking himself, "Was it upon emerging from such a place, under a similar sky, that a kind of gorilla, who was a hunter like a beast and a painter like a man, understood for the first time that he would have to die?" ["Est-ce au sortir d'un tel lieu, sous un firmament semblable, qu'une sorte de gorille chasseur comme les fauves et peintre comme les hommes, comprit pour la première fois qu'il devrait mourir?"]²³ Then, crossing the Place du Panthéon, empty of officials after the ceremony, he recalls a conversation about concentration camps with the deeply religious Catholic writer Georges Bernanos: "With the camps, Satan has reappeared visibly in the world," Malraux remembers saying to him, and he also recalls Bernanos's own funeral a few years later (482).

Finally, he tells of walking through Paris on his way to a committee meeting—a committee composed of former deportees, members of the Resistance—to discuss a project for a monument to Jean Moulin. As Malraux walks down the rue St. Jacques (it obviously can not be on the same night as the night of the ceremony, but we are still in the neighborhood of the Panthéon), he begins a long meditation on the experience of deportees: "I have been thinking about the camps for twenty years" ["Il y a vingt ans que je pense aux camps"] (482). He has read a great many testimonies of deportees, and he evokes incidents of humiliation, torture, and the Nazis' attempt to rob their victims of their status as men ["leur qualité d'hommes"]. To a reader today, this sounds like an allusion to Primo Levi's *Se questo è un uomo* [*If This Is a Man*] (currently mistranslated as *Survival in Auschwitz*), which had appeared in Italy in 1947 and been reissued there in 1963, shortly before Malraux started the *Antimémoires*. It appeared in French translation for the first time in 1967. But in the French context, Malraux may have been thinking primarily of Robert Antelme's *L'espèce humaine* (1947), one of the first camp memoirs to be published by a *résistant*; Antelme, like Levi, places the question of what it means to be human in the face of extreme suffering and humiliation at the center of his reflections. The Nazis' attempt to dehumanize their victims ultimately failed, Malraux suggests, because killing a person will not necessarily rob that person of his or her humanity: "The extermination camps, by trying to transform men into beasts, made one begin to understand that being human does not consist only in living" ["Les camps d'extermination, en tentant de transformer l'homme en bête, ont fait pressentir qu'il n'est pas homme seulement par la vie."] (496). The fact that Malraux makes no distinction between extermination camps, generally reserved for Jews, and concentration camps like Ravensbrück or Buchenwald, where most *résistants* were taken, was not unusual in the mid-1960s; nor was the absence of any mention of Jews as the designated targets of Nazi persecution. Malraux was writing the *Antimémoires* during the high point of "repressed memory" in France regarding the persecution of Jews and France's participation in it. His reflections, while restricted to deportees who were members of the Resistance, nevertheless strive for a solemn, self-consciously philosophical level of generalization about the human condition.

When he reaches the meeting room, he finds the discussion among former *résistants* becoming heated: Where should the monument to Moulin be placed? What kind of design should it have, abstract or figurative? Should there be an open competition to find the right sculptor? Following the philosophical meditations on evil and humanity, the discussion here strikes Malraux (and the reader) as almost comical: "la comédie du monument" (499). But it also makes him wonder: How could men and women who had seen the worst (all of the *résistants* present had been deported), who had come back from hell, put so much passion into disagreements about petty details? "What dismays me is to see Lazarus coming back from the dead to argue over the shape of their tombs." ["Ce qui m'angoisse, c'est de voir Lazare revenir de chez les morts pour discuter avec irritation de la forme des tombeaux."] (498). I read these remarks as a self-reflexive commentary by Malraux on the inadequacy of any effort—including, presumably, his own—at public commemoration. The monument to Moulin becomes a "comedy," even when planned by those whose memories of suffering are the most genuine, the most compelling. Perhaps, Malraux suggests, the reason—and the paradox—is that their memories of suffering have been erased by what came after, by life itself: "It's the insidious power of life, capable of erasing everything. . . . Life had covered up these survivors as the earth had covered up the dead." ["C'est la puissance insidieuse de la vie, capable de tout effacer. . . . La vie avait recouvert ces survivants comme la terre avait recouvert les morts."] (499). What obsesses him is the thought that absolute evil ("the shadow of Satan") had been visibly present in the world during several years, yet even those immediately under its sway seem to have forgotten it.

In the end, it is not a monument—nor, it would appear, a public ceremony like that of the Panthéon, nor even, perhaps, a public speech like his own funeral oration—that will keep the memory of suffering, and of the heroism that sometimes accompanied it, alive. Rather, it may be the shared recollections produced in conversation in certain rare circumstances and, a thing even more rare, the written record of such a conversation by a writer equal to the task. After most of the contentious committee members have gone, Malraux remains alone with four survivors of Dachau and Ravensbrück, a woman and three men, one of them a priest. How, he asks them, did they experience the return to life, the return to humanity from hell? For once, the one who does most of the talking is a woman—the first time this occurs in any work by André Malraux.[24] He calls her Brigitte, withholding her last name; but some readers today may recognize Brigitte Friang, a Gaullist *résistante* and journalist who worked with Malraux immediately after the war and again when he became Minister of Culture in 1958 and who later wrote several books, including one on Malraux. There, she explains that Malraux based this part of the *Antimémoires* on individual conversations he had with her and others.[25] In particular, he had several long interviews with her which eventually led to her writing her own memoir of deportation, *Regarde-toi qui meurs* (1970).

Brigitte Friang, as portrayed by Malraux, sounds at times very much like Charlotte Delbo, another *résistante* who had been deported and who had started to publish her stunning books of testimony in the early 1960s (her best-known memoir, *Aucun de nous de reviendra* [*None of Us Will Return*] first appeared in 1965).[26] Like Delbo, the Brigitte of the *Antimémoires* describes those who came back from the camps as only seemingly alive, seemingly returned to normal:

> Nous sommes toutes revenues à l'état de cadavres. Après un temps assez court, passé généralement dans la relative solitude du lit, nous semblions . . . rétablies. Et les nôtres croyaient que nous étions redevenues leurs semblables moralement aussi. Mais nous étions les semblables des copines, et de personne autre. La famille, c'était comme le lit: chaud et étranger.[27]

> We all came back looking like corpses. After a fairly short time, generally spent in the relative solitude of our beds, we seemed . . . recovered. And our loved ones thought that we had become once again like them, morally as well. But we were like our camp buddies, and like no one else. The family was like the bed: warm and foreign.

In this conversation, Malraux is a listener—he asks an occasional question, while it is the others who speak and remember. But of course it is he who records, or more exactly who shapes their statements according to his own obsessions and preoccupations—these former *résistants* sometimes sound like Malraux's fictional heroes. And it is he who places their testimony at the end of his book—or almost at the end, for the book actually ends with a page devoted to a return visit to Lascaux, twenty years after his first visit in 1944. Malraux explains that so many visitors had flocked to the cave that it had had to be closed to the public to keep the original paintings from being destroyed. Some Sundays, a guard tells Malraux, as many as fifteen hundred people showed up. From now on, they would still be able to see the paintings, but only as reproductions in the museum—here is a link to Malraux's works on art, which preceded the *Antimémoires*. Lascaux, a prehistoric testimony to the human need for art, is here placed in counterpoint to the history of atrocities that dominated the twentieth century.

Should we conclude from the final segment of the *Antimémoires* that Malraux scorned politics and public ceremonies, even where the memory of great events—and great men—was concerned? That would probably be an exaggeration. I do believe, however, that in concluding his book the way he did, Malraux was putting official public memory into critical perspective, and he was also suggesting, perhaps, that in the long run—the run of eternity, he might say in his grand style—art is more important than politics. The work of art, as Malraux often stated, speaks to the individual viewer or reader, not to assembled crowds. Although Lascaux was closed, the paintings would be preserved and reproduced for individual viewing; like books, they had become endlessly reproducible.

In the end, it is works of art, including the *Antimémoires* themselves, that take precedence over public discourse, and even over the illustrious dead who produced them. Malraux lies with Moulin in the Panthéon, visited only by the occasional tourist. But the *Antimémoires* endure.

ᚠ 4

History, Memory, and Moral Judgment after the Holocaust

MARCEL OPHULS'S *HOTEL TERMINUS: THE LIFE AND TIMES OF KLAUS BARBIE*

> The hell with "teaching" the Holocaust! Denounce and be angry!
> —*Marcel Ophuls*

> Memory loves a movie.
> —*Patricia Hampl*

*I*N AN ESSAY PUBLISHED more than forty years ago, Theodor Adorno asked the question: What does it mean to "work up," to "process," or—as the English translation puts it—to come to terms with the past? "Was bedeutet: Aufarbeitung der Vergangenheit?" ["What does 'Coming to Terms with the Past' Mean?"]. The word "Aufarbeitung," Adorno wrote in 1959, had already become a highly suspect *Schlagwort*, a slogan, for it did not imply a "serious working through [*verarbeiten*] of the past, the breaking of its spell through an act of clear consciousness."[1] Working through, which is here contrasted with the suspect "working up," is Freud's word for overcoming resistance to difficult material: To work through such material [*durcharbeiten*] requires effort. Although Adorno himself did not use the Freudian term (instead, he said *verarbeiten*, yet another word for working up or processing), the translators got his meaning right. For Adorno insists, in this essay, on the difference between a genuine working through of the past in the psychoanalytic sense (further on, he defines psychoanalysis as "critical self-reflection") and a mere "turning the page" on the past which is actually a desire to wipe it

77

from memory. That kind of working up is false and ineffective, as well
as self-deceptive: "The attitude that it would be proper for everything
to be forgotten and forgiven by those who were wronged is expressed
by the party that committed the injustice," Adorno notes with dry
irony (115).

In the West Germany of 1959, those words had a special significance. Although the Adenauer government had recognized, early on,
Germany's responsibility for the Nazi persecution of the Jews and had
signed an agreement in 1952 to pay reparations to Holocaust survivors, the general mood in the country was not in favor of remembering. As many historians have noted, the main goal in West Germany after the war was " 'normalcy' at all costs."[2] The assumption of
responsibility for the "Jewish question" did not, it has been argued,
carry with it a full recognition of the "Nazi question": the role of
National Socialism and of anti-Semitism in German life and politics
before the war, and their prolongation within the postwar period.[3] In
East Germany, the situation of memory was even worse, as Jeffrey
Herf has shown.[4] Adorno's essay reminded his fellow Germans that
their desire to "get free of the past," while understandable (for "one
cannot live in its shadow") could not be satisfied as long as "the past
one wishes to evade is still so intensely alive" (115).

The solution, according to Adorno, was enlightened pedagogy on a
mass scale, a pedagogy at once "turned toward the subject"—focusing
on individual psychology and aiming for increased self-consciousness
and "subjective enlightenment" on the part of individuals—and turned
toward objective arguments about history: "Let us remind people of
the simplest things: that open or disguised revivals of fascism will bring
about war, suffering, and poverty. . . ." (128). That particular reminder
is useful even today—though one may wonder whether Adorno was
not being overly optimistic in trusting in the power of rational argument, based on self-interest, to counteract the emotional appeals of
racism, xenophobic nationalism, and militant religious fundamen-
talism, which all come today in various stripes.

Adorno's idea about the need for critical self-reflection is an excellent starting point for a discussion of Marcel Ophuls's Academy
Award-winning documentary, *Hotel Terminus: The Life and Times of
Klaus Barbie*. This film explores the ethical conundrums that arise
when one attempts to confront, both critically and self-reflectively, the

immense historical phenomenon of the Holocaust, and (even more difficult) when one attempts to make one's way around the conflicted memories that the Holocaust has produced in both the public and private spheres, in Europe and the Americas.

This may sound like an excessive charge to place on the shoulders of a single film, or filmmaker. But I hope to show that *Hotel Terminus* lives up to the task.

The film was first screened at Cannes in 1988 and was immediately recognized as a major work, winning the Academy Award the following spring for best documentary. It is readily available on video (unlike most of Ophuls's other films), but in movie theaters it had very short runs, both in Europe and in the United States; surprisingly few people have seen it.[5] Aside from being a difficult and brilliant work, I think it is a film that makes many viewers on both sides of the Atlantic uncomfortable. It is that lack of comfort that will be my focus in discussing the film.

But first, a bit of historical background. Klaus Barbie, born in 1913 in Bad Godesberg in the Rhineland, into a family that came from the Saar region near the French border, was head of the German Security Police (SIPO-SD) in Lyon during the German Occupation of France from November 1942 to late August 1944. Known as "the butcher of Lyon" because of his cruelty, Barbie was responsible for the torture and deportation of many hundreds of Jews and members of the Resistance during that period. In particular, he was known as the man who had arrested and tortured to death the best-known hero of the Resistance, Jean Moulin. After the war, Barbie disappeared from view; it came to light much later that for several years he had worked for the American Army's Counter intelligence Corps (C.I.C.) in Germany, which was deep into the Cold War almost as soon as World War II had ended. In 1951, the C.I.C. helped him escape from Europe via the "rat line," the notorious escape route for former Nazis organized by members of the Catholic Church. In 1952 and again in 1954, he was tried for his war crimes in France and condemned to death *in absentia*.

In the early 1970s, Barbie was tracked down in South America. Under the false name of Klaus Altmann, he was living at ease with his family in Bolivia and Peru, involved in shady business deals and very close to the military rulers in La Paz. In the late 1970s, pressure built up for his extradition to France, thanks in large part to the efforts of Beate and Serge Klarsfeld. But Altmann, interviewed by French newspaper and television reporters, denied categorically that he was Barbie; and he was confident in the protection of the Bolivian government. The French government, under conservative president Giscard d'Estaing, was not overly eager to press the matter. It was only in February 1983, after changes in regime both in France (where Socialist president François Mitterrand was elected in 1981) and in Bolivia (where President Siles Zuazo replaced the military junta in late 1982), that Barbie was flown back to France and incarcerated at Montluc Prison in Lyon, the scene of his own earlier exploits (this was for symbolic reasons—he was transferred out of Montluc into a more secure prison a week later).[6]

The arrest and return of Klaus Barbie to Lyon, more than forty years after he first arrived there and set up his headquarters in the luxurious Hotel Terminus (which gave its name to Ophuls's film), caused an immense uproar in France. His trial took over four years to prepare, and at times it was not certain that it would take place. The trial—which unfolded over an eight-week period between mid-May and early July 1987—was a watershed in the history of French memories of World War II and in the history of French jurisprudence as well, for the case brought about a new definition of "crimes against humanity" in French law. By an interesting coincidence, the trial took place the same year as the publication of Rousso's *Le syndrome de Vichy*, which ended with the claim that the memory of Vichy had become, since the early 1970s, a national obsession.[7]

What were the reasons for the French "obsession"? Probably the most important was the disappearance of Charles de Gaulle from the political scene and the demythologizing of the Gaullist version of wartime France as a "nation of resisters." The Gaullist myth of a France united against the occupant—all save for a few traitors who received their just punishment—had served a useful unifying function in the decades following the war, but it was definitively laid to rest in the early 1970s. Robert Paxton's 1972 book *Vichy France* (translated immediately into French) documented the Vichy regime's more-than-eager collaboration with the Germans, as well as the deep ideological and political divisions that had existed in French society during the decades preceding the war; Marcel Ophuls's groundbreaking 1971 film, *The Sorrow and the Pity*, based on dozens of interviews with people who remembered those years, showed the wide range of choices, most of them less than heroic, made by the citizens of France during the Occupation.[8]

The other important reason for the obsession with Vichy was the emergence of a new extreme right party in French politics (Jean-Marie Le Pen's Front National), along with a French brand of Holocaust negationism represented by Robert Faurisson and others. This provoked a strong reaction, from liberal intellectuals as well as from a wider segment of the population.[9] At the same time, a certain part of the extreme left embraced the negationist theses as a way of supporting the Palestinians against Israel. Whatever the exact position one adopted, the Holocaust loomed large—this at a time when the accelerating memory of the Holocaust was becoming an international as well as a French phenomenon.

During the four years that preceded the Barbie trial, the national obsession was given ample opportunity to grow and develop. The list of charges against Barbie required plaintiffs and witnesses, producing an immense amount of testimony and public attention.[10] As we saw in Chapter 2, the trial also brought to the fore a painful aspect of the collective memory of the Resistance around the person of Jean Moulin, whose arrest along with six other Resistance leaders in June 1943 was known to be the result of a betrayal. Internal dissensions within the Resistance—among Gaullists, communists, and several other factions—were gleefully emphasized by Barbie's defense team, headed by the militant lawyer Jacques Vergès. Vergès, who had represented a number of Algerian terrorists in the 1960s and later, was pursuing his own agenda in defending Barbie: He wanted to use the trial as a way of putting France itself on trial, not for what it had done under Vichy but for the tortures it had practiced during the Algerian war. Furthermore, Maître Vergès sought to exacerbate possible conflicts between Jewish plaintiffs and plaintiffs who had been tortured or deported as members of the Resistance. At stake here was an important point of jurisprudence, for at first the prosecution excluded all charges *except* those brought by Jewish victims. Barbie's crimes against *résistants* came under the heading of war crimes rather than crimes against humanity, and had therefore expired under the statute of limitations. Besides, in his trials of the 1950s Barbie had already been condemned for a number of war crimes, and he could not be tried for the same crimes twice.

Maître Vergès was overjoyed when, acting on the request of various Resistance groups, the French Supreme Court of Appeals [*Cour de Cassation*] ruled in December 1985 that certain charges could be maintained even though they featured crimes of torture or deportation against *résistants*, not only those against Jews. In effect, this ruling changed the definition of "crime against humanity" in France, and was criticized for that reason by a number of intellectuals. Alain Finkielkraut, for example, argued that the ruling played into the hand of Vergès, for it seemed to say to the Jews: "You ask us to suffer with you, but your memories are not ours, and your narcissistic lamentations do not bring tears to our eyes."[11] According to Finkielkraut, by extending the definition of crimes against humanity, the ruling actually fomented rivalry among group memories and group suffering. In his view, the murder of the Jews in the Holocaust was a universal concern, not simply a "narcissistic lamentation;" therefore, the definition of crimes against humanity did not need to be expanded.

Of course, Alain Finkielkraut is Jewish.

That is a horrible thing to say, isn't it? But it is what Jacques Vergès, and not only he, would say (and did say, in different words) in response to Finkielkraut's argument. Or so Finkielkraut would say. Or so I say that Finkielkraut would say.

With those multiple twists in mind, we are ready to look closely at Marcel Ophuls's *Hotel Terminus*.[12]

Other People's Memories

The film opens with a dark screen, then the names of the American producers appear with piano music on the soundtrack: Someone is playing, haltingly, the opening bars of the slow movement of Beethoven's *Pathétique* sonata. After another credit line and another stop and start in the music, a black-and-white photograph appears: three men in medium close-up, evidently at a party, laughing. The one on the left, a young man, has his arm around the shoulder of the one in the middle, who holds up a wine glass in a toast. The man in the middle is wearing a party hat and holds an upraised cane in his other hand. The camera zooms in on him, the music fades, and we hear a

Klaus Barbie (center) and friends. Copyright 1988
The Memory Pictures Company.

man's voice speaking English with a German accent: "We had a New
Year's Party almost fifteen years ago, and Barbie was sitting at the end
of the table." The camera cuts to a medium close-up of a youthful,
jovial-looking man sitting on a sofa, and his name and occupation flash
on the screen: Johannes Schneider-Merck, import-export. "And then
I said that this bastard Hitler had, you know, betrayed the idealism of
German youth. He jumped up, furious, and shouted, 'In my presence,
nobody insults the Führer!' " In the middle of this sentence, the
camera cuts back quickly to the close-up of the man with the party
hat, who is now identified as Klaus Barbie, then back to a close-up of
Schneider-Merck; the attentive viewer may have noticed that this jo-
vial interviewee is the young man in the opening photo, with his arm
around Barbie.

The fact that Ophuls chooses to open his motion picture (in living
color) with a black-and-white still photograph is significant. The photograph, an informal snapshot taken decades after Barbie's crimes in
Lyon and more than a decade before his trial and the making of this
film, emphasizes the passage of time and the huge distance between
the historical subject of the film (the Nazi criminal Barbie) and those
who speak about him or try to follow his tracks forty years later. The
snapshot, freezing one intermediate moment (and a New Year at that)
in that huge temporal lapse, may be a figure for memory—or more
exactly, for the multiple, necessarily incomplete memories, of many

people ranging over time and place, that will constitute the substance of the film.[13]

Schneider-Merck continues his story: "His face turned red, it was like something exploded in him—it was something he really believed in, there was no arguing: 'The Führer is number one,' you know, and I'm sure that in his prison cell in Lyon, he has got . . ." Schneider-Merck, laughing, draws a frame with his fingers to suggest a photo, and the camera cuts to a close-up of the Christmas decoration on the side table next to him; another voice, that of the interviewer Marcel Ophuls, has said something, but one cannot catch the words. Schneider-Merck: "Has he got a photo?" Ophuls: "I don't know!" and both men laugh. "Maybe we should send him one for Christmas!" Schneider-Merck jokes. The camera now cuts to a view of a prison, evidently the prison in Lyon, and the film's title appears over the image.

In the meantime, some music has been playing. Exactly at the moment when Schneider-Merck, mimicking Barbie, says, "The Führer is number one," the pure voices of the Vienna Choir Boys are heard singing a plaintive song in German. To French or American viewers, the song is probably not familiar—but to most Germans it is well known, a folk song, a love song. "Wenn ich ein Vöglein wär / und auch zwei Flüglein hätt / Flög ich zu dir / Weils aber nicht kann sein / Weils aber nicht kann sein / Bleib ich allhier." ["If I were a bird and had two wings, I would fly to thee. But since that cannot be, but since that cannot be, I will stay here."][14]

Speak of multiple twists: A former close friend, now one no longer, recalls Barbie's love of the Führer and shares a laugh with the filmmaker. Schneider-Merck, involved in an unspecified kind of import-export, will explain later that Barbie and his pals cheated him out of half a million Deutschmarks, which he had entrusted to them as part of a currency speculation. No one in this tale has very clean hands, certainly not its narrator.[15] Yet the viewer, like the filmmaker, has shared a laugh with him at Barbie's expense. Upon reflection, the viewer may wonder: What exactly did Schneider-Merck mean, at that party long ago, when he said that Hitler had betrayed the idealism of German youth? "He had, you know, betrayed. . . ." But what do we know? Did Hitler betray German youths' idealism by leading them into the war? Or by losing the war? Did their idealism embrace Nazi ideas, for example, about the danger of the "Jewish race"?

Schneider-Merck addresses his "you know" not to us, but to Marcel Ophuls, son of the German Jewish emigré filmmaker Max Ophuls—Max was born in Saarbrücken, Barbie's *land*, in 1902, and left Germany with his wife and young son (Marcel, five years old at the time) in 1933. Marcel Ophuls knows German folksongs, as well as French ones and American ones. "I don't have any roots," he has said about himself, "but I have ties. . . . very deep ties to the Anglo-Saxon world and to America. I have traditional ties through my mother and father to Germany."[16] Does Marcel Ophuls know what German youths' idealism was, and how Hitler had betrayed it? Later in the film, while interviewing one of the former American intelligence agents who had employed Barbie after the war, Ophuls asks him, somewhat aggressively: "What is a Nazi idealist ?" The agent had called Barbie, in a memo he wrote for the State Department in 1947, "a Nazi idealist"—now, almost forty years later, he tells Ophuls that he does not remember what he meant by that phrase, but wishes he could rewrite it. "Yes, perhaps especially right now," Ophuls replies cruelly.

But he is not cruel to Schneider-Merck; in fact, he shares a joke with him. We too laugh—until we start to wonder why we are laughing.

Then there is the music. Does the beautiful old love song allude, ironically, to Barbie, who longs to fly to his beloved Führer? Or does it allude, with different degrees of irony, to anyone whose wings have been clipped: Barbie in his prison cell, idealists who have been betrayed, import-exporters of doubtful integrity who have been cheated, Jews who were expelled from home? The next song we will hear in the film, a few sequences after this, is another folk song sung by the Vienna Boys' Choir: *Ade nun mein lieb Heimatland* [*Farewell now, my beloved homeland*]. It was sung by political exiles after the 1848 Revolution as well as by those who left or were made to leave after 1933.[17] Ophuls puts it on the soundtrack over images of the village of Izieu, near Lyon, from where forty-four children were deported to Auschwitz in April 1944 on Klaus Barbie's orders—the most damaging of the charges brought against him at his 1987 trial.[18]

"Farewell now, my beloved homeland." After shots of the village and the building where the children lived, we see black-and-white photos of some of the children: a little brown-haired girl, a young boy. There follows a montage of voices without music, talking about Barbie; then the song starts again—but this time we are in the border city of Trier, where Klaus Barbie went to high school. As the camera pans over the city with the song on the soundtrack, the filmmaker's voice is heard, reading a letter written by Klaus Barbie in 1934: "Like my mother, I am a child of the Eifel [region]." The camera cuts to the old German farmer Johannes Otten, who knew Barbie as a child and calls him affectionately *der Bub*, "the boy." In the Izieu sequence we have just seen, a French farmer said he remembered "the little Jews" of the children's home, with the same song playing on the soundtrack.

Is Ophuls suggesting, with that parallelism, that the boy Barbie and the children of Izieu were alike? That the "butcher of Lyon" was once a lovable boy who had to leave his homeland? Are we supposed to feel sorry for him (Otten recalls that Barbie's father, a teacher, became very violent and beat the boy when drunk), the way we feel sorry for the children of Izieu? Or is the parallelism ironic, suggesting not similarity but difference: Barbie was a boy who left home, but he grew to a ripe old age in exile; the children of Izieu were gassed upon arrival at Auschwitz, and it was Barbie who had sent them there.

Similarly, we might ask what role the *Pathétique* sonata plays in the opening sequence. Later, several people who knew Barbie in Bolivia will remark that he was a fine musician, a masterful pianist. Is Ophuls giving us, ironically, the familiar trope about "Nazis who listened to Beethoven after a day's work of killing"? Is he mocking the torturer who plays the most clichéd melody of Beethoven, and stumblingly at that? Or is he seriously wondering what relation can exist between sublime music and crimes against humanity?[19]

The film does not answer these questions, certainly not explicitly. This does not mean that it adopts a position of moral relativism—Ophuls has stated that he is "very Manichean."[20] But the moral judgments the film proposes must be arrived at through work and struggle by both filmmaker and viewer. On the filmmaker's part, the work and struggle are not only in the filming but in the montage. "I intervene enormously in the editing, for it's there that the narrative is formed," Ophuls said in an interview about this film. "*Hotel Terminus* is by far the most difficult thing I've done in my life. I'm quite pleased and optimistic to have been able to come out of it alive, I really thought I'd drop dead in that godforsaken editing studio in Billancourt."[21] He wrote five different scripts at the editing stage and barely considers the film finished.

The brilliance of Ophuls's editing lies in its capacity to pose uncomfortable questions for the viewer—or, to put it another way, in its capacity to force the viewer into uncomfortable subject positions in relation to the material. Never—or at least, never for long—do we have a chance, in this film, to bask in righteous indignation or moral superiority, not even toward a villain like Barbie. The extremely rapid and complex montage of soundtrack and images not only demands close attention but creates a destabilizing effect on the viewer's understanding, on his or her moral certainties, and even, I would say, on his or her sense of self: "Whom do I believe and who do I think is lying? Whose ideas do I share? Whom do I identify with? Where are my loyalties?" These are among the questions that Ophuls obliges the viewer to confront with his editing. Like all of his documentary films, *Hotel Terminus* is what theorists call an interactive documentary, whose standard form is the interview, or generally multiple interviews.[22] In *The Sorrow and the Pity*, Ophuls had already perfected his technique of "dialectical montage" in editing the interviews. Dialectical montage here consists of cutting up the individual interviews and juxtaposing them with parts of others, so that the statements of one witness are qualified, or even totally contradicted, by those of another witness (or several others) in quick succession. In some cases, it is the insertion of documentary footage, or of an unrelated film clip or a musical soundtrack, that produces the dialectical effect, qualifying visually or aurally what is being said by the interviewee. Since Ophuls refuses voice-over or "voice of God" commentary in his films, whatever meaning the viewer derives must be gotten from his juxtapositions; if the juxtapositions are rapid as well as contradictory, the viewer is kept off balance.

Contributing to the viewer's sense of instability, narrative and visual fragmentation are much more present in *Hotel Terminus* than in *The Sorrow and the Pity*. Geographically and temporally, *The Sorrow and the Pity* focuses on the city of Clermont-Ferrand between 1940 and 1944, whereas *Hotel Terminus* moves among five countries (France, Germany, the United States, Bolivia, and Peru) on three continents, covering a period of more than forty years. In *Sorrow*, the languages are almost exclusively French and English (with a few short sequences in German); in *Hotel Terminus*, we hear substantial amounts of German (with some dialects) and Spanish, as well as French and English, including English spoken with a wide range of foreign accents. As for *dramatis personae*, the final credits for *Hotel Terminus* list ninety-five people seen and heard in the film—and since some items on the list are plural ("citizens of Marburg"), the number we actually see and hear is even greater, 100 or more. *The Sorrow and the Pity*, only seven minutes shorter, lists thirty-five interviewees. For anyone not familiar with at least some aspects of the Barbie case, and even for someone who is, a first reaction to *Hotel Terminus* may be nothing short of bewilderment at the succession of voices and faces, not to mention musical motifs, landscapes, and inserted film clips or photographs. If the filmmaker had to struggle with his editing, so does the viewer.

Paradoxically, however, this is not a flaw in the film. On the contrary, by means of his montage, Ophuls creates what I would call a *good* public use of memory, as opposed to manipulative, overtly instrumental uses. *Hotel Terminus* presents an unusually wide range of individual memories (or lack of memories, whether genuine or feigned) referring to a man who, by the force of circumstance, looms large historically. Around the figure of Barbie, individual memory, collective memory, and historical memory converge, and often clash: The film's subtitle turns out to be serious as well as parodic—this really is a film about the "life and times" of Klaus Barbie, on a world stage. Ophuls's editing emphasizes both his and the viewer's difficulty in confronting and evaluating the testimonies he gathers (or fails to gather, in some cases). But the issues as he presents them are not undecidable; they are merely not to be resolved without a struggle.

Is the struggle only intellectual, a matter of critical judgment? Ophuls has stated, somewhat haughtily, that his films are not intended for people with less than a high-school education. But he added, in the same interview, that the "man in the street" is often more canny [*malin*] and attentive to difficult works than he is given credit for being.[23] In fact, the viewer is summoned not only to evaluate critically, but to situate him or herself affectively, as a subject—an ethical subject as well as the subject of aesthetic perception—in relation to the film's rendering of "other people's memories." I want to suggest that Ophuls achieves this by putting himself into the action, in front of the camera as well as behind it.

The Filmmaker's Self

As film theorists have pointed out, the interactive documentary allows for a wide range of interventions on the part of the filmmaker, who can participate more or less noticeably in the interviews. At one end of the interactive spectrum is what Patricia Hampl has called the "memoir film," where the filmmaker and his or her friends and family are the real subject of the story.[24] At the other end is what Bill Nichols calls the "masked interview," where the filmmaker is neither seen nor heard in the final cut, but has in fact instigated the conversation and simply edited signs of him/herself out of it.[25]

In a film whose proclaimed subject is a historical event or personage, one would expect a relatively unobtrusive presence on the part of the filmmaker, closer to the "masked interview" than to the memoir film. Ophuls, however, has—with increasing insistence and provocativeness from *Hotel Terminus* on—played against this expectation. Already in *The Sorrow and the Pity*, his presence was clearly felt. Although that film showed only a handful of *images* of the filmmaker, he was present in almost every interview as a voice: respectful toward some, witheringly ironic toward others, and adopting a wide range of tones in-between. The range of attitudes communicated by Ophuls's voice is one indication of the film's moral spectrum: At the positive (respectful) end, we find Pierre Mendès-France, who joined de Gaulle in London after escaping from a French prison, and the peasant Grave brothers, members of the Resistance who were denounced and deported; at the negative (ironic) end is Marius Klein, the merchant who put an ad in the papers around 1941 to inform people that despite his name, he was not Jewish. Between these extremes, Ophuls's expressive voice modulates from that of neutral information-seeker, as when he inquires of the owner of a movie theater what kinds of films played during the Occupation, to that of calm adversary, as when he corrects some "facts" advanced in defense of the collaborationist Prime Minister Pierre Laval by his son-in-law. These interview techniques were one element that made *The Sorrow and the Pity* a groundbreaking documentary—its influence on Claude Lanzmann's *Shoah* is obvious in this regard, as in some others.

Hotel Terminus uses the same interview techniques, but adds to them a new set of procedures that emphasize the filmmaker's visual presence and subjective responses. Recalling the many scenes in *Shoah* where Lanzmann appears in the frame, we might see in Ophuls's self-representations a piece of reverse influence: He started filming *Hotel Terminus* just around the time that *Shoah* came out (1985) and has himself drawn a parallel between his subjective interventions and Lanzmann's.[26] (He also interviews Lanzmann briefly in the film, in what appears to be a homage and a gesture of solidarity more than anything else). But Ophuls has suggested, as well, that it was the subject he was dealing with that dictated his (and Lanzmann's) choices: "I feel frustration, bitterness, and revolt, and because I believe that documentaries should reflect the mood of the moment, it's all up there on the screen."[27] Can one make a film about other people's memories of Klaus Barbie without putting one's own self and emotions into the film? Ophuls's answer is No.

I propose to call those moments of self-representation and subjective expression where the filmmaker's self comes strongly into play the *expressionist moments* of the film. While this is a somewhat loose definition, it allows us to discount those scenes where Ophuls is visible without any "strong" affect involved. As suggested by Ophuls himself in the remark I quoted above, frustration and anger are the strongest affects displayed, but there are a few others. In my view, these expressionist moments are the most original—as well as the most problematic—moments in the film, aesthetically and thematically. Furthermore, it is in these moments of visually highlighted subjectivity that Ophuls points the viewer to the central moral issues raised by his work.

Old Nazis

The first expressionist moment consists of three sequences in succession, linked by a single theme. The series occurs quite early in the film, just after the lengthy segment Ophuls devotes to Jean Moulin and the problem of his arrest and betrayal. Returning to an earlier interview with Daniel Cordier, a distinguished-looking man who was Moulin's young assistant in 1943 and is now his respected biographer, Ophuls asks him, off-screen: "Do you think that the Moulin case has overshadowed other tortures: the Holocaust, deportation, the death camps?" Cordier answers that indeed, Barbie owes his "glory, in quo-

Ophuls gets the door slammed in his face. Copyright
1988 The Memory Pictures Company.

tation marks," to Moulin—otherwise, he was just an ordinary torturer.
"Atrocious but ordinary," Ophuls ventures. "Yes, atrocious, monstrous,
but altogether ordinary—he did what thousands of other Nazis did or
would have liked to do." As Cordier speaks this sentence, the camera
cuts to a view of Ophuls from the back, reaching the top of a staircase.
On the landing, an elderly man stands in the doorway, expecting him.
Ophuls (after a quick cut that elides any preliminaries) addresses him
in German: "I'd like to ask you—what crimes against the Reich could
a two-year old girl commit?" The man gestures with his hand as if to
say "not that again," and starts to shut the door, then opens it partially
and says: "That little girl . . . I didn't even look." At this point, an
identifying tag appears on the screen: "Karl-Heinz Muller, former Gestapo chief in Toulouse." Muller continues: "Whoever was there,
signed. If I had separated the two-year old girl. . . ." Then, abruptly:
"Oh what's the use!" and shuts the door as Ophuls cries "Bitte!"
["Please!"] Ophuls turns toward the camera, with an odd smile on his
face; in the meantime, a chorus on the soundtrack has started, in English: "Joy to the World, the Lord Has Come!" "Fröhliche Weih-
nacht". ["Merry Christmas"], Ophuls says to the door, as the camera
cuts to a sign that reads "Frohes Fest" ["Happy Holiday"] in a store
window.

In a perceptive essay on this film, Richard J. Golsan refers to this
scene as one of several filmed in Germany, in which "Ophuls abandons

any real pretense of objectivity" and uses "heavy-handed techniques to make his case."[28] Indeed, the irony of the Christmas carol, and more generally of the Christmas motif here and throughout the film, may be called heavy-handed. But what, exactly, is the "case" Ophuls is making in this scene? That old Nazis continue to live among their neighbors, undisturbed? That old Nazis do not like to be reminded of their crimes? Neither of those cases had to be made, I think, to European or American audiences *circa* 1985. If that were solely—or even principally—the point of the scene, Ophuls's efforts would seem to be wasted, or at the very least not cost effective: too much effort for the point. But what if the point of this scene were something different; for example, the encounter between an old Nazi and an aggressive Jewish filmmaker who does not even introduce himself or ask to be admitted before launching into a "question" designed to get the door slammed in his face? What if the point were precisely to lead to the odd smile with which the filmmaker glances at the camera as he is left standing there? And what if, furthermore, the point of the scene were to prod the viewer to exclaim: "Hey, you staged all that! That was a *mise-en-scène!*"

In a long interview with a French film journal in 1988, Ophuls stated a general rule of documentary film: "One shouldn't do any staging [*mise en scène*]."[29] Critics who find his irony too heavy-handed are responding to what they perceive as Ophuls's transgression of this rule.[30] The reason for the rule is important, for it distinguishes the documentary genre from fiction. The seriousness and authenticity of documentary as a representation of reality demands that the filmmaker eschew techniques of "make-believe." As if he were replying to this criticism, Ophuls adds in the same interview: "In *Hotel Terminus*, the only moments where there is staging it's comedy, and it's so obvious that I hope people will be amused by it."[31] In other words, there is no deception involved since the staging is obvious.

Ophuls does not consider the scene with Muller as a *mise-en-scène*, because he could not really plan or control it: There was a possibility that Muller would not slam the door in his face.[32] The example he mentions in the above interview is a scene later in the film, clearly staged, in which he and his German assistant Dieter Reifarth mimic one of the many refusals they are receiving from people in Bavaria who claim they never knew Barbie and have nothing to say. The scene is broadly farcical, with Ophuls playing a Munich lady who is at first very interested when she hears of a documentary being made, but as soon as she finds out it what it is about, retreats behind feigned absence of memory and lack of knowledge about politics. Ophuls has explained, in various interviews, that in *Hotel Terminus* his main difficulty was how to deal with people who either claimed forgetfulness and ignorance or else constantly lied and "manipulated." The farcical scene of mimicry in Bavaria (one of the major "expressionist moments" in the film) was one way he found to express his frustration. "There's no contradiction in handling often tragic subjects in depth and the idea of game playing. On the contrary, I see no other way out," Ophuls told an interviewer in 1995.[33]

In psychoanalytic terms, we might speak of such "playing" as a defense against overwhelming feelings of sadness and anger. In a 1988 essay titled "The Sorrow and the Laughter," Ophuls tells the story of a woman he once met in London, whom he employed to dub one of his films into English. She was a survivor of several Nazi and Soviet concentration camps, and "between takes she would tell me of her own experiences. . . . Most of her stories turned out to be uproariously funny, I'm sorry to say."[34] But of course, he is not sorry at all. Mrs. Pravda's (that, he claims, was her name: Mrs. Truth) way of coping with tragedy is exactly his own. Immediately following the above remark, he states what can be considered one of his aesthetic credos: "The reason Ernst Lubitsch's *To Be or Not to Be* is the greatest film ever made on National Socialism is that he debunks it, makes it ridiculous." As for his own films, "Through the method of investigative sarcasm, you can make a point against the horror but also demystify the horror at the same time."[35]

Aside from being an outlet for personal feeling, "playing" in a documentary is a sign of self-consciousness about the form. As Ophuls put it to his 1995 interviewers, it is a way of "stressing the form, putting it up front"—a tendency he sees as "part of the maturing process."[36] In this self-reflexive mode, which Bill Nichols mentions as one of the canonical modes of the contemporary documentary genre, the filmmaker "speaks to us less about the historical world . . . than about the process of representation itself."[37] By mimicking the woman who refuses to be interviewed, Ophuls emphasizes his own role, as well as his own difficulties, as a documentary filmmaker. I would say, however, that in this process he *also* "speaks to us about the historical world." For he prefaces his little farce scene with a somewhat less farcical direct address to the camera: "This is February something or other 1986, and we are still in Bavaria. . . . I represent Memory Pictures. . . ." Here, metacommentary about the process of representation merges with commentary about the historical world: Ophuls suggests that the willed forgetfulness of some Germans in 1986 refers not only to the "Nazi past," the years before and during the war, but also (maybe especially) to the continuing survival of Nazism. It is significant that this sequence, explicitly dated (February 1986), was shot during the early days of the historians' debate [*Historikerstreit*] that was being waged heatedly in the German press at that very time, a debate that concerned precisely the origins and the historical meaning of Nazism.[38]

Of course, we could say that the farcical scene is heavy-handed, like the scene with the old Nazi—but the question about the "case" Ophuls is making can be asked here as well, and even more so the question of his own position with regard to it. If his "case" is that we should condemn all those who claim to have forgotten the past (and who include, as the film makes clear, not only former Nazis but many others, of various ages and nationalities), then we might see Ophuls's heavy-handedness as a method of forcible recall, with all the aggressiveness and sadism that such methods imply. Clowning an old Munich housewife with a dubious past, the filmmaker affirms his own superiority, just as he does in more overt fashion in other scenes where he confronts reluctant or "forgetful" individuals (like the former American agent Robert Taylor, who called Barbie a "Nazi idealist") with past actions they would rather not think about. One critic has compared Ophuls's role to that of a psychoanalyst bringing repressed memories to light.[39] But the sadism of such scenes suggests a different comparison, one that Ophuls himself has made. He has compared his role to that of an "interrogator," noting the "cruel enjoyment" [*jouissance méchante*] that both he and the viewer could take from his playing that role[40]—precisely the role that, as we hear over and over from witnesses, Klaus Barbie was so good at. But if we allow that association to surface, then the notion of the filmmaker's "heavy-handedness" takes on a new, more troubling, meaning. A "heavy-handed" interrogator is close to a torturer. The filmmaker's "heavy-handedness" thus becomes both a sign and a cause of the viewer's discomfort—and I would guess that Ophuls intended it as such, whether consciously or not.

In a quite amazing passage in his 1988 interview, Ophuls remarked on a certain similarity between himself and Klaus Barbie: "It's true that there is, between Barbie and me, at least one point of identification (or maybe several. I too yell a lot, but I don't torture. . . .), it's the cosmopolitan aspect. Both born in Germany, followed by a diaspora. His is the diaspora of the torturers, mine is the other one. But our knowledge of languages, of the way people think in other countries. . . . He's a man of considerable intelligence, a man who knows the mentality of those he deals with, and who used his knowledge professionally. . . . Well, me too."[41] If the viewer has enjoyed Ophuls's sadism, whether overt or farcical—and inevitably, one has, as Ophuls knows—then the viewer must also say, "Me too."

Odd and uncomfortable couplings, whose implications go far. I do not mean toward a facile conclusion about "complicity between victim and perpetrator," but rather toward the question of what it takes to genuinely "work through" a subjective relation to the Holocaust. Ophuls's film suggests—and brilliantly enacts—the proposition that any attempt to deal with that question involves making one's own fears, angers, and prejudices visible, both to oneself and others. That means, for a filmmaker, not standing behind the protection of the camera, with the illusion of objectivity and the inevitable superiority that that affords, but putting oneself at least occasionally in front of it, even if it makes one look bad—like a sadistic interrogator, or like an "aggressive Jew" who gets the door slammed in his face—or, simply, weak, sad, or ridiculous.

That brings us back to the old Nazi Karl-Heinz Muller, and the silly grin on Ophuls's face as he stands by the door. He looks at once sheepish and triumphant, for if he could not fully predict what would happen in this scene, he was ready for the rebuff and knew it would yield "something to show"—otherwise, why would he have asked Muller that question, with no preliminary *politesses?* But Ophuls also looks, by the same token, manipulative, somewhat obnoxious (does he have to play "Joy to the World" just then?), and angry. Anger impedes control, whether of one's own behavior or that of others.

The theme is "failed encounters with old Nazis living in retirement." Ophuls repeats it with the two sequences immediately following this one, in a crescendo of anger and loss of control, matched by increasing emphasis on his own role. After Muller, he tries to interview a man named Steingritt, who worked for Barbie in Lyon (participating in the arrest of Jean Moulin) and was tried after the war and served time in jail. We see Ophuls gesturing to the cameraman to follow him as he climbs the steps in the hallway of Steingritt's apartment building. Steingritt, who has come downstairs, puts a piece of paper up to block the camera; Ophuls chases him into the stairwell and is finally stopped by the closing of the elevator door as Steingritt rides away. "Why won't you talk to me? You don't even know what I want to ask?" Ophuls keeps saying. "Leave me in peace, I've served my time. And stop filming!" Steingritt responds. The sequence ends with a striking image: Ophuls staring at the closed elevator door, whose glass reflects his own silhouette and the outside door, then walking out of the building as "Joy to the World" starts up again.

In this scene, the emphasis is less on the filmmaker's superiority or aggressiveness than on his weakness. The old Nazi gets the better of him—he blocks the camera's view and attacks Ophuls verbally. Rather than being in the position of sadist, Ophuls appears here in the position of victim: the other man will not allow him to ask a single question. Of course, in one sense Ophuls is still in control, since he controls the camera and the editing, but what he chooses to show us is the scene of his own humiliation and lack of control. The look on his face this time is not smirking, but grim.

The third sequence in what I am calling the initial expressionist moment ("failed encounters with old Nazis") is the longest, and it stages the filmmaker's self in the most complex way of the three. It begins with Serge Klarsfeld, who has acted as the "expert informant" about all three of these former Nazis in intercut shots, and who explains that Bartelmus, Barbie's assistant for Jewish affairs in Lyon, was tried after the war but condemned to only ten years in prison—which proves, says Klarsfeld, that crimes against Jews were not considered as serious as war crimes at the time. The camera cuts to a road with a sign indicating entrance to a town, then to rooftops, a row of houses, a street sign: *Friedhofstrasse* [Cemetery Street]. Offscreen, we hear Ophuls's voice, very low and polite: "Frau Bartelmus?" A woman's voice answers. He would like to speak with Herr Bartelmus, Ophuls tells her. Yes, she knows, she answers, but her husband has no com-

Ophuls is left standing by the elevator. Copyright 1988
The Memory Pictures Company.

ment. Cut to Ophuls, wearing a raincoat and matching cap, walking
in a vegetable garden. Bending over rows of vegetables, as if he were
searching for a hidden squash or pepper, he calls out repeatedly, in a
loud voice: "Herr Bartelmus? Herr Bartelmus?" A double mug shot,
front and profile, of a brutal-looking man, evidently Bartelmus at the
time of his postwar trial, appears on the screen. A woman's voice,
coming from in front of the vegetable garden offscreen, asks Ophuls
what he's doing there. Looking for Bartelmus, he answers. "You won't
find him there," she says coolly, then asks him to leave the premises—
private property. The camera cuts to her balcony, and we see her from
afar as Ophuls leaves the garden and stands below: a youngish woman,
born after the war.

The camera is now behind Ophuls, as he looks up at her—a balcony
scene, with the filmmaker as Romeo, but this Juliet is indifferent. "His
past [*Vergangenheit*] doesn't interest you?" Ophuls asks. "No, it doesn't
interest me," she answers. Cut to a man's voice, then a close-up of an
elderly man in profile, shaking his head—he is speaking in Bavarian
dialect: "I'm not at all interested, not at all interested." The camera
cuts to another youngish woman, a gas station attendant who has just
filled up Ophuls's car. "You're doing it for the sensationalism, that's
what I think," she says as she walks back to the pump, then takes the
money handed to her by Ophuls's assistant; Ophuls and another assistant stand looking at her. "Old people should be left in peace, not

Looking for Herr Bartelmaus in the cabbage patch. Copyright 1988 The Memory Pictures Company.

hounded from place to place," the woman continues. Cut to the old man who is "not interested." We hear Ophuls's voice, evidently asking about something he has just said that we have not heard: "What do you mean?" "You're selling pictures," the man answers. "And what about the children who never grew old?" Ophuls asks, as the camera cuts to a young girl opening the door of a ground-floor apartment. "Do you think it will help the children if you make an old man's last years difficult?"—it's the gas station attendant speaking again, and the camera pans over to her in medium close-up, with Ophuls and his assistant listening.

Cut now to an extreme close-up, the eyes and nose only, of the frontal mug shot of Bartelmus we saw previously, with Ophuls's voice on the soundtrack: "So your husband had nothing to do with arresting Jews?" Mrs. Bartelmus, unseen, replies as the camera pulls back to show the whole face in the photograph: "I can't say Yes or No. It was something that happened not only in Lyon, and it wasn't just Barbie who was responsible. Frenchmen too were involved." The camera cuts to another black-and-white photo: two French policemen on the left, one on the right, and between them a young man wearing a suit and matching cap, with a scared look on his face. This is evidently a wartime roundup, a *rafle*, and the French police are in charge.

What has happened here? The sequence starts like the other two, with Ophuls rebuffed and angry; sarcastically, he clowns the bumbling but clever detective looking for his prey in a vegetable patch (his attitude and his raincoat may remind one of Inspector Columbo, one of Ophuls' heroes, as he has stated in interviews).[42] In the balcony scene, he gets a young German woman to state that the old Nazi's past does not interest her, presumably producing a negative effect on the viewer. Then, in the gas station, the situation turns: Ophuls himself becomes the accused. "You're selling pictures." Do the accusations make the accusers look bad—ordinary Germans denying responsibility, still not interested in the past? That may well be. But in a telling way, the accusations hit home: Ophuls *is* making a picture, and he will sell it. Are the murdered children of Izieu only an alibi, a justification for "selling pictures"?

At the opening of *Hotel Terminus* at Cannes, Ophuls recounts in "The Sorrow and the Laughter," he was confronted during intermission by a tearful elderly woman, "small and rather stout" and full of gratitude—she wanted to tell him about the nightmares and sleepless nights his film had revived in her. His own reaction, however, was one of embarrassment, and a desire for distance from this victim. "Ever since, much against my will, I've become 'specialized' in films about old Nazis, collaborators, and their victims, I've tried learning to cope with such encounters," he writes stiffly. Victims of the Nazis who see his films tend to "project their own desperate feelings" into them, reacting to his own "mostly professional involvement in intensely emotional ways," he adds. "How could I explain to that lady in the lobby . . . , after she had rolled up the sleeve of her summer blouse to show me the concentration-camp number tattooed on her wrist . . . that my main satisfaction was that the audience had *laughed* in the right places and my main concern was that it would continue reacting favorably to my film?"[43] This anecdote, told by Ophuls, puts him in a curiously unattractive light. Instead of siding with the grateful survivor, he insists on his difference from her: his own involvement in the material is "mostly professional"—his main concern is that his film meets with critical success.

This may, of course, be an elaborate defense on Ophuls's part—a defense against his own "desperate feelings" (he has spoken of "fits of paranoia" he experienced while making the film)[44] as well as against the pain of identifying with a concentration-camp survivor. But in addition to being defensive, Ophuls's statement confirms the accusations thrown at him by the "ordinary Germans" at the gas station: He is acting out of self-interest, "selling pictures."

It is precisely in order to counter this accusation, we may surmise, that Ophuls brings us back, at the end of the sequence, to Bartelmus, the brutal man in the mug shot. The filmmaker may be selling pictures, but this man's past should not be forgotten. In a final twist, however, Mrs. Bartelmus's rejoinder brings both Ophuls and the viewer up short: "The French too were involved." Yes, they were, and Ophuls gives us the photo of the roundup with French policemen, bringing the sequence to a close.

The filmmaker is not innocent, and neither are the French, yet Barbie and his henchmen are guilty. Barbie and his henchmen are guilty, even though the filmmaker is not innocent and neither are the French. However one turns the phrase, the truth that emerges is uncomfortable. But it is the truth we are asked to grapple with here.

If I have dwelt at such length on this first "expressionist moment" and on the associations it calls up, it is not only because I admire Ophuls' complex artistry. It has been to show that the moments of the filmmaker's highlighted self-representation in this film are also the moments when questions of moral judgment are posed in the most acute and compelling way. These questions concern not only the enormously difficult subject of guilt and responsibility in the Holocaust and of the proper way to approach it today, but also the role of documentary filmmaking in representing those very questions. This is not to say that the same questions do not arise at other moments in the film, for they do. But they attain particular force and are explored with particular acuity in those scenes where the filmmaker's subjectivity is expressed not through indirect means (by the editing, music, placing of witnesses in the frame, and all the other cinematic means at his disposal) but directly, visible on screen as a corporeal presence. It is when the filmmaker himself becomes a "social actor" (the name given to people filmed in a documentary) that the moral *and* aesthetic issues raised by the film are most clearly highlighted.

"Un film de juif"?

As a final example, which will also lead us toward a conclusion—and, as it were, to the heart of the matter—I want to focus on a brief but

intense expressionist moment from the second half of the film. It occurs as Ophuls is tracking Barbie's escape to Bolivia after the war, by
way of the so-called "rat line" operated out of Rome, which furnished
many Nazis with falsified travel documents. Ophuls interviews Ivo
Omrcamin, a Croatian living in the United States who was closely
involved with the operation of the "rat line." In a typical dialectical
montage, Omrcamin's statements are intercut with those of a very
different interviewee, Brooklyn District Attorney and former Con-
gresswoman Elizabeth Holtzman—a handsome woman dressed in
blue, sitting at an oval table in her office. Ophuls is only heard with
Omrcamin, but he is in the frame with Holtzman. At one point,
Omrcamin says, in his heavily accented English, "There is that segment of the Jews who will never stop before turning the last stone,
and such Jews are helped by immense riches in this country [who]
want to prosecute Barbie." Ophuls's voice, smooth, encouraging, asks
one of those questions he is famous for, letting witnesses reveal the
ugliest things about themselves: "You think they're a vengeful people
. . . ?" "Oh, yes," says Omrcamin. Ophuls repeats, "The revengeful
ones." Omrcamin, looking pleased, adds emphatically, pumping his
arm up and down, "To fabricate the crime and then accuse somebody
of having committed those crimes—and hang them!" Ophuls's voice,
strangely quiet, responds: "I see."

Next we are back in Elizabeth Holtzman's office, and the camera
slowly zooms from a full view of Ophuls, sitting facing Holtzman and
seen in half profile, to a close-up of Holtzman as Ophuls asks, very
slowly, in a low voice: "Do you ever get the feeling, Ms. Holtzman,
that, um, only . . . Jews and old Nazis are still interested in . . . Jews
and old Nazis?" Her reply is quick: "Actually, not. Actually, the whole
problem of Nazis in America was brought to my attention by a non-
Jew who was horrified, as a human being, that, for example, our government could protect Nazi war criminals living here and allow them
to stay here." After another dialectical cut to Omrcamin, who accuses
Holtzman of opportunism—that she wants to get reelected in
Brooklyn, where the "vengeful Jews" live—Holtzman continues,
speaking straight into the camera: "There is a view that somehow the
Holocaust is simply a Jewish problem—when indeed the dangers of
the Holocaust affected millions of non-Jews as well. And the threat
that it represents today is to *all* humanity, not only to Jews."

Holtzman functions, in what looks almost like a deliberately staged scene, as the spokesperson for the moral and philosophical credo of the film, its ethical center: the Holocaust concerns all humanity, not only Jews. She says this in reply to Ophuls, who, in the quietest, most depressed moment of the film, wonders whether "only Jews and old Nazis" are still interested in that event. He has just been told, by the negationist Croatian exile, that the Holocaust is a Jewish invention. Unable to reply anything except "I see," Ophuls turns to Elizabeth Holtzman, a fellow Jew. She reassures him that not only Jews are interested in the Holocaust and makes an eloquent case for the universally human relevance of that historical event. But just to destabilize matters, Omrcamin indicts her for acting out of crassly political motives.

So here we have the moral heart of the matter: Whose concern is the Holocaust? Ophuls, in a 1988 interview with Jean-Pierre Jeancolas, stated that he was constantly aware, during the shooting of the film, "including during my fits of paranoia in the streets of Germany, France, and Bolivia," of something that bothered him greatly: "I felt the aspect of 'Ah! a Jewish film!' [*un film de juif*] weighing on me."[45] "Un film de juif" is more exactly translated as "a film by a Jew, for Jews"—in other words, not a film of *human* concern or interest, but merely another piece to add to the storehouse of group memories and to the skirmishes of identity politics. What really bothered him, Ophuls explained, was the thought that this "Ah! a Jewish film" feeling existed "on both sides of the camera"—not only on the part of those he interviewed, which would be understandable, but on the part of those who assisted him, in Germany and elsewhere: "It drove me crazy, at times."

Whose concern is the Holocaust? Who should remember, or want to remember, the Holocaust? The gas-station attendant in Germany says, "Leave the old men in peace, don't exploit them for your profit." Marcel Cruat, a French billiard player in Lyon, tells Ophuls right at the beginning of the film, "Personally, I'm not one for vengeance, and forty years is a long time." Besides, his own family was not touched by the deportations, "if you see what I mean." Much later, Paul Schmitt, the warden of the Montluc prison who first received Barbie when he was returned to France, tells Ophuls: "If you want my opinion as an average Frenchman, *un français moyen*, forty years is a long time—if they had wanted to kill him earlier, they would have."

Are the memory of the Holocaust and the demand for justice purely matters of self-interest, then? That is what the negationist Omrcamin claimed: The Jews care about the Holocaust because they are "the revengeful ones"—and besides, there was no Holocaust. Elizabeth Holtzman contradicted him, reassuring the filmmaker that his film was not just a "film de juif." But earlier, we heard the "average" French billiard player affirm that he had nothing against Barbie because his family was not "affected by the deportations." And soon we will hear Barbie's Bolivian bodyguard and friend, Alvaro de Castro, telling Ophuls (in the next-to-last of the great expressionist moments in the film) that Barbie had some Jewish friends in Bolivia—those who were not angry, who did not keep a grudge, "sin rancore." Ophuls, who has just lost his temper with de Castro ("Look at at me! Do you know that I'm a Jew? Do I look Jewish? Did Barbie teach you how to recognize a Jew?") will repeat, incredulous: "The Jews are not full of anger? This is what Barbie thought?" De Castro: "So he said." But we next hear an anecdote from a German acquaintance of Barbie: He once saw Barbie attacked and almost hurled to his death from a balcony by a German Jew, who recognized him and screamed that his whole family had been wiped out by the Nazis.

Klaus Barbie, as he was boarding the plane that took him back to France, gave a last television interview in Bolivia, which Ophuls reproduces. The white-haired old man, unbowed and unrepentant, says in excellent Spanish: "I have forgotten. If they haven't forgotten, it's their concern. I in any case have forgotten." That brings us right back to where we started: "The attitude that it would be proper for everything to be forgotten and forgiven by those who were wronged is expressed by the party that committed the injustice." That was Adorno, in 1959; and that was Klaus Barbie, in 1983.

And what do people say in the first decade of the twenty-first century? The Omrcamins and the David Irvings (Irving, a professional historian, is all the more reprehensible for his negationist views) are still with us, as are the "average citizens"—of France, of Germany, of Bolivia, of the United States—who think that all moral judgments are a question of self-interest. These average citizens are not "assassins of memory," as Pierre Vidal-Naquet has called the negationists. But they are impatient. They want to "turn the page on the past" before working through it.

On top of the stairs with Simone Lagrange. Copyright 1988
The Memory Pictures Company.

Fortunately, there are also others—like the non-Jews who first
alerted Elizabeth Holtzman to the problem of Nazi war criminals in
the United States, or like Jews who write denunciatory books about
the genocide in Rwanda in the 1990s or about King Leopold's genocide in the Congo a century ago.[46]

Ophuls knows this too. At the end of *Hotel Terminus*, after the trial
and condemnation of Klaus Barbie—for he was tried, however belat-
edly, and condemned to life imprisonment for crimes against humanity—the filmmaker stands at the top of the stairs with Simone
Lagrange, one of the witnesses he truly respects, a survivor of Auschwitz who was arrested with her parents by Barbie's men when she was
a schoolgirl. She and Ophuls have just climbed the narrow staircase
to her old apartment while talking about two of the neighbors she
remembers from that time: Madame Serre, who still lives in the
building and whom we saw a few minutes earlier conversing with them
from her upstairs window (yet another balcony scene), and Madame
Bontout, now deceased. When Barbie's men were leading the family
down the stairs, Simone Lagrange says, Madame Serre stayed carefully
behind her locked door. Madame Bontout (Mrs. Goodall—how lucky
Ophuls is with names) opened her door and tried to pull the young
girl inside, only to receive a slap in the face that sent her reeling. As
the filmmaker and the woman stand perched on top of the staircase,
another woman's voice (the voice of Jeanne Moreau) informs us that

"this motion picture is dedicated to the late Madame Bontout, a good neighbor."

From which one might conclude two things. It is better to be a good neighbor than a bad neighbor, even if it gets you a slap in the face. And in order to have the right to say that, one must earn it—which means that, like the filmmaker, one must be willing to engage in critical self-reflection, just as Adorno said. Only then will we viewers, individually and collectively, be able to "put the past behind us and turn the page."

That would be the cautiously upbeat ending. But following Ophuls's own dialectical lead, I want to end on a somewhat less stable and less comforting note, by returning to Ophuls's anecdote about his encounter with the Auschwitz survivor at the screening of *Hotel Terminus* in Cannes. As we recall, Ophuls distanced himself from the emotional victim, affirming his own cool professionalism. And he went even further. After the woman, in an angry outburst, screamed, "I want all Germans killed, they're all alike," Ophuls bid her goodbye: "At that point, I was unable to repress the urge to tell that unhappy woman that the intermission was over, that my wife was waiting for me in the theater, and that *my wife is German.* I know I shouldn't have done it."[47] Why not? Because it was sadistic? The woman, silenced, walked back into the theater, where she started a commotion with her shouts: "They should all be killed!" Then other members of the audience got into the act, berating the woman, supporting her, or bringing up their own memories of the Resistance. Finally, it was Ophuls himself who, in an effort to calm things and get the film back on the screen, announced that in his opinion, "any concentration-camp survivor was entitled to any opinion she might have about Germans," or about anything else.

Earlier, he wanted nothing more than to affirm his difference from this woman; now, he took her side. This intricate dance of closeness and distance, identification and disavowal, may be a more just image on which to conclude than that of a page finally turned. For the viewer as for the filmmaker, questions persist: Where do I stand? Whom do I resemble?

Maybe, where memory of the Holocaust is concerned, no "turning of the page" is yet possible.

Or is that just a Jewish obsession?

5

Anamnesis: Remembering Jewish Identity in Central Europe after Communism

ISTVÁN SZABÓ'S *SUNSHINE*

*T*HE LARGE MAJORITY OF Central European Jews were wiped out in the Holocaust—this is a fact that needs no repeating. During the four decades of European communism, very little discussion was possible in the Soviet-dominated countries about the fate of the Jews under Nazism, and even less discussion was possible about the problems and dilemmas of Jewish identity among the survivors who had remained in Central Europe. The communist version of World War II was that it had been an "antifascist struggle," and the specific persecution of Jews was almost never mentioned.[1] Many Holocaust survivors emigrated after the war, especially from Poland and Hungary, where anti-Semitic outbreaks in 1946—shocking, even if rare—indicated a certain lack of welcome in their homeland. Those who stayed, whether out of choice or necessity, often downplayed or even hid their Jewishness during the communist years, adopting what the sociologist Henri Tajfel calls the "minority behavioral strategy of rejection" as far as their Jewish identity was concerned.[2] Changes of name to disguise Jewish origins by families who had survived the war were common, even in Western European countries. In France, more Jews changed their name in the immediate postwar years than before; in Hungary, where "Magyarizing" of names had begun as early as 1900 for patriotic reasons, many Jews who had not yet adopted "Magyarized" names did so after the war.[3]

106

Hungary, furthermore, presented a special case because, despite destruction and emigration, close to 100,000 Jews remained in the country throughout the postwar decades, most of them living in Budapest. While few worshipers were to be found in the run-down synagogues during those years, the rabbinical seminary (the only one in Eastern Europe) continued to train rabbis. The majority of Hungarian Jews, however, lived in some form of silence, if not downright amnesia, about their identity and history. Tony Judt, among other historians, has observed that assimilated Jews in Eastern Europe who lived under communism were reluctant to recall the history of Jewish persecution during the war and "often made considerable efforts to hide their Jewishness—from their colleagues, their neighbors, their children, and themselves."[4] This refusal of memory was encouraged by the official histories, which sought to deny the role of the "home" governments in the roundup and deportation of Jews, laying the blame exclusively on the Germans.

In Hungary, it was only in the 1970s that Jews' silence about their past began to be broken with an occasional novel or memoir, including Nobel Prize–winner Imre Kertész's autobiographical novel, *Sorstalanság* (*Fatelessness*), published in 1975. The first Hungarian film to focus on the experience of Jews facing deportation was the 1983 *The Revolt of Job* (directed by Imre Gyöngyössy and Barna Kabay), which tells the story of an old, childless Jewish couple in a village who adopt a Christian orphan boy in an attempt to create a heritage after their deportation and death; the story was based on Gyöngyössi's own childhood.

Following the fall of the Berlin wall in November 1989, the thin stream of Jewish memory about the Holocaust in Hungary became, by comparison, a veritable torrent. In the past decade and a half not only writers, poets, and filmmakers, but historians and sociologists (some Jewish, others not) have produced important works about the role and fate of Jews in modern Hungarian history as well as about the pressures and contradictions of Jewish identity in Hungary and in Central Europe after the Holocaust and after communism.[5]

István Szabó's 1999 film *Sunshine* is one such work. This English-language film, with a largely Anglophone cast, was made for an international as well as a Hungarian audience (it was dubbed into Hungarian).[6] While it garnered praise and mixed reviews in the United

States and England, it was in Hungary that the film really had an effect. It aroused passionate commentaries in the Hungarian press, especially among Jewish intellectuals, whether they were self-identified as Jews or assimilated ("of Jewish origin," as the euphemism goes). Szabó (born in 1938), one of Hungary's best-known filmmakers, speaks neither as a historian nor a philosopher: *Sunshine* is not a manifesto or a programmatic statement. But this visually and aurally sumptuous film, epic in scale and ambition, raises compelling questions about the dilemmas of Jewish memory and Jewish identity in Central Europe, and about the filmic representation of traumatic collective histories. The debate over the film revolved largely around the way today's Hungarian Jews see themselves and their past history, and wish others to see them.

A Family in History: 150 Years

Like all historical epics, *Sunshine* aims to tell a story about individuals that a spectator can identify with, and at the same time give an accurate representation of a complex and extended collective history. Szabó has stated in interviews that he is fascinated by "how people's private lives have been influenced by history and politics."[7] *Sunshine* can be seen as the culmination or combination of several of his earlier films in German and Hungarian, which focused on individual lives in smaller segments of the long historical period treated in this film.

Sunshine sums up the history of Jews in modern Hungary by telling the story of a single family over four generations. Emmanuel Sonnenschein, while still a boy, leaves the village where his father, the local tavern keeper, has been killed by an explosion in his distillery, and makes his way to the capital. While no exact dates are mentioned, we are evidently in the mid-nineteenth century, after the revolutionary flames of 1848 have died down and just before the period of Hungary's greatest economic and cultural flowering under the Dual Austro-Hungarian Monarchy (1867–1918).[8] Emmanuel, a poor devout Jew, takes with him to Budapest the precious black notebook that contains his father's secret recipe. By the time the story begins in earnest—when Ralph Fiennes makes his appearance as Emmanuel's young-adult son—the Sonnenscheins have become rich through Emmanuel's distillery, which produces the tonic he calls "a taste of sunshine" [*A napfény ize*, the film's title in Hungarian].

While the film's narrative mode is that of the historical epic, Szabó introduces a mediating presence from the start: The story is told with voice-over narration by the last male descendant of Emmanuel Sonnenschein, his great-grandson Ivan. Ivan's voice (in English, the voice of Ralph Fiennes, who plays all three roles of son, grandson, and great-grandson) opens and closes the film and intervenes at various moments. Although the voice-overs are not emphasized, and few critics commented on them, they designate the film as a memory film, for the story is told not by an impersonal camera-narrator but by a specific individual who is also a participant in it. Ivan was not yet born when the story begins, but we are reminded by his interventions that this is his family's story as he sees it.

After the prologue, the film divides neatly into three historical periods; extending the meteorological metaphor suggested by the title, we can call them the "sunlit age," roughly 1890–1914; the "stormy age," roughly 1914–1944; and the "overcast age," 1945 to our day.

When Emmanuel's two sons, Ignatz and Gustave, reach young manhood in the 1890s, the era of Hungarian prosperity and cultural achievement is at its height, and Jews play a prominent role in it. Historians have often described the "assimilationist contract" that linked the liberal nobility to Jewish industry and finance in the period of the Austro-Hungarian Monarchy. The liberals, inspired by the ideals of the Enlightenment as well as by Magyar patriotism, sought to modernize a backward, quasi-feudal country and to create a unified nation despite the number of minority ethnic groups scattered over its large territory. The "assimilationist contract" gave Jews, especially those living in Budapest, an opportunity to participate fully in the liberals' modernization project, and in the creation of a modern Hungarian identity and culture. In return, as the historian András Kovács explains, "Hungarian Jews were expected to demonstrate total loyalty to the Hungarian state, to accept the political hegemony of the nobility, and to strive for complete assimilation within the Hungarian community."[9]

Ignatz Sonnenschein becomes a jurist and is quickly promoted to the high position of a Central Court judge; but since "a Central Court judge cannot have a name like Sonnenschein," as his Christian patron (a liberal politician) tells him, he changes his name to the more Magyar-sounding Sors, which means "fate" in Hungarian. His brother Gustave, a doctor, does likewise, and so does his cousin and adopted sister, Valerie, who soon becomes his wife (the Sonnenschein men's relation to women is a problematic aspect of this film, which I will discuss later). Drafted into the officer corps as a military judge during World War I, Ignatz remains a lifelong loyalist to the Emperor, Franz Joseph. Gustave follows a more radical route, joining the Socialist Party and later the Revolutionary government of Béla Kun (1919). After the fall of the Kun regime, he is forced to leave Hungary.

Magyarizing one's name in the period before World War I did not have the same anxious connotation (hiding one's Jewishness for fear of persecution) that it would acquire during the 1930s and during the postwar period. Change of name was practiced not only by Jews but by other ethnic minorities in Hungary—Slovaks, Croats, and Germans—who wanted to affirm their loyalty. For Jews, who had acquired their Germanic names in the eighteenth century under the Hapsburg Emperor Joseph II, Magyarizing their name was a sign of patriotism as well as of belief in the promises of assimilation. It did not necessarily imply a renunciation of Jewish self-identification or of Jewish practice, although Jews in Budapest generally practiced a Reform brand of Judaism in opposition to the Orthodox practice of most provincial Jews. By changing their name when they do, Ignatz, Gustave and Valerie are not giving up their Jewishness, but rather affirming their Hungarianness.

The vexed question asked by this film is whether—and how—one can be both Jewish and Hungarian after the Holocaust. For as it turned out, the "assimilationist contract" was much more fragile than it seemed to the Jews of Ignatz and Gustave Sonnenschein/Sors's generation. The contract did not foresee—and could not, ultimately, withstand—the economic crisis and the aggravated nationalism that followed the dismemberment of the Hapsburg Empire after World War I, when Hungary lost two-thirds of its territory. Nor did it foresee the revolutionary upheavals in Russia and in Hungary (where the short-lived Kun regime, dominated by assimilated Jews, was brutally put down by the authoritarian regime of Miklós Horthy), or the rise of Nazism and radical anti-Semitism in Germany, not to mention the massive destruction of Hungarian Jewry during the war and the quasi-total repression of Jewish self-consciousness in Hungary during the communist decades.

Many Jews, seeing the handwriting on the wall, emigrated from

Hungary in the 1920s and 1930s. Those who stayed faced increasing hostility and persecution by their own government, culminating in the Jewish laws of 1938 and 1939, which virtually excluded Jews from Hungarian economic, cultural, and political life. Ignatz Sors does not live to see that day, for he dies shortly after World War I; but his two sons, István and Adam, experience virulent anti-Semitism while they are still teenagers. Adam, who takes up fencing after being attacked by his own schoolmates, becomes a national and Olympic champion, and an ardent patriot. By that time, however, Jewishness and Hungarian patriotism coexist only in a highly problematic fashion. When Adam is told that in order to be allowed to join the officers' fencing club (which has the best fencers) he must convert to Catholicism, he does so—accompanied by his brother and by the women they will marry.

In the character of Adam, Szabó explores a psychology that already fascinated him in his Oscar-winning 1981 film, *Mephisto*, and that became the focal point of the film that followed it, *Colonel Redl* (1984): that of the "pariah" parvenu, who, once he is accepted—albeit grudgingly—by a group or an institution, becomes loyal to the point of losing all ability to judge his situation or that of the institution itself, and who gets morally and physically destroyed in the process. This psychology exists to some degree in all of the Sonnenschein/Sors men, but it is most clear in Adam. At the Berlin Olympics, he is oblivious to everything other than winning for Hungary—oblivious to the huge swastika banners, the crowds in uniform, the disquieting atmosphere, none of which escape his aristocratic Christian trainer. Married to a Jewish woman, the trainer soon emigrates from Hungary; upon hearing of this, Adam calls him a traitor. The rigidity of this character is beautifully captured by Fiennes' performance.

In 1941, the Hungarian government—an ally of Germany—conscripted most Jewish men into forced labor service, where they were subjected to treatment that ranged from harsh to homicidal. Adam is tortured to death in a forced labor camp by Hungarian gendarmes, when he insists on wearing a white armband (signaling that he is a convert) and on identifying himself as "Adam Sors, an officer in the Hungarian army and Olympic gold-medal winner." As István Deák points out in his historical review of the film, the fate of Adam is modeled on that of the Hungarian fencing champion Attila Petschauer, a Jewish convert to Catholicism who was beaten to death in a forced labor camp.[10] Adam's teenage son, Ivan (our narrator) watches helplessly as his father is stripped naked, beaten, strung up on a tree and doused with cold water, slowly turning into an ice statue—refusing unto death to call himself a Jew.

In March 1944, the Germans invaded Hungary and started the systematic deportation of Jews from the provinces, an operation administered and carried out by Hungarian officials and police. Two thirds of Hungary's Jews, close to half a million people, perished through deportation and other forms of murder. The systematic deportations never reached Budapest, which accounts for the relatively large number of Jews (when compared to Poland, for example) who remained in Hungary after the war. However, in the last winter of the war, Budapest Jews were hounded by members of the pro-Nazi Arrow Cross Party led by Ferenc Szálasi, who had replaced Horthy as head of the government in October 1944. Adam Sors's remaining family are murdered by the Arrow Cross in Budapest; the only survivors are Ivan and his grandmother Valerie, who return to an empty apartment in 1945. To signal the end of the war, Szabó inserts archival footage showing bombed-out buildings and dead horses on the street, which people cut up for food.

Ivan's story, developed in the last part of the film, brings us up to the present. Like many young Jews after the war, Ivan becomes an ardent communist. In fact, Ivan is technically not Jewish, being the son of two converts—but Szabó is historically accurate in suggesting that for a few years at least, many surviving Jews in Hungary subscribed to the communist regime and occupied high positions in it.[11] Ivan works for the dreaded secret police, the AVO—until his boss and friend Andor Knorr (played by William Hurt), a survivor of Auschwitz, is arrested on trumped-up charges of "Zionist conspiracy" and tortured to death by the communist regime. We are in 1952, just as the anti-Jewish Slansky trial is starting in Czechoslovakia and the "doctor's plot" is about to be launched in the Soviet Union. Ivan quits the police, eventually becomes a leader of the failed 1956 revolution, and spends several years in prison. In the 1960s, after Valerie's death, he finds a letter addressed by his great-grandfather Emmanuel to his son Ignatz, advising him to stay true to himself and his origins. Taking this letter to heart, Ivan changes his name back to Sonnenschein—

and for the first time in his life, he announces in a final voice-over, he "breathes freely" in the streets of Budapest. In a huge temporal leap, the film's last sequence is of Ivan walking with the crowds in present-day Budapest, on a recently created pedestrian street. As the final credits roll, the camera slowly and lovingly pans over the city, with its river and bridges and the hills of Buda.

The debates that raged in the Hungarian press about this film at its release in 2000 were almost without exception focused on its ending: the meaning, implications, and plausibility of Ivan's taking back his Jewish/Germanic name. This debate is fascinating for what it tells us about contemporary Hungary and about the situation of Jews there. Before discussing it, however, I want to consider in some detail the aesthetics of Szabó's film, which combines realist representation with a modernist self-consciousness that underscores the problem of identity at the heart of the film.

Realism and Repetition

Szabó's interest in both history and modernist cinema was already evident in his earliest films, which made him famous before he was thirty. His first feature films in Hungarian were all to a greater or lesser degree autobiographical, focusing on the period from 1944 to the early 1960s, which corresponded to his recurring protagonist's childhood, adolescence, and university years in Budapest; they also corresponded to some of the most dramatic years in modern Hungarian history, comprising the year of the Holocaust in Hungary (1944–1945), the arrival of Russian troops and the beginning of the communist regime, the failed revolution in 1956, and the relative "normalization" of the 1960s. Szabó's 1966 film *Apa* [*Father*], which was recognized as having clear affinities with French New Wave cinema (especially the films of Truffaut), tells the story of a young boy whose father dies in 1945 and who comes of age in the postwar years; his 1973 film *Tűzoltó utca 25* [*25 Firemans Street*] is at times difficult to follow for a non-Hungarian audience, employing modernist techniques of fragmentation, dream sequences, and temporal zigzags that allude to various moments of Hungarian history between the two World Wars. In his German trilogy, made in the 1980s, Szabó covers the years between the 1890s and the late 1930s in Central Europe, but the chronology of the films does not correspond to historical chronology: The first film, *Mephisto* (1981), covers the rise of Nazism in Germany, starting around 1930 and ending just before the outbreak of World War II; the second film, *Colonel Redl* (1984), leaps back to the final decades of the Hapsburg era in Austria-Hungary, ending with the outbreak of World War I; the last film of the trilogy, *Hanussen* (1988), covers the period from the end of World War I to the Nazis' rise to power in 1933.[12]

Whereas these films were destined primarily for a European audience, which could be presumed to know the historical background so that mere allusions to it sufficed, *Sunshine* aims for a broader public. Paradoxically, the film has to assume a fairly large amount of contextual historical knowledge on the part of the viewer, even while providing such knowledge in a form that will be historically accurate (or at least, not glaringly inaccurate), cinematically appealing, and not too confusing to follow. The historian István Deák has vouched for the film's historical accuracy, give or take a few details. Inevitably, however, Szabó must rely on a certain schematicism and simplification, if for no other reason than the huge temporal sweep of the narrative. Characters tend to function as types, rather than as fully developed figures; plot and narration are linear, avoiding the complex chronologies of Szabó's early films.

Like the traditional epic, and like realist fiction, *Sunshine* relies on repetition and parallelism to establish a pattern and reinforce its themes. Repetition occurs both on the level of plot and characters and in the *mise en scène*, including decor, lighting, and music. The family's apartment and the building in which it is located are one major repeated element, used to great effect: the physical deterioration of these spaces tracks both the family's and Hungary's decline. The visual evolution from the comfortable, replete bourgeois interior of the Hapsburg years to the threadbare dinginess of the communal apartment in the Stalinist years communicates a huge amount of historical information in cinematic terms. Similarly, colors are used to mark the film's movement from sunshine to darkness and back to at least a partial sunshine. In the middle section, when the family sits listening to the announcement of the first Jewish Law on the radio, the screen is almost black, the figures barely visible. One of the most memorable moments, visually, occurs toward the beginning, when the courtyard of the Sonnenschein house is suddenly covered with golden wild-flowers, like a carpet of "sunshine." The moment is captured in a photograph of Valerie, snapped by Gustave as she sits on a bench in the middle of the flowered courtyard, trying to remove a thorn from her foot; this black-and-white photograph becomes a recurrent image in the film, evoking a moment of youthful happiness as the family's history becomes more somber.

The musical score by Maurice Jarre is also highly patterned, with the leitmotif borrowed from Schubert's *Fantasia in F Minor for Two Pianos* accompanying the family's evolution. Played by Valerie and Ignatz as young lovers, the Schubert piece becomes the Sonnenschein theme music, sometimes fully orchestrated, at other times reduced to a single piano. In the sequence of Adam's murder, there is no music at all, while in the concluding sequence, when the Sonnenschein name is revived, the Schubert melody swells to full orchestration. Szabó makes use of other musical motifs as well; the Hungarian folk song "Spring Wind" *[Tavaszi szél]*, which is played at Valerie and Ignatz's wedding and recurs often, underlines the family's love of Hungary and its deep sense of "Hungarianness," according to Szabó's published commentary.[13]

On the level of plot and characters, repetition is used to underline the film's major themes of assimilation and identity. The choice of a single actor to play the three generations of protagonists emphasizes the similarities in character and situation as well as the physical resemblance of the three men. However, it also highlights the pitfalls of repetition as a thematic trope. A number of reviewers in England and North America criticized the film for being too schematic or heavy-handed (in other words, excessive in its repetitive patterning) and found particular fault with the recurrence of Ralph Fiennes.[14] In the final sequence, when Ivan reads his great-grandfather's letter, we see the latter's face and then two other faces of Ralph Fiennes as Ignatz and Adam, mouthing the words while the third Fiennes holds the letter. This degree of redundancy seems excessive, all the more so since Ignatz and Adam have not been shown to have understood or followed the message they are transmitting ("Know yourself; don't abandon your religion").

In other instances, however, repetition communicates a meaning visually that is not stated verbally. Early in the film, for example, we

Ignatz meets the Emperor. Courtesy of Serendipity Point Films, Inc.

see Ignatz dressed in military uniform, approaching a palace which the voice-over tells us is that of the Emperor Franz Joseph: It is World War I, and Ignatz, a military judge, is going to have a private audience with the Emperor. The meeting lasts only a minute and is perfunctory, but Ignatz is deeply moved. Afterward, approaching the staircase, he touches his shoulder where the Emperor briefly placed his hand, like a teenager who has been touched by a rock idol. (Interestingly, István Deák finds this detail one of the rare false historical notes in the film; the Emperor would never have touched a commoner in such a familiar way).

One of the hostile critics of the film in Budapest remarked that the scene with the Emperor was put into the film to please American audiences, who "like palaces."[15] While the jibe may have a grain of truth in it, the palace scene is actually crucial to the film's theme of assimilation/accommodation, and it is repeated with variations in both Adam's and Ivan's stories. Adam, after his Olympic victory, enters a similar grand building, also dressed in uniform, and receives a military decoration; afterward, he descends the staircase, ramrod stiff, moved beyond words. Ironically, it is this same military stiffness and loyalty to the "homeland" that will get him killed a few sequences later. The scene of Adam's decoration thus both "repeats" his father's meeting

Ivan and Carole meet on the grand staircase. Courtesy of Serendipity Point Films, Inc.

with the Emperor and foreshadows his own death; more importantly, it exacerbates the theme of assimilation. What in Ignatz is an understandable loyalty to a system that has encouraged his advancement (at least, in his own eyes) becomes a tragic blindness in his son, who remains loyal even to a system that seeks his destruction.

There is yet a third decoration scene, which pushes the accommodation theme even further. Ivan, on Stalin's birthday, is decorated along with other police officers in a public ceremony in the Opera House (another grand building), and is chosen to give the formal speech of thanks. Standing on the stage in his uniform before a large crowd, Ivan shouts his words in a monotone: "Comrade Stalin has shown us the way!" His eyes stare ahead, oddly recalling the boy's stare at his father being tortured. Afterward, he is shown descending a grand staircase—but there is no pride in his face, only his usual pained look. This sequence "repeats" the two earlier ones, but turns the wheel once more; whereas his father and grandfather were men of will and power, Ivan is an automaton. His face constantly frozen into an anxious mask, he is the embodiment of trauma.

George Schöpflin has remarked, in a thoughtful review of the film, that Szabó's heroes are singularly devoid of irony. This strikes Schöpflin as a fault, aesthetically and historically; for the typical defense of the Jewish "insider/outsider" against the daily small (or large) humiliations he had to endure even in the best of times was, precisely, irony. The irony of the Jewish insider/outsider acted, according to Schöpflin, as a corrective to the "kitsch and sentimentalism" that always threatened the "intense emotions generated by nationalism."[16] This ironic distance from their own assimilation, he claims, is precisely what the Sonnenschein men lack.

Indeed, one is hard put to find a Szabó hero, in his oeuvre as a whole, who displays the kind of "corrective" irony Schöpflin describes, at once self-deprecating and subversive of the system to which the insider/outsider belongs (and does not belong). The protagonist of *Colonel Redl* may come closest to it. A poor boy from Galizia who is plucked from his home and sent to Imperial military school, where he rises to a high rank thanks to the patronage of a member of the General Staff, Redl is a typical "pariah" parvenu, in terms of class rather than ethnicity. Some fellow officers claim he is Jewish, but the film indicates that he is not; however, one of his good friends is the Jewish Army doctor Gustave Sonnenschein! This name has obviously been with Szabó for a long time. In an undeniably self-ironic, subversive move, Redl, appointed as the head of military intelligence, writes and files a negative report about himself, which leads to his downfall.

There is no such ironic subversion in *Sunshine*. There is, however, a different kind; all the Sonnenschein men engage in socially transgressive sexual behavior. Already in *Redl*, the main subversion of the hero consisted in his homosexuality; similarly, in *Mephisto*, the conformist actor who is willing to accommodate to the Nazi regime transgresses Nazi racial laws by his ongoing love affair with a black woman. In *Sunshine*, sexual transgression is repeated from generation to generation. Ignatz marries his first cousin and adopted sister Valerie, against his father's wishes; Adam, the proper patriot, engages in an adulterous love affair with his brother's wife. True, it is she who pursues him and he hates himself for yielding to her, but it is significant that their first sexual encounter takes place immediately after he descends the grand staircase with his decoration, as if to "correct" his rigid conformism and propriety. Similarly, it is while descending the staircase after his praise-of-Stalin speech that Ivan has his first encounter with Carole, the married blond policewoman who teases him about his anxious look ("the sad man," she calls him); in the next scene she shows up in his office, where they make breathless love on his desk.

Transgressive sexuality presents itself as the subversive counterpart to "good boy" integration into the system, a possibility of individual self-affirmation outside institutional or political norms. In this equation, women function as outsiders to authority, possible vehicles of freedom—but they are also, by the same token, outside the political realm and outside history. In his interview with the Hungarian journalist Dora Mülner ("Itt vigyázni kell"), Szabó stated: "Women stand with two feet on the ground. . . . They are much closer to nature, to every part of nature, including blood, than men. . . . For that very reason, they are less likely to fall prey to the attractions of ideologies and of history, they are more able to safeguard their identity than men."[17] A compliment, but also a sexist stereotype.

Furthermore, the women in *Sunshine* are not only outside politics (a positive trait in this context), but appear to be outside ordinary ethical standards as well. Adultery is not only a societal transgression; it is also a personal betrayal, and the women in *Sunshine* become increasingly crass. As in other repetitive patterns in the film, the progression is downward as the generations advance. Valerie, who leaves Ignatz for another man after World War I, declaring him too much of a conformist to the Empire, returns to him when he becomes an outcast during the Kun regime; Adam's sister-in-law, by contrast, never regrets betraying her husband with his own brother. As for Carole, she betrays not only her husband but her lover Ivan: Despite their passionate lovemaking, she drops him immediately when he falls from official grace; and when they meet by chance on the subway years later, she escapes, refusing to have any contact with him.

On the other hand, and perhaps in keeping with his theory about women's firmer grasp of reality, Szabó makes the old Valerie (beautifully played by Rosemary Harris) into the moral center of the film. Enduring through all four generations (the young Valerie is played by Rosemary Harris's daughter, Jennifer Ehle), Valerie expresses the ethical norms of the film when she tells Ivan that politics and history are not the important things in life; what really matters is the appreciation of life's beauty, despite the destructiveness of history. If there is a "message" in the film, this affirmation of individualist values—and of art, for Valerie is for a time a professional photographer—may well sum it up.

But what about Jewish identity and Jewish memory? We will get to that question by way of self-reflection.

Self-Reflection and Self-Revision

Just as repetitive patterning and linear narration are hallmarks of historical realism and of the epic mode, so self-reflection and the disruption of linear narrative are hallmarks of modernism. But self-reflection, in *Sunshine*, is not merely a modernist device; it is a veritable reexamination of a painful history, at once personal and collective.

Self-reflection as a formal device emphasizes the constructed (as opposed to "natural") status of the artwork, and Szabó uses it in significant ways in all of his films. In *Sunshine*, he exploits the difference between black-and-white still photography and colored moving image to highlight the relation between life and art. This is done most explicitly with the photograph of Valerie removing the thorn from her foot. We first see her in "living color," as part of the ongoing narrative; but the instant after Gustave clicks the shutter, we see the black-and-white photo on the screen. Szabó thus points to the transformation of the living scene into an artwork, enduring but deprived of color and movement. The same transformation occurs later with other scenes, photographed by Valerie. The photo of Valerie reappears at several key moments in the film, marking the march of time and the falling away of the family's history from that idyllic moment of "sunshine." Adding yet one more aesthetic layer, the pose in the photo is that of a standard type of Hellenistic sculpture, the Spinario or "thorn-puller." Szabó indicates this in a scene showing Adam's visit to the Pergamon Museum in Berlin after the Olympics, when he is charmed by an antique statue of a boy in exactly his mother's pose. Szabó obviously modeled the photograph on the statue, but in the film, the statue "follows" the photograph. This is one more way of putting into question the relationship between art and life, as well as the relationship between and among different forms of artistic representation. It is also a way for Szabó to link his film to a long tradition of European art films, from Murnau to Godard, which invite comparisons between the film image and painting or sculpture.[18]

Szabó's use of formal self-reflection highlights another dichotomy as well—not between art and life, but between history and fiction, or documentary and fictional film genres. He inserts archival newsreel footage into the fictional sequences of *Sunshine*, sometimes splicing his

Valerie, removing a thorn from her foot, assumes the Spinario pose. Courtesy of Serendipity Point Films, Inc.

main characters into the archival film. The black-and-white footage, marking every historical moment from World War I to 1956, introduces a documentary element into the fiction.[19] Paradoxically, however, this guarantee of historical reality interrupts the color narration and subverts its realism; the fiction is "de-realized" in the process, shown to be (only) fiction. Conversely, the spliced-in presence of Ralph Fiennes in historical footage puts the authenticity of documentary film into question.

Szabó introduces an explicit piece of self-reflection about historical representation in film through the character of an opportunistic director who makes propaganda films for whatever government is in power. The unnamed film director (played by the Hungarian actor Péter Halász), who is interrogated by Ivan after the war, made propaganda films purporting to show Soviet atrocities on the Russian front. We actually see an excerpt from one of his films viewed by Ivan; but when pressed by Ivan, the director admits that the film was staged and filmed in a small town near Budapest. The presumed documentary was a fake; and he never did travel to the Russian front—the director tells this to Ivan as a plea in his favor. "You shit!" is Ivan's comment. The complications here are quite wonderful, since this fake documentary was evidently made by Szabó to be used in his realist historical epic—hence, it is both fake and "real," a fictional creation masquerading as a false documentary. Szabó often uses such *mises en abyme*

Adam visits the museum and comes upon a Spinario sculpture. Courtesy of
Serendipity Point Films, Inc.

(in this instance, a film within the film) in his work, and their presence
is always thematically significant. The director in *Sunshine* reappears
later, filming Ivan when he receives his decoration, then filming him
again in the midst of the revolutionary crowds in 1956. It is because
of his film that Ivan ends up in jail after the uprising is put down.

What is the difference between documentary, fake documentary,
and historical realist fiction? What constitutes authenticity in film, and
how can we tell when a film lies? What is the responsibility of a
director to his audience, to his sponsors, to himself? How can one
survive, make films, and succeed in not being "a shit"? These are
among the questions raised by the self-reflexive sequences in *Sunshine*.

But there is more, and it is here that the question of Jewish memory
comes to the foreground. Self-reflection in *Sunshine* functions not only
in the usual way, as a formal pointer to the film itself, but also inter-
textually: *Sunshine* can be read as a thematic rewriting of Szabó's 1966
film, *Father*. In both films, the story is refracted through the main
character whose presence is signaled by voice-over narration, rather
than through an omniscient camera. Some of the archival newsreels
in *Sunshine* were also used in *Father*: the dead horse on the street in
Budapest in 1945 and the blown-up bridges on the Danube are among

the opening shots of the earlier film. There are a number of other visual allusions to *Father*; in particular, the shot of a single dilapidated streetcar on top of a hill with tracks leading up to it, which appears in black and white in *Father* and is shot exactly from the same angle in *Sunshine*—the only difference being that here the streetcar is new (the time is the 1950s, not 1945) and is shot in color. This visual quotation cannot be coincidental—the image is too carefully arranged for that.[20] Finally, the few black-and-white sequences in *Sunshine* that are pseudoarchival, shot by Szabó and featuring Fiennes, can also be considered as allusions to *Father*, which was shot in black and white.

Most interesting from our point of view, however, is that *Sunshine* makes explicit what is only implied in *Father*—namely, that the young protagonist is (or was) Jewish. Joshua Hirsch, in a perceptive essay, has analyzed the "repressed" Jewish story in *Father*.[21] The protagonist of that film, a young boy who lives through the war in Budapest, is identified as Catholic, but a number of indications, akin to Freudian slips, suggest that he comes from a Jewish (or formerly Jewish) family. What is repressed in *Father*, manifesting itself only as symptoms, becomes explicitly represented in *Sunshine*. Hirsch mentions as one "symptom" in the earlier film the fact that the protagonist's father was hunted by the Arrow Cross in 1944—this is recounted to the boy by his mother, but she leaves unstated why the Arrow Cross (whose main activity in 1944 was rounding up Jews) pursued him. Later, the young Takó asks his mother: "Did you ever think of leaving Hungary?" and she replies that his father did not want to leave, since he was "very Magyar." Again, no explanation is offered, but if one reads this exchange in light of Adam's story in *Sunshine*, its repressed meaning becomes clear. This repression may correspond to Szabó's own attitude toward his family's Jewish background; in the long interview he gave to an Italian critic in 1976, Szabó mentioned the autobiographical elements in *Father* without ever mentioning the protagonist's—or his own—ethnic or religious background. In recent interviews, as well as in the 1994 essay by David Paul, Szabó's family's Jewish background is explicitly mentioned.[22] This is clearly more than an individual choice—it is part of a collective remembering of Jewish identity after the taboo of the communist period, a taboo that may have been imposed by the regime but that also corresponded to the desire of most Hungarian Jews.

The anamnesis, or lifting of repression, that characterizes the relation between *Sunshine* and *Father* is beautifully brought out in the visual representation of the yellow star that Hungarian Jews were forced to wear after the Nazi occupation in March 1944. In *Father*, the yellow star appears only in a *mise en abyme*, during the shooting of a feature film in Budapest in the 1950s: a crowd of extras wearing the star (including Takó, who is presumably not a Jew) are marched over a bridge in a reenactment of what actually happened in 1944, while a temperamental director yells instructions at them through a megaphone. This oblique visual reference is all that we see of the Holocaust in Hungary in *Father*. The one character who is identified as a Jew in the film, Takó's girlfriend, talks to him at some length about her family's persecution during the war and about her problems of identity as a Jew and a Hungarian; but the camera shows only her face as she speaks, not the past she evokes. (Symptomatically, however, her narrative occurs during a walk she takes with Takó along the Danube, which evokes the shooting of Jews into the river by the Arrow Cross in 1944). In *Sunshine*, by contrast, the Holocaust representation is direct: Szabó shows not only the sadistic murder of Adam in the labor camp, but also archival footage of a line of Jews wearing the yellow star, being herded on a street in Budapest.

The Hungarian historian István Rév, writing about the "prehistory of post-Communism," has remarked that for him, "dealing with history is not a scholarly task; it is an existential undertaking," a way of examining the "possible available relations to the perpetually remade past."[23] The self-reflexive elements in *Sunshine*, and especially its revisionary relation to Szabó's earlier film, suggests that this evocative phrase can apply to the work of the filmmaker as well.

What's in a Name?

Change of names, whether of persons or places, is not new in Hungary. After the communist takeover in 1948, all of Budapest's major boulevards, streets, and squares were renamed, sometimes more than once: Andrássy Boulevard, named after a nineteenth-century statesman, became Stalin Boulevard, then People's Republic Boulevard; Király Street, referring to the King, became Mayakovsky Street, and so on. After 1989, the old names were given back. Proper names, István Rév has noted, are "related to efforts toward securing unambiguous identity."[24] That goes as much for sites as for people.

Why, then, was the ending of *Sunshine*—Ivan's taking back his original family name—so shocking (one commentator called it "astounding") to some Hungarian viewers? Szabó offered his own interpretations of the ending in interviews. For him, the film's real theme is that of personal identity; by taking back his Jewish-sounding name, Ivan breaks the pattern of accommodation to authority, with its attendant alienation of self, that was begun by his grandfather. "The obligation to accommodate, the terrible desire to fit in, transmitted from father to son, is what the story's last hero, Ivan, breaks with," Szabó stated to a Hungarian journalist. And in the same interview, he explains: "the protagonist finally understands who he is, and assumes that identity. That is much more important than the change of name. Ivan realizes that in order to be part of society, he does not have to renounce his self."[25] In an interview with a Canadian journalist, he generalized this theme to include not only Jews, and not only Hungary: "The film is about an identity crisis. . . . This is not only a Jewish problem. Millions of people suffer from the same question. Who am I? Should one, for the promise of a better life, cut off one's roots? I used the Jewish family simply as an example, because I know that world. I think that similar worries exist among the Turks in Germany, and one sees this problem in England, Ireland, and Kosovo."[26]

Well, yes. But not exactly. As Szabó well knows, the Jews in Hungary are not really comparable to Turkish "guest workers" in Germany, nor to Asian immigrants in England. The specificity of Hungarian Jews until the Holocaust (and since then, but much more problematically—that is the point) is that they *felt* Hungarian. They were not exiles; Hungary was their home. Furthermore, as Szabó shows in his film, they played an important historical role in the modernization of Hungary and in the creation of modern Hungarian identity. Jewish intellectuals—writers, journalists, publishers—played major roles in Hungarian cultural life, and the liberal professions were at times more than 50 percent Jewish. The Jewish laws of the late 1930s were designed precisely to do away with this Jewish "domination." They suddenly informed the Jews, even upper-class, assimilated, or converted Jews like Adam Sors, that they were not true Magyars, that in true Magyar eyes they were pariahs.

For over forty years after the Second World War, Jews who had survived and had decided to remain in Hungary persuaded themselves (with just a bit of effort) that anti-Semitism, as well as Jewish identity, were things of the past: Jewishness was irrelevant in communist Hungary. Many Jews born after the war did not even realize until much later that their family was Jewish: "How I learned that I was a Jew" became practically a canonical subgenre of autobiography in the early 1990s.[27] During the communist period, the word "Jew" could hardly be printed in the newspaper, nor were anti-Semitic writings publishable. It is true that the official anti-Zionist discourse of the Soviet bloc, starting in 1949 and revived periodically thereafter, was often a convenient cover for anti-Semitism, in Hungary as elsewhere. Still, Hungarian nationalism and the anti-Semitism that has traditionally accompanied it were not overtly endorsed by the communist regime.

After 1989 and the lifting of official censorship of the press and of book publishing, traditional anti-Semitic discourse once again became possible and actual. Of course, the same was true of other discourses, including Zionist and anti–anti-Semitic ones. The MDF, the center-right party that came to power in the 1990 elections, tolerated an extreme xenophobic and nationalist wing which eventually split off and formed its own party, the "Magyar Truth and Life Party" (MIÉP) led by the writer István Csurka. Csurka still edits *Magyar Forum*, the party's weekly newspaper, which is unabashedly anti-Semitic. Evicted in the 1994 elections, which brought the Left to power, the MIÉP bounced back in 1998 and was quite close to the new governing party, the once liberal but increasingly conservative and nationalist "Young Democrats" (FIDESZ) led by Viktor Orbán. In the 2002 elections, the "Young Democrats" were in turn ousted in favor of the Socialists, who may themselves be ousted in 2006.

Meanwhile, in 1999, the Hungarian public heard, for the first time in more than half a century, a member of the government refer to the "Jewish question" in Hungary; this provoked a certain indignation, whereupon a government spokesman published an open letter in a newspaper, explaining the Minister's meaning—not anti-Semitic, he said. But commentators pointed out that historically, the term "Jewish question" always had an anti-Semitic connotation in Hungary: It referred to the "overrepresentation" of Jews in the country's elite.[28] In 2002, before leaving office, the Orbán government erected its own version of postwar history in the "Terror House" museum on Andrássy Boulevard (former headquarters both of the Arrow Cross and of the Communist secret police), which accords one-tenth as much space to the Arrow Cross atrocities committed during the war as it does to the excesses of the Communist years. The museum's flyers emphasize that the Arrow Cross ruled only for "a few months" whereas the Communists ruled for decades. István Rév, analyzing these texts in detail, shows that the history they present absolves Hungary from all responsibility in the persecution of Jews, ascribing it exclusively to the Nazis, including the "Hungarian Nazis" who were the Arrow Cross. Hungary is presented only as a victim of outside forces from 1944 to 1989: first the Nazis, then the Soviets. Referring to the Arrow Cross as Nazis suggests that they were more German than Hungarian; as for the Soviets' Hungarian followers, the museum suggests that most were Jews bent on "revenge." Rév points out the factual inaccuracies and ideological biases (not always obvious to non-Hungarians) that underlie this "fantastic" account: "A script, and a rather familiar one, is put forward as a normal (normalized), that is, obvious, neutral presentation of history."[29]

Despite these troubling manifestations, however, it would be a mistake to compare contemporary Hungary to the 1930s, let alone the 1940s. For one thing—leaving aside the hugely different world situation—the majority of Hungarians do not appear to be in favor of anti-Semitism; for another, the Jews of Hungary have reacted vigorously, on the whole, to the reemergence of anti-Semitism from under the rug. Many assimilated Jewish intellectuals who had never spoken, or even, one surmises, thought much about their Jewish ancestry have in recent years begun writing or speaking about it. As one such intellectual remarked in 1993, "I have no contact with Jewishness, but now that there are anti-Semites I affirm that I'm a Jew."[30] The scholarly study of the Holocaust in Hungary, begun years ago in the United States by Hungarian Jewish refugees (notably Randolph Braham), has in the past decade become established in Hungary as well. In 2004, the Socialist government opened a Holocaust Memorial Center in Budapest, constructed at great expense, which aims to present public programs related to the history of Hungarian Jews.[31]

Aside from assimilated Jews who have a tenuous or nonexistent link to Jewish practice, Hungary today has a thriving Jewish community (more exactly, a plurality of communities), located chiefly in Budapest: Synagogues, Jewish schools, and Jewish cultural journals indicate a significant and visible Jewish presence. While being a Jew in Central

Europe is never simple, one might refer to a growing number of Jews in Hungary as "unproblematically self-identified Jews" (well, almost unproblematically). According to the latest sociological studies, there has been a return in recent years to a certain degree of Jewish practice (minimally, celebration of the Passover seder and attending synagogue on Yom Kippur) among young people, even among those raised by parents who had totally abandoned identification as Jews.[32]

And where does Szabó's film (released in Hungary in 2000, while the conservative Orbán government was still in power) fit in? *Sunshine* is clearly not about the "unproblematically self-identified" Hungarian Jews. Nor, one might say, was it chiefly addressed to them, though many went to see it and wrote about it enthusiastically; the Jewish cultural monthly *Múlt és Jövő* devoted almost a whole issue to discussions of the film in January 2000. Rather, the film's addressees were assimilated Jews who, like Szabó himself—or like his protagonist Ivan Sors—had only recently begun avowing (publicly or privately) their Jewish ancestry. By a fascinating but not altogether surprising twist, the critics who most passionately attacked *Sunshine* in Hungary belong precisely to this group.

"I left the movie sad and puzzled," wrote one well-known journalist in the liberal (formerly Socialist) daily, *Népszabadság*. Szabó's answer to the search for identity is, according to her, the "worst possible" one, for it supports those (that is, the anti-Semites) who "contest our inherited Hungarianness." If Ivan Sors can find his true identity only by becoming Sonnenschein, why should not all the Kovács and Kis (common Hungarian names, meaning "Smith" and "Little") whose families changed their name generations ago be advised by the anti-Semites to take back their Kohn name?[33] In fact, the extreme right-wing press has taken to "outing" assimilated Jews by digging up their family's original Germanic name; the anxiety expressed by the journalist alludes to this nasty habit.

A similar anxiety is found in what may have been the most detailed and sweeping critique of the film, published in the highly respected cultural weekly *Élet és Irodalom (Life and Literature)*. The author, Péter György, a well-known intellectual, criticizes Szabó for bowing to global market pressures in producing a film chiefly for an "American" audience. For the sake of this audience, György claims, Szabó has simplified Hungarian reality and presented a negative view of Hungary: His film does not show any "decent," ordinary, non-Jewish Hungarians, nor any extraordinary ones who sheltered Jews during the war. This is the image "the world will have of our Hungarian history, and this one-sidedness pains me," writes György. But his biggest worry, a veritable *cri de coeur*, is that "Israelite" and "non-Israelite" Hungarians will be driven apart by the "example" proposed in the film's ending. Szabó is wrong to insist on Jewish "difference" with Ivan's change of name, György maintains. Take the great modernist poet Miklós Radnóti: "He was born Glatter, he became a Catholic, and he is a Hungarian poet as Radnóti." Would not Szabó himself be outraged if "some nobody" suddenly started referring to the poet as Glatter?[34]

Fascinating question. Could a Miklós Glatter be a great Hungarian poet? György's answer seems to be "no," for only a "nobody," a creature beneath contempt, would think of referring to Radnóti as Glatter.

What György does not say, because it is known to all who read him, is that Miklós Radnóti was murdered in 1944 by Hungarian soldiers while on a forced march with a group of other Jewish prisoners. One occasionally hears that the Arrow Cross, not regular soldiers, killed Radnóti; in fact, it was noncommissioned officers of the Hungarian Army who shot him and fellow prisoners, when they were too weak to continue their march.[35] For all his Hungarianness and love of Hungary and the Hungarian language (Radnóti refused all his adult life to call himself a Jew or a Jewish poet, and converted to Catholicism in the early 1940s), he suffered the same fate as thousands of other Hungarian Jews. His posthumous volume of poetry, containing some of his greatest poems, written in his last months while in captivity, bore a title *(Tajtékos ég)* that has been translated into English as "Foamy Sky"—a sky with puffy clouds. As it happens, the first image we see in *Sunshine*, while the opening credits roll, is of a bright blue sky with foamy clouds. A mere coincidence? Perhaps. Or perhaps an unconscious association, for Szabó certainly knows Radnóti's poetry, and Adam Sors's fate is strikingly similar to Radnóti's—as it is to the fate of many others. The problem that *Sunshine* struggles with is the problem so sharply posed by the lives and works of the thousands of murdered Hungarian Jews who had thought of themselves as full-fledged citizens.

Tamás Ungvári, one of the many well-known intellectuals who responded to György's article, puts it well: Szabó's film opens up sen-

sitive wounds. It is about people who "chose a fate [a play on words
on the name "Sors," also in György's title], but whom that fate did
not choose. Another fate chose them, one they did not choose."[36]
Ungvári is pessimistic. The world over, he writes, combined identities
have become the rule: African-American, Catalan-Spanish, Breton-
French, Scottish-English. The only combination that its own society
tolerates with difficulty is that of Jewish-Hungarian. (Ungvári may be
idealizing the situation of Catalan-Spaniards or Breton-French, but
we can let that pass).

Although its anxious critics read Szabó's ending as equally pessimistic ("assimilation has failed, there is no way for a Jew to be just
Hungarian"), the film in fact seems to offer a more optimistic possibility. To be "outed" as a Jew is hostile and humiliating, but to come
out of the closet—to take back one's Jewish name willingly—is liberating. Ivan "breathes freely" in Budapest at last as Sonnenschein; he
does not leave Hungary, but makes his life there. The film's final pan-
orama of Budapest, beneath a muted sky, suggests that the beauty of
the city so closely identified with the Sonnenscheins' history may con-
sole Ivan for the losses and humiliations his family has suffered.

To an American viewer, even a Jewish-American born in Hungary,
this ending seems quite plausible. One can be Hungarian even with a
Jewish name; pluralistic democracy can work in Hungary. In sum, a
multiculturalist dream which I (being of a postmodern persuasion) am
drawn to applaud. Yet, for reasons quite different from those of the
Hungarian critics, I am a bit troubled by Szabó's ending. The dream
is tenuous, even as a dream. The change of name is secondary, Szabó
has stated; what matters is the recovery of roots and of a suppressed
identity. But at the end of this film, Ivan has *nothing but* the name to
tie him to Jewishness or to his family's past. He is the baptized son of
two Catholic converts, and he has thrown out all traces that might
constitute a cultural archive. Photographs, letters, all the papers carefully saved by the faithful (Catholic) family servant during the war,
even the famous black notebook that was at the origin of the family
fortune—Ivan discards them all. The notebook falls to the ground,
unseen and unrecognized by him, then joins the rest of the archive in
the garbage van. The past, it would seem, has nothing to offer, and
the future is equally blank: Ivan has no progeny, as far as we can see.
He is the last of the Sonnenscheins, alone in the city crowds.

Yet, the ending of the film is clearly meant to be upbeat. The pan over Budapest, the swelling music, Ivan's final voice-over announcing that he feels free, all indicate a hopeful mood. A triumph of individualism and an affirmation of the individual artist, as some commentators have suggested?[37] Perhaps. But I cannot help thinking of the final image of Szabó's last film before *Sunshine*, *Sweet Emma, Dear Böbe* (1992), which is bitterly ironic. What if, instead of reading the final image of *Sunshine* as a promise, we were to read it as ironic: not Szabó's dream, but a delusion of his traumatized hero? It all depends, finally, on how one interprets Ivan's statement, at the end, that he wants to follow in his grandmother's footsteps and photograph the world around him. Valerie appears here as the artist and individualist who represents the film's values. Since Ivan has shown not the slightest inclination for artistic expression up to this point (circa 1961, when he is more than thirty years old), this could be pure fantasy on his part. But since the voice-overs in the film designate Ivan as its narrator, we can also interpret the film itself as confirmation or "proof" that he has realized his project, the way *A la recherche du temps perdu* can be read as the realization of the novel planned at the end by Proust's narrator. In that case, the sudden jump at the film's end to the Budapest of 1999, "after communism," could be an indication of Ivan's future in relation to 1961 and of his present situation as a filmmaker.

Of course, this still leaves open the question of how one can recreate a family history after discarding the family archive. Is a change of name enough to "secure an ambiguous identity," as Rév suggests? Does Ivan discard the archive (the tool of historians) in order to rely, as an artist, only on his personal memories and on the memories transmitted to him by his grandmother in fashioning his story? Must artistic creation reinvent the past, rather than documenting it? What is the relation between memory and identity, between recollection and artistic creation, between personal remembrance and a collective "perpetually remade past"?

Like the Danube that flows through Budapest, full of Jewish ghosts, *Sunshine* is a beautiful and deeply moving film that poses insoluble questions. These questions will preoccupy us, in various ways, in the chapters that follow.

6

Revision: Historical Trauma and Literary Testimony

THE BUCHENWALD MEMOIRS OF JORGE SEMPRUN

> . . . the dream of every writer: to spend his life writing a single
> book, constantly renewed!
>
> —*J. Semprun,* L'écriture ou la vie

$\mathcal{P}$SYCHOLOGISTS HAVE BEEN studying trauma and its relation to memory since the late nineteenth century, ever since the beginning of the discipline. Charcot, Janet, and others who worked at the famed Salpêtrière clinic in Paris (including Freud, who spent several crucial months there in 1885–1886) elaborated the first theories of traumatic dissociation and recollection in relation to hysteria.[1] After World War I, when the treatment of veterans of trench warfare gave rise to the concept of war neurosis or shell shock, trauma studies acquired a historical as well as a psychological dimension. In the past half-century, as the memory of the Holocaust has come to occupy an ever-larger space in public consciousness and in the academy, the study of trauma has become a subject for philosophers and literary and cultural critics as well as historians and psychologists. The catastrophe of September 11, 2001 (not to mention all the other catastrophes of the last decade) has, of course, added yet another layer to contemporary trauma studies and studies of collective memory of atrocity.

The cultural historian Dominick LaCapra proposed a few years ago to distinguish what he called structural trauma from historical trauma. Structural trauma, according to this distinction, is general and "transhistorical," appearing "in different ways in all societies and all lives."[2]

The trauma of birth and separation from the mother would be one example; the anxiety of being "thrown into" the world, as Heidegger put it, would be another. Historical trauma, by contrast, is specific, located in time, and "not everyone is subject to it." War, racial or ethnic persecution, and genocide are examples that come to mind. LaCapra argues, persuasively, that we should not conflate these two kinds of trauma, as some theorists tend to do: the Holocaust was not an extreme version of a general human condition of abandonment, but a historical event with victims, perpetrators, and bystanders. While we can never "free" ourselves of structural trauma, we can try to work through the legacies of historical traumas and even, perhaps, avoid them.

I agree with LaCapra about the need for fine distinctions; indeed, I believe that yet another one is needed. LaCapra assumes the collective nature of historical trauma, without exploring how the collective is related to the individual; and also without distinguishing what we might call *personal* historical trauma from *collective* historical trauma. If a child is abused or dehumanized by a parent in Middletown, USA, circa 1944, that experience can be qualified as traumatic, and in LaCapra's terms it would come under the heading of historical trauma, since it is not part of the human condition. But such personal historical trauma differs from the abuse and dehumanization that children and adults suffered in concentration camps in that same year of 1944; one major difference is that in the former case the event is experienced by a single person at a given time and place, whereas in the latter it is experienced by thousands at a given time and place.

Of course, no two people experience the same event in exactly the same way. Collective historical trauma is experienced by individuals, one at a time, and this fact has important consequences for the concept of testimony. Every testimony is unique; it reports what the speaker has personally witnessed or lived through. Giorgio Agamben has noted that Latin has two words for witness: *testis*, whose primary meaning is spectator or bystander, and *superstes*, which also means spectator or bystander but primarily means survivor.[3] Although the English word "testimony" is derived from the first, almost always when we speak of testimony in a nonjuridical sense we have the second word in mind; it is the survivor, not the uninvolved spectator, who presents his or her testimony of the traumatic event.

Testimony is always of necessity individual; but if it refers to a collective historical trauma, it will, also of necessity, be about more than the experience of a single person. Even while it represents (in the sense of re-presenting, making visible) the unique perspective of the one who says "I," testimony in such a case also represents in the sense of being exemplary, of "standing for." The single witness, even while recounting his or her own experiences, represents all those who were in a similar position in the same time and place. Jean-Paul Sartre, in *What Is Literature?* refers at one point to his and his generation's discovery of what he calls historicity—that is, the realization that one's individual life was inexorably linked, down to its smallest details, to the lives of countless others. Sartre locates this discovery (which he says struck most Frenchmen with "stupefaction") around 1930:

> Starting around 1930, the world economic crisis, the rise of Nazism, the events in China, the Spanish Civil War opened our eyes; it seemed as if the ground was going to fall from under us. . . . And our life as an individual, which had seemed to depend on our efforts, our virtues and our faults, our good and bad luck, and on the good or bad will of a very small number of people, seemed to us to be governed down to its minutest details by obscure and collectives forces; and its most private circumstances seemed to reflect the state of the whole world.[4]

Although it does not deal specifically with the questions of witnessing or of historical trauma, I find this statement wonderfully suggestive in relation to them. The feeling that one's "private circumstances" can "reflect the state of the whole world" describes, I think, the particular aspect of the relation between individual testimony and collective historical trauma that I am trying to pinpoint. The witness who recounts his or her own story represents, in both senses of the word, multitudes who did not survive to testify or who may have survived but have remained speechless. Represents always imperfectly, incompletely, to be sure—but these adverbs apply to the witness's relation to his or her own story as well.

This representative role places upon the survivor-witness of collective historical trauma an unusually heavy burden of responsibility. Every witness, by definition, promises to tell the truth of his or her experience, to the best of her or his recollection, just as every auto-biographer implicitly or explicitly undertakes to do the same. But when one is seeking to tell the truth about an extreme experience that was lived through by many others as well as by oneself, the responsibility is far greater than usual. To lie or to cheat, under such circumstances, is ignominious—consider the disgrace that immediately followed when it was proven that Binjamin Wilkomirski had fabricated his "childhood memories" of the Holocaust (a case I will discuss in detail in Chapter 6). Even merely to err or misremember in such a case can be a source of shame or embarrassment.

Avishai Margalit, in his philosophical reflection on the ethics of memory, calls the survivor-witness of collective suffering a "moral witness" and an agent of collective memory; he does not, however, explore the complicated status of testimony itself, as an act of narration that purports to tell the truth about past experience.[5] As we know, and as countless experimental studies have shown, faulty memory and error are the human lot: People of irreproachable moral character and the best intentions inevitably distort details, forget or invent whole episodes, and commit other "sins of memory" in recounting their past, whether to themselves or to others, in writing or in speech.[6] But here, it seems to me, is where the full force of literary testimony makes itself felt. For one sign of the "literariness" of a testimony is precisely its awareness of the pitfalls of memory and human error, its self-consciousness, and what one might call its *performance*, of the problems of testimonial writing about trauma. There are, of course, many ways to define the "literary." Not every written text is literary, even if it has been published; conversely, one need not be a professional writer in order to produce a powerful work of literary testimony.

The writer I will discuss here *is* a professional writer; and he has written not one but a whole series of self-consciously literary testimonies about his experience in a Nazi concentration camp.

Jorge Semprun, a Spaniard whose family left Spain at the outbreak of the Spanish Civil War (although upper-middle-class and Catholic, the family was strongly Republican), was twenty years old in the fall of 1943 when he was arrested as a member of a foreign contingent of the French Resistance and deported some weeks later to Buchenwald. He remained in Buchenwald for more than a year, from January 1944 until the liberation of the camp by Allied soldiers in April 1945. He then returned to Paris, and spent many years as a clandestine operative for the Spanish Communist Party, trying to oust Franco. It was not until he was forty that he published his first book.

Before he entered the Resistance, Semprun was a philosophy student in Paris, well versed in Spanish, German, and French literature and harboring literary ambitions himself. As he has often explained, however, he made a conscious decision after returning from Buchenwald to "forget" the camp—it was his only way to go on living. In the early 1960s, he began an autobiographical novel, *Le grand voyage* [The Long Voyage], published in 1963. The book won a major literary award (the Formentor Prize) and was translated into many languages. It recounts the protagonist's journey to the Nazi camp, in a boxcar jammed with other prisoners. The outstanding feature of this novel, noted by all of the numerous critics who have written about it, is Semprun's handling of narrative time. While the time of the journey is clearly delineated as five days, the narrative often switches, sometimes in a single sentence, to the time before the journey (including the narrator's childhood) or, more unusually, to the time after his liberation from the camp, including the many years that preceded the writing of the book.

Lawrence Langer, in his early study *The Holocaust and the Literary Imagination*, compared Semprun's numerous and abrupt temporal shifts to Proust's. They "complicate memory by making it an act of anticipation as well as recollection, thus adding to the familiar 'remembrance of things past' a seemingly impossible 'remembrance of things to come.' "[7] Actually, in Proust's novel the "remembrance of things to come" is not at all impossible, for the Proustian narrator is perched at the top of a temporal edifice from which he can command the whole sweep of the past, moving his gaze and his narrative up and down and sideways at will. The narrator of *Le grand voyage*, emphasizing repeatedly that he is writing many years after the journey, exploits the same possibility. While this could be seen, as in the case of Proust, as a sign of narrative mastery and control (Colin Davis sees it as a sign of the narrator's "Marxist certainty," since the book was written while Semprun was still a member of the Communist Party),[8] it is also possible to interpret the frequent temporal shifts as a sign of traumatic disturbance. Thus, Sidra Ezrahi has suggested in her reading of this novel that "the simultaneity of past, present, and future . . . fixes the Holocaust in the eternal present . . . the concentrationary reality which has invaded the psyche remains there inexorably."[9]

Although clearly autobiographical, evoking events and memories that Semprun would return to in many of his subsequent works, *Le grand voyage* was subtitled *roman*. Semprun has been careful to label some of his imaginative works as novels, while others (six on the latest list of publications) bear either no label or are subtitled *récits* (narratives). It is these "non-novels" that interest me here, in particular the three that I have called Buchenwald memoirs: *Quel beau dimanche!* (1980) [*What a beautiful Sunday!*], *L'écriture ou la vie* (1994) [*Literature or Life*], and *Le mort qu'il faut* (2001) [The necessary dead man, not yet translated]. These works all qualify as autobiographical, according to the minimal criteria proposed by Philippe Lejeune: the author's name is identical to the names of the narrator and of the protagonist.[10] It is true, however, that since he used several pseudonyms during his years in the Resistance and in the Communist Party, Semprun's names have been multiple. Furthermore, as he has stated both in these books and in published interviews, he takes certain liberties that could be called novelistic even in these testimonial works; for example, he gives real people false names and even invents certain characters. In *L'écriture ou la vie*, he explained in an interview, he telescoped two French officers he met right after liberation into a single character, "because that shortcut [*raccourci*] is more effective than simple reality." But he added that he always observes an "absolute limit": "never to facilitate the work of negationist critics. Each word is weighed so that it is impossible to put into question, on the pretext that such and such a detail is false, the veracity of my testimony as a whole."[11]

Here, then, is the crux of literary testimony: Semprun as survivor-witness claims incontrovertible veracity for his testimony as a whole; but Semprun as writer claims the right to take certain liberties when they are "more effective than simple reality." Is this an unfortunate contradiction, a breach of responsibility, or a fruitful paradox? To put it somewhat differently, what does "effective" mean in the above statement? The French expression Semprun uses is "porter davantage" [*ce raccourci porte davantage que la simple réalité*], which, if one wanted to be very literal, could be translated as "carries more than simple reality." More of what does it carry? "Raccourci," which means both shortcut and condensation, refers to the fictional liberty taken by the

writer of the testimony; but we may consider the word itself as a
"shortcut"—or, if you will, a metaphor—for *écriture*, a writing that is
not merely a recording of events but a difficult engagement with language and meaning. The German word for poetry, *Dichtung* (literally,
a "thickening") points toward the same metaphor—poetry as "condensed" language. Semprun's claim, then, would be that writing in this
sense, while it may be inexact as regards positive facts, leads to greater
and more complex understanding, presumably both on the part of the
writer and the reader.

In *L'écriture ou la vie*, the work in which he is most explicitly concerned with the problem of testimonial writing, Semprun formulates
this claim repeatedly. "Only the artifice of a masterly narrative will
prove capable of partially conveying the truth of the testimony," he
writes at the beginning, recalling his first thoughts after liberation.[12]
A hundred pages later, recounting a heated conversation among survivors who wonder whether anyone will ever understand the horrors
they experienced, he repeats the idea: "How do you tell such an unlikely truth, how do you impel one to imagine the unimaginable, if
not by elaborating, by reworking reality, by putting it in perspective?
With a bit of artifice, then!" (135/124]. Later still, discussing the
problem with his former professor in Paris, he states the idea again:
"I don't want to do a simple testimony [*simple témoignage*]." He continues: "I need a narrative 'I' that draws on my experience but goes
beyond it, capable of opening the narrative up to fiction, to imagination. . . . fiction that would be as illuminating as the truth, of course.
That would help reality to seem real, and truth to be believable [*vra-
isemblable*]" (175/165). These words, presumably spoken in 1945, seem
to be anticipating *Le grand voyage*, an autobiographical novel written
in the first person, published many years after this scene but many
years before the book we are reading. Semprun's play with narrative
time is evident here, as he may be projecting back to 1945 preoccupations that were not acted on, or even formulated, until much later.

While it is paradoxical (and Semprun takes pleasure in emphasizing
the paradox), the notion that fiction can tell the truth more effectively
or more profoundly than straightforward factual narrative is not at all
startling; indeed, even the notion that testimony, whether literary or
not, inevitably comprises elements of fiction is by now a common-
place—we are all postmodernists in that regard; we know that every

narrative is constructed, no matter how "simple" or "artless" it may appear. Nevertheless, I would suggest that Semprun's repeated insistence on the necessity of artifice in literary testimony about the Holocaust is worth exploring in depth. What is the nature, or the meaning, of artifice in this context? What is its relation to memory, to repetition, and to trauma? One thing that makes Semprun such an interesting writer is that he himself has thought about these questions and has incorporated them, more or less explicitly, into his work. It will be useful, therefore, to consider one example in detail—but before that, we need to take a brief detour to consider psychoanalytic views about repetition and trauma.

Freud's most developed reflection about repetition occurs in *Beyond the Pleasure Principle*, written shortly after World War I. He begins with a question: Why do victims of shell shock return persistently to the trauma of the war in their dreams? Given that dreams are wish-fulfillments, how can one explain the compulsive repetition, in the dream, of a deeply unpleasant experience? He then proposes two rather different explanations for what he calls the compulsion to repeat. On the one hand, it manifests a desire for mastery; by repeating the original trauma in his thoughts or dreams, the subject seeks to overcome it, to actively assert his control over it. In this sense, the repetition is akin to children's play, and here Freud mentions his famous example of the "Fort-Da" game, in which the toddler whose mother has disappeared tries to master his anxiety by repeatedly throwing away and then retrieving a toy. On the other hand, the compulsion to repeat is a sign of the death instinct, the desire of the organism to return to its original inorganic state. Repetition, therefore, seems to be a two-faced phenomenon, implying either activity and mastery or passivity and death.

More recently, some analysts, reviving the terminology of Pierre Janet as well as Freud, have distinguished between two kinds of memory: traumatic memory, which is characterized by compulsive repetition and inflexibility, and narrative memory, characterized by fluidity and variability.[13] The subject of traumatic memory is essentially passive, locked into a repetition that abolishes the difference between past and present; the subject of narrative memory is essentially active, able to situate the traumatic memory in the past and therefore to gain some emotional distance from it. If traumatic memory is like melancholy, imprisoned in the past and unending in its deadening effect, narrative memory is like mourning, a process that ends with the resumption of life and a turn toward the future.[14] Or, in yet another pair of Freudian terms, if traumatic memory is an acting out, then narrative memory is a working through, an ongoing process that may last a lifetime.

How does this relate to writing about historical trauma? Sidra Ezrahi, in an article titled "Representing Auschwitz," has defined two approaches to writing and theorizing about the Holocaust, whether in testimony, fiction, or criticism—one she calls absolutist or static, and the other relativist or dynamic. "The static or absolutist approach," she writes, "locates a non-negotiable self in an unyielding place whose sign is Auschwitz; the dynamic or relativist position approaches the representation of the memory of that place as a construction of strategies for an ongoing renegotiation of that historical reality."[15] Ezrahi suggests, at the end of her article, that these two approaches are in fact "part of the same dialectic," but I think they can also be mapped onto the analytic distinction between traumatic memory and narrative memory. In that case, the static or absolutist approach would be governed by unchanging repetition, while the relativist approach would be governed by repetition with a difference, what Ezrahi calls renegotiation. To keep in mind its relation to repetition, however, I am going to call it revision—that is, a process whereby the memory of a traumatic past event is not merely repeated but continually reinterpreted in light of the subject's evolving preoccupations and self-understandings. I also like this word because it contains "vision," hence a new way of seeing something one has seen before.

Now we can come back to Semprun. I would like to propose, by means of an extended example, that artifice in Semprun's testimonial works is the poetic equivalent of revision in the sense I have just defined and also to show that this process, which implies a mastery or overcoming of trauma ("only the artifice of a masterly narrative can tell the truth of the testimony"), is neither simple nor unproblematic—and that Semprun knows that as well.

Revising the Entry into Death

Next to his particular handling of narrative time—which he has called "this manner of writing in a temporal to-and-fro, between anticipation and turning back"[16]—I would say that revision is Semprun's characteristic signature as a writer. This is probably most evident in *L'écriture ou la vie*, whose very structure is based on revision. Revision also becomes an explicit theme in this book, as Semprun looks back at some of his earlier works, notably at one or two novels, and explains why he invented certain characters (like the "guy from Semur" in *Le grand voyage*, who acts as a listener/witness to the narrator's memories in the boxcar), or why he transformed some real-life companions into fictional characters with different traits. Such explicit commentary on what was "invented" in a work of fiction shows a self-consciousness that occasionally borders on self-parody. Thus, after one such explanation, Semprun concludes: "There's the truth reestablished, the total truth of that story which was already truthful" (*EV* 47/37). The possibility of arriving at "total truth" once and for all is, of course, put into question by the very enunciation of that sentence. As if to confirm the instability, Semprun reports, much later in the book, a conversation he had with Carlos Fuentes shortly after the publication of *Le grand voyage*. Speaking about the Spanish translation of Semprun's book, Fuentes, playing on the adage of *traduttore/traditore* [translator/traitor], tells him he should have done the translation himself, for that way he could have allowed himself to "betray your original text to try to go further." After that, he could have translated the Spanish version back into French and so on endlessly, since the experience is inexhaustible. Thus, Fuentes concludes, "you would have realized the dream of every writer: to spend his life writing a single book, endlessly renewed!" (*EV* 285/275).

This charming episode suggests, in a humorous mode, what also has a more somber implication and is stated that way elsewhere in the book: The experience of Buchenwald can never be exhausted because it is the experience of death—not only the death of others but one's own. In the beginning of *L'écriture ou la vie*, Semprun describes his first encounter with liberating soldiers, three British officers who stare at him with horror. Seeing their panic-stricken eyes, he understands that he looks like a ghost, indeed that he is a ghost, a revenant: "For I had not really survived death. . . . I had not escaped it. Rather, I had crossed through it, from one end to the other" (*EV* 24/15). No wonder that for many years, he chose "deliberately and systematically" to forget the camp and to forget writing as well. Once he started, however, the task became endless, open to endless revision.

Does that imply, as Fuentes suggested, that it is open to the author's multiple betrayals of his own texts?

This question brings me to the detailed example I have been promising, an episode that Semprun recounts no less than four times in the three Buchenwald memoirs—once in *Quel beau dimanche!*, twice in *L'écriture ou la vie*, and once again in *Le mort qu'il faut*—over a period of more than twenty years. We may assume that this episode had, or has acquired over the years, a crucial importance for the survivor-writer. It should come as no surprise, therefore, that the episode concerns the moment of his entry into the camp—or what we could call, remembering what he says about being a revenant, his moment of crossing over the threshold of death. My contention is that the full import and meanings (with emphasis on the plural) of this episode can only be understood if one reads it serially, in its repeated and revised versions from work to work. Somewhat to my surprise, none of the critical commentaries I have read on Semprun has undertaken such a project, or even noticed the repetition of the episode, let alone its importance.

Let's start, then, with *Quel beau dimanche!* This is a book devoted chiefly to Semprun's growing disaffection from Communism during the early 1960s; but the "beautiful Sunday" of the title refers to a day in Buchenwald in 1944 (as well as being a homage to Aleksandr Solzhenytsn's *One Day in the Life of Ivan Denisovich*). Using "a typical Sunday in Buchenwald" as its temporal anchor, the narrative leaps forward and backward in time, in Semprun's characteristic manner. The episode of the entry into the camp is recounted about a quarter of the way into the book, and is introduced in a section that begins with the question of his name. A former fellow inmate from Buchenwald, who happens to be his driver as he travels on a mission for the Spanish Communist Party in 1960, calls him Gérard: "But Gérard is a false name that makes me jump."[17] The autobiographical narrator then explains that Gérard had been the name given to him in the Resistance, along with the false profession of gardener. In the course of this explanation he shifts several times from the first to the third person, as if the grammatical disturbance were a symptom of his uncertain identity: "In Buchenwald, he was no longer Gérard Sorel, except for the Frenchmen who knew me from the prisons in Auxerre and Dijon, and the transit camp at Compiègne. I wasn't a gardener either" (*QB* 94/101). After this, suddenly, comes the memory of arrival:

Le nuit de mon arrivée au camp, j'avais fini par me trouver planté devant un type, assis à une table, avec des crayons et des fiches devant lui. Deux minutes avant, je courais tout nu . . . le long de couloirs en ciment, d'escaliers labyrinthiques. . . . Je ne savais plus très bien où j'en étais, après la longue série de brutales cérémoniales initiatiques de cette nuit d'arrivée à Buchenwald. (QB 94–95)

On the night of my arrival in the camp, I had finally ended up in front of a guy, seated at a table, with pencils and file cards in front of him. Two minutes earlier, I was running naked . . . along cement hallways, labyrinthine staircases. . . . I no longer knew quite where I was, after the long series of brutal initiation ceremonies of that night of arrival in Buchenwald. (*WB* 101)

The emphasis here is on shock, the "brutal initiation" into a hitherto unknown world. The man seated at the table asks him for his profession, in German:

"*Beruf?*" m'a-t-il demandé. Je lui ai dit que j'étais étudiant, puisque je n'étais plus jardinier. Le type a haussé les épaules. "*Das ist doch kein Beruf!*" s'est-il exclamé. Ce n'était pas un métier, semblait-il. J'ai failli faire un calembour d'hypokhâgheux. "*Kein Beruf, nur eine Berufung!*" ai-je failli dire. Pas un métier, seulement une vocation. . . . Mais je me suis retenu de faire ce jeu de mots d'hypokhâgneux germaniste. . . . Je n'ai donc pas fait mon calembour vaseux et j'ai insisté sur ma qualité d'étudiant. Alors, prenant son temps, le type m'a expliqué qu'à Buchenwald il valait mieux avoir un métier manuel . . . Gérard alors a pensé que le seul travail manuel dont il maîtrisait les rudiments, c'était celui de terroriste. . . . Mais je n'en ai rien dit et le type, en désespoir de cause, m'a inscrit comme étudiant. (*QB* 95–6)

"*Beruf?*" he asked me. I told him I was a student, since I was no longer a gardener. The guy shrugged his shoulder. "*Das ist doch kein Beruf!*" he exclaimed. That was not a profession, it seemed.

I almost made a college boy's pun. *"Kein Beruf, nur eine Berufung!"* I almost said. Not a profession, merely a vocation. . . . But I held back from making that verbal joke, typical of a first-year student of German. . . . So I didn't make my inane joke and insisted on my status as a student. Then, taking his time, the guy explained to me that in Buchenwald it was better to have a manual trade. . . . Gérard then thought that the only manual work he was acquainted with was that of terrorist. . . . But I said nothing about that and the guy, giving up, registered me as a student. (*WB* 102–3)

The anecdote proper ends here. We notice the shifts in pronouns again: Clearly, the main focus is on identity. The newly arrived prisoner, stripped naked and then clad in haphazard rags, is asked to say what, or who, he is, and he clings to his former identity as a student. When challenged, he thinks of making a clever joke to show off his knowledge of German, but then holds his tongue. Although he has his way in the end and is registered as a student, the prevailing mood is one of disorientation and uncertainty. The paragraphs of commentary that follow the anecdote prolong this mood:

Mais seize ans après, ça me fait sursauter que Barizon m'appelle encore Gérard. C'est comme si je cessais d'être moi, d'être Je, pour devenir le personnage d'un récit qu'on ferait à propos de moi. Comme si je cessais d'être le Je de ce récit pour en devenir un simple Jeu, ou Enjeu, un Il. Mais lequel? Le Il du Narrateur qui tient les fils de ce récit? Ou le Il d'une simple troisième personne, personnage du récit? Quoi qu'il en soit, je ne vais pas me laisser faire, bien sûr, puisque je suis le rusé Dieu le Père de tous ces fils et tous ces ils. (*QB* 96)

Sixteen years later, though, in Nantua, it makes me jump that Barizon still calls me Gérard. It's as if I ceased being me, being I, to become a character in a story that would be told about me. As if I ceased being the I of this story to become a simple Game, or Stake, a He. But which one? The He of the Narrator who holds the threads of this narrative? Or the He of a simple third person, a character in the story? In any case, I'm not going to let

myself be pushed around, of course, since I am the crafty God
the Father of all these sons [or all these threads] and all these
he's. (*WB* 103)

The quasi-avalanche of puns in this passage (*Je, Jeu, Enjeu; fils, fils,*
ils), all relating to identity, indicates the anxiety of the narrator who
seeks to reassure himself that he is in control of his self and of his
text. The unexpressed question is not only "Who am I?" but "What
is my relation to the tale I am telling?" Is he really a crafty God, fully
in charge of his material?

It is worth noting that the event that triggers the memory of his
arrival in Buchenwald—his old campmate Barizon calling him
Gérard—is situated in 1960, before Semprun wrote his first book.
Although by the time he is writing this book, *Quel beau dimanche!*, he
is a well-known writer, the conversation with Barizon is set much
earlier, at a time of multiple identities as a Communist Party operative
on his way out of the party. The memory of his arrival in the concentration camp, with its brutal stripping away of identity, is thus over-
determined by his other preoccupations with identity at the time the
memory surfaces.

Fourteen years later, in his next autobiographical text about Buchenwald, *L'écriture ou la vie*, Semprun returns twice to the episode of
arrival in the camp. In fact, this episode becomes a major structuring
element of the book. Its first appearance is toward the beginning, in
a chapter whose narrative time is situated in April 1945, shortly after
the liberation of the camp. As before, the incident is introduced as a
suddenly remembered memory; this time, however, it is recounted not
only to the reader but to an interlocutor within the narrative. Lieutenant Rosenfeld, a German American officer in Buchenwald after
liberation, is interviewing former inmates who were involved with the
administration of the camp, including Semprun. Rosenfeld (whose
name suggests that he is Jewish, though Semprun does not comment
on this fact) looks at the number and the red triangle on Semprun's
jacket, and engages conversation: " 'You're a student, I suppose. But
of what?' asked Lieutenant Rosenfeld. That reminded me of something, some distant episode" (*EV* 91/81). In fact, the episode was not
so very distant from this scene in ordinary time—it took place about
fifteen months earlier. But since it relates to his initiation, a time when

he did not yet know Buchenwald, it evidently feels very far away. Oddly, the memory has made him smile, without knowing it. Rosenfeld asks him whether philosophy makes him smile (Semprun has just told him he had been a philosophy student), and it is in reply to that question that the narrative of the episode begins: "I had run down the long underground passage. Barefoot, on the rough concrete floor. Stark naked, I might add: naked from head to toe. Naked as a worm" (*EV* 92/82). There follows a detailed, two-page flashback to an even earlier moment ("Before, there had been the uproar, the dogs"), then everybody being herded into the shower room, hours of waiting, being shaved from top to bottom and plunged into a disinfectant bath. "It was after all these ritual purifications that we were sent running through the underground passage" (*EV* 94/83–84). The shift from first person singular to plural indicates that this is not only Semprun's story, but that of a whole group. Then comes another page of detailed description of the clothes they received, ill-fitting and mismatched. Finally, he finds himself in front of the prisoner who is filling out identity cards of the new arrivals.

What was related in one paragraph in *Quel beau dimanche!* (from arrival to standing at the table) has been expanded here to almost five pages. Paradoxically, it is the later text that contains the more detailed memory.

The actual encounter with the inmate who registers him takes about the same amount of space as in the earlier book, but it is strikingly different. First of all, the man who was designated simply as "le type," "the guy," is here described in some detail: "About forty years old. Gray hair. Eyes, extraordinarily blue; extraordinarily sad, too" (*EV* 95/ 85). As before, the man asks him his profession; and as before, when he replies that he is a student—specifying, this time, "of philosophy"— the man says that is not a profession, *"Das ist doch kein Beruf!"* At this point, the narrative veers from repetition and expansion to outright self-contradiction: "I couldn't help making a second-year Germanist's pun for his benefit. '*Kein Beruf aber eine Berufung!*' I was quite pleased with my witticism" (*EV* 95/85). Having emphasized, in the 1980 version, that he had held his tongue, here he emphasizes the very opposite! The contradiction could not be more blatant. There is also a more minor contradiction: whereas earlier he had called himself a "first-year student" [*hypokhâgneux*], here he makes himself a year more advanced *[khâgneux]*, perhaps in accordance with the arrogance of his behavior—a behavior that seems all the more in contradiction with his surroundings, since the humiliation that preceded the exchange has just been described at great length. After this, the account follows the earlier one: The young man insists, stubbornly, that he is a student of philosophy, and the anecdote ends with "the guy with the blue gaze" making a gesture of impatience and sending him on.

Then the narrative returns to April 1945. Rosenfeld, who has listened to the story with interest, remarks: "It's a good beginning." Beginning of what? Semprun asks. " 'Beginning of the experience,' he said. 'And of the account you could give of that experience!' " (*EV* 97/86). Thus, while in this second telling we again have a story of initiation with an emphasis on the new inmate's stubborn clinging to his former status as a student, the main emphasis is not on personal identity—there are no shifts in pronouns, no reflections on his name—but rather on how to tell the story, how to bear witness. Rosenfeld's remark suggests that the substance of the experience is indissociable from its telling; this confirms Semprun's own view, repeated variously throughout the book, that only a self-consciously literary writing can render the truth of the camp experience. At this moment, he replies to Rosenfeld that he considers the story he has just told him too "anecdotique" for a good beginning; instead, one should begin with "the essential part of this experience," which was the "experience of radical Evil." Rosenfeld catches the allusion to Kant's *radikal Böse*, making Semprun wonder whether he too is a philosophy student. Semprun then repeats to the American lieutenant what he had said to himself after his encounter with the British officers: "Death is not something we brushed up against. . . . We lived it. . . . We are not survivors, but revenants. . . ." (*EV* 99/89). Note that he is now speaking in the plural, not only about himself as before. And he says it not to himself but to another "student of philosophy," who functions as a privileged listener and even a partner in the shaping of the testimony.

Let us return for a moment to the detail of the flagrant contradiction, concerning what Semprun said or did not say to the man who registered him. Why has he so obviously contradicted himself in recounting this part of the episode? A writer as self-conscious as Semprun could not *not* have reread his earlier version—he often quotes passages from his other works, and *Quel beau dimanche!* will be mentioned later in this book, in connection with this very episode. The contradictory detail is evidently intentionally planted (or at least, tolerated) in the repeated version of the anecdote. Is it meant to say: "The detail is unimportant, it's the meaning of the experience as a whole that counts"? Perhaps. But I have also suggested that the meaning of the whole has shifted in this second version from the problem of personal identity to that of witnessing, and from individual trauma to collective historical trauma ("we are revenants"). In that light, the episode, while "anecdotique," is not at all trivial. Its very repetition, from one work to another much later one, indicates that it is important.

The contradictory detail may also be interpreted as an implicit commentary on the nature of memory over time, both as concerns the writer and the reader. Semprun, the "crafty God the Father," may be whispering to the reader who knows his work: "If you're clever, you'll catch me in flagrant contradiction. Which is the 'true' version? It doesn't matter, because details aren't what matter. Memory vacillates as one grows older—but even if the details are wrong, the testimony as a whole is reliable." We could say that the text here *performs* the vacillation or unreliability of memory over time, which has been much studied by experimental psychologists recently. In fact, Semprun plays a complicated game with memory and narrative time: *Quel beau dimanche!*, published in 1980, recounts an episode that took place more than thirty years earlier (January 1944), which the narrator suddenly remembered in 1960, about halfway in time between the original event and its telling. *L'écriture ou la vie*, published fourteen years after *Quel beau dimanche!*, recounts the same episode, but expands the introductory details (the "ritual" of arrival and depersonalization) from one paragraph to several pages; and it shifts the *moment of recall* of the episode to April 1945, less than a year and a half after the event. So while the writing of *L'écriture ou la vie* takes place much later than the writing of *Quel beau dimanche!*, the act of recall is situated much earlier. Which of the two contradictory accounts, then, is the factually accurate one? Perversely, or playfully, or because he no longer knows, Semprun withholds this information from the reader.

Is it possible that Semprun made this mistake unconsciously, never noticing the contradiction? If, for the sake of argument, we allow that hypothesis, it reinforces the point about the vacillation of memory.

What changes is the role of Semprun as author and witness. In the first instance, everything, including the vacillation of memory, is part of the author's artifice. In the second, he made a mistake—although it is not clear whether the mistake occurred the first time he told the story or the second, since both tellings came many years after the event. Considering Semprun's frequent reminders that as author he is fully in charge, and his frequent allusions to artifice, I tend to think that he knew exactly what he was doing. Charlotte Delbo, another non-Jewish deportee known for her literary testimonies, wrote as an epigraph to her book about Auschwitz, *Aucun de nous ne reviendra [None of Us Will Return]*, that although she was no longer sure that everything she said was true *[vrai]*, she was certain that it was truthful *[véridique]*. It is as if Semprun wanted to remind us that in his account too, factual truth and truthfulness do not always coincide—and sometimes, the factual truth will never be known.

The real surprise, however, a veritable *coup de théâtre*, is still to come: The last chapter of *L'écriture ou la vie*, titled "Return to Weimar," begins with the word "No": "No, that's not what he wrote!" (*EV* 287/278). Almost two hundred pages after the retold anecdote, Semprun returns to it once more, and he corrects not the small contradictory detail about what he said or did not say, which remains unresolved, but a major "fact" he has already told twice. What we find out now, from a "forty-year old man" who speaks to him in German, is that the scribe who registered him did not write the word "student" on his identity card: "He didn't write down 'student,' but something completely different!" At this point, increasing the suspense, Semprun takes a leap backward to explain the situation: this new scene occurred in March 1992, forty-seven years after his "last day in the camp." He had never returned to Buchenwald, refusing all invitations, but in 1992, following a dream in which he heard the torch singer Zarah Leander singing a love song (like the ones broadcast on the loudspeaker on Sunday afternoons in the camp), he changed his mind. Returning to Buchenwald would, he hoped, allow him to finish his long-delayed book, *L'écriture ou la mort* [sic], which he had begun (as he already told us earlier) on April 11, 1987, the day of Primo Levi's death by suicide. But before the text returns to Buchenwald, it takes yet another lengthy detour, as Semprun reflects on the three books he brought along on the journey; one of these was a volume of poems by Paul Celan, and Semprun mentions in particular the poem about Celan's visit to Heidegger, "Todtnauberg." The poet, Semprun writes, hoped for "a heartfelt word" *["un mot du coeur"]* from the philosopher, which never came. He suggests that Celan's suicide shortly after the failed visit was somehow its consequence: "no heartfelt words had held him back" (*EV* 300/291).

Just as earlier the reflection on writing and witnessing had led to the experience of death, here the reflection on the death of Celan (and of Levi, linked to the writing of this book) leads to further thoughts on writing and testimony, as well as on Semprun's own approaching death. Standing in Buchenwald in March 1992, with his two step-grandsons who have accompanied him on the visit, Semprun remembers the odor of burned flesh issuing from the crematoria and realizes that he is among the last witnesses with personal memory of that odor: "A day would come, relatively soon, when there would no longer be a single survivor of Buchenwald left. . . . No longer would anyone be able to say, with words springing from physical recollection and not some theoretical reconstruction, what it was like. . . ." (*EV* 301/292).

Finally, he comes once again to the original anecdote—which I am now tempted to call the primal scene of entry into Buchenwald—picking up the thread left hanging twenty pages earlier, when the "bearded quadragenarian" had said "No." Semprun summarizes, in a brief paragraph, the story of his arrival that he has just told to his two step-grandsons; he also reminds us that he had already told the story to Lieutenant Rosenfeld half a century earlier. So here we have the third version of the sequence, very short this time, but with all its elements intact: "The exhaustion, the thirst, the shower, the disinfection, the dash . . . stark naked through the underground passage" (*EV* 306/297). This underground passage begins to take on the aspect of a birth canal, from which he emerged another man.

Semprun repeats, once again, the "fact" he had told earlier (as well as in *Quel beau dimanche!*): The scribe wrote "student" on his registration card. But that is when the guide steps in with his "No, that's not what he wrote!" " 'I've read your books,' he told me. 'You mentioned this already, in *Quel beau dimanche!* So, knowing that you were coming today, I went looking for your registration card in the Buchenwald files. . . . Here's a photocopy of it!' " Semprun takes the paper from him with trembling hands: "No, he hadn't written *Student*, the unknown German comrade. No doubt guided by some phonetic association, he'd written *Stukkateur*" (*EV* 307/298). This word, relatively rare in German, refers to a worker in stucco—not a simple plasterer, but a skilled craftsman. Unlike students—or, for that matter, writers—these workers combined artistry with manual labor: "Stucco workers had come from Italy, centuries earlier, during the Renaissance. ... They had decorated Fontainebleau and the châteaux of the kings of France. ..." (*EV* 308/299). Thanks to this professional identity bestowed on him by the "unknown German comrade," Semprun concludes he may have been spared deportation to another, harsher camp: "that absurd and magical word, *Stukkateur*" (*EV* 309/300) had very possibly saved his life.

Here is a dramatic reversal, if ever there was one. The delayed discovery of a factual error he had cherished for over fifty years leads Semprun to reinterpret the whole meaning of the episode: It now appears to him above all as an example of human solidarity. The anonymous comrade who had saved his life, he reflects, had acted according to "a generous idea of humanity" (*EV* 311/302). He had acted in conformity with the *idea* of communism, no matter how bloody its actual history had been. This reflection on Semprun's part is at least a partial revision of the harsh critique of communism that had governed *Quel beau dimanche!* It also obliges Semprun to rethink the reasons for his own survival in Buchenwald. What would have happened if the inmate had simply shrugged his shoulder and registered him as a student?

But the dramatic reversal has other meanings as well, relating both to testimony and to artifice. As far as testimony is concerned, it functions as another performative. What is performed here is not the vacillation of memory, as in the contradictory detail, but rather the limitation of individual knowledge: one can live for fifty years with a version of one's own history that turns out to be false. Significantly, the "correction" is here supplied by an attentive reader who has taken the trouble to confront the witness's testimony with the historical document. We could think of this moment as a veritable allegory of testimony: The witness can be mistaken, even though his account is given in good faith; the testimony is always addressed to another person, who thus participates in it; the other's participation may lead to new understanding, and hence to revision of the testimony.

Given the particular form of the other's intervention in this instance, we might also see here an allegory of testimony's relation to history: A testimony is always, necessarily, one incomplete version of an event; although a complete history may never be known, the historian's task is to confront, wherever possible, the testimony with other documents in order to arrive at a closer approximation of the facts. Despite his repeated claim to artifice, Semprun does not deny the possibility of historical knowledge or the existence of historical fact.

François Maspero, whose father, the well-known Sinologist Henri Maspero, died in Buchenwald, has done documentary research that puts into doubt some of the dates mentioned by Semprun in *L'écriture ou la vie*, where he recounts seeing Henri Maspero next to Maurice Halbwachs, the great theorist of collective memory and Semprun's former professor, who also died there.[18] Semprun affirmed to me in a personal conversation (July 8, 2004) that he is certain he saw the two men sharing the same bunk, although he is no longer sure of the exact date. This example is a striking instance of the difference between a historical reading, which considers the factuality of what is reported, including details such as dates, to be of primary importance, and a literary reading, which may emphasize the overall meaning of an episode (in this case, the death of two great scholars in Buchenwald) and accord less importance to the precision of some details. François Maspero's desire for strict historical accuracy is all the more understandable given that Henri Maspero was his father, whom he lost as a young boy and whose last days he would like to reconstruct with all the precision possible. Here is an instance when the legitimate claims of testimony run headlong into the equally legitimate claims of historical research. Memory, and its failures, must be respected, but so must historical fact.

And what about artifice? It too is inscribed into the episode of delayed discovery, for as the reader realizes, Semprun as *author* has known all along what he has saved for last. When he recounted the scene in 1980, in *Quel beau dimanche!*, we can assume that he was genuinely mistaken about what the German comrade wrote on his card; but the repetition of the mistake in the first part of *L'écriture ou la vie* was obviously an artistic decision, for even if he had already written that account before returning to Buchenwald in 1992, he could easily have corrected his error in the final version of the manuscript. Instead, he chose to delay the reporting of his discovery until the end, thus underlining the constructed nature of his narrative and his own role as master of artifice. He acts here exactly like the Proustian narrator, who saves until the last volume of his immense novel the long-delayed discovery that, as a child, he had misinterpreted a gesture by his neighbor Gilberte: What he had taken to be an obscene insult was in fact an erotic invitation.[19]

Semprun's delayed discovery, like the Proustian narrator's, is a sign of the text's textuality, its character as writing, as *écriture*. At the same time, it is a sign of the possibility of endless rewriting of a traumatic event. The episode of his arrival and registration in Buchenwald was the moment of Semprun's entry into a world of death. His obsessive rewriting of the event, with its variants, its expansions and contractions, and its unresolved contradiction, as well as its structure of delay, signals both the traumatic nature of the experience and the impossibility of ever exhausting its meanings. In a published conversation with Elie Wiesel, which took place around the same time as he was writing *L'écriture ou la vie*, Semprun stated: "The more I write, the more my memory returns. . . . Whence my theory that it's an inexhaustible writing, at once impossible and inexhaustible. One cannot say it, but one will never have said it all."[20]

'Impossible and Inexhaustible': The Obligation to the Dead

In the last of his Buchenwald memoirs (not yet translated into English), *Le mort qu'il faut*, published in 2001, Semprun returns for a fourth time to the scene of initiation. This time, the narration of the memory of the event is situated in the camp itself, before liberation, in the very midst of death. And it is addressed *to* a dead man, or rather, to one of those living-dead who in the camp were called "Muslims" ["*Muselmänner*"]. *Le mort qu'il faut* recounts an episode occurring on a Sunday in December 1944, which did not find its way into *Quel beau dimanche!* The communist inmates who largely ran the camp had gotten wind of a telegram from Berlin inquiring about Semprun, and arranged to have him spend a night among the dying in the hospital, so that he could switch identities with a dead man (a young Frenchman close to him in age and occupation, "le mort qu'il faut" or the necessary corpse) in case the Gestapo was after him. This baroque plan ended in ironic deflation. It turned out the Gestapo was not after him and there was no need for the elaborate plot, but in the meantime Semprun has given us the story of his relation to the dead man, François L., whom he calls "my *Doppelgänger:* another myself, or myself as another."[21]

Semprun had first noticed François L., already reduced to the state of a *Muselmann*, a few weeks earlier in the latrines of the Small Camp, the camp for invalids where he went to visit his old professor Maurice Halbwachs on Sundays. (A strange, one is almost tempted to say happy, coincidence, for a writer concerned with testimony and memory to have been present at the deathbed of Maurice Halbwachs, the theorist of collective memory). The young *Muselmann* drew his attention because the number on his ragged jacket was almost exactly the same as Semprun's—it meant, he speculated, that the young man must have arrived on the same train, and gone through the same rituals: "This being must have been running very close to me in the underground hallway . . . In the end, naked, shaved all over, showered, disinfected, bewildered, he must have found himself in front of the German inmates who were filling out our identity cards" (*MF* 41–422). Here is the beginning of the fourth recounting of the primal scene in Buchenwald. The addressee is not yet François L. but the reader; a page later, however, Semprun tells us that he began telling stories to the young *Muselmann*, who remained motionless and silent, a heap of rags. It is this creature, at once his *Doppelgänger* and totally other, separated from him by his impending death, who became the first listener of Semprun's reminiscences, in a place so "pestilential" (44) and marked by death that no Nazi guard ever ventured there (56): "In sum, I paid him in tobacco so that he would listen to me tell him the story of my life" (44). And it is this same young *Muselmann*, whom he eventually succeeded in engaging in conversation because of their mutual love of Rimbaud, who became the addressee of his anecdote about the unknown German comrade. Delayed by a hundred pages in the book, recounted in flashback as Semprun lies next to the dying young man on his hospital bed, here then is the second half of the fourth version of the primal scene:

François, dans la baraque des latrines du Petit Camp, . . . avait beaucoup apprécié ma discussion avec le vétéran communiste allemand, demeuré anonyme, inconnu, qui ne voulait pas m'inscrire comme étudiant de philosophie, *Philosophiestudent*. 'Ici, ce n'est pas une profession, me disait-il, *kein Beruf!*' Et moi, du haut de l'arrogance imbécile de mes vingt ans, du haut de ma connaiss-ance de la langue allemande, je lui avais lancé: '*kein Beruf, aber eine Berufung!*', pas une profession mais une vocation! De guerre lasse, avais-je dit à François, voyant que je ne voulais rien com-prendre le détenu allemand m'avait renvoyé d'un geste irrité. Et il avait sans doute tapé sur sa vieille machine à écrire: *Philoso-phiestudent*. François appréciait l'anecdote. (*MF* 149)

François, in the latrine barrack of the Small Camp, . . . had greatly appreciated my discussion with the veteran German com-munist, who remained anonymous, unknown, who didn't want to register me as a student of philosophy. 'Here, that is not a pro-fession,' he said to me, '*kein Beruf!*' And I, from the height of my idiotic arrogance of a twenty-year old, from the height of my knowledge of the German language, had riposted: '*kein Beruf, aber eine Berufung!*', not a profession but a vocation. Knowing when he was licked, I had said to François, the German inmate had sent me off with an irritated gesture. And he had doubtless typed on his old typewriter: *Philosophiestudent*. François appreciated the anecdote.

To anyone who has read *L'écriture ou la vie*, let alone both that book and *Quel beau dimanche!*, the artifice of this passage is obvious, maybe even puzzling. After the enormous importance he had accorded to the delayed discovery in the 1994 book, Semprun's choice here to keep the focus strictly on what he knew in December 1944, with no "cor-rection" either here or later, may appear odd. Unless, of course, that is precisely the point: here is a detail directed at the attentive reader, the reader who, like the "bearded quadragenarian," compares one text to another. In fact, what follows immediately after this makes full sense only to a reader who knows the earlier versions of the story: Semprun recounts that François told him he too had answered *Student*—but the inmate who was filling out his card had merely shrugged his shoulder. "The German inmate had not made any comment nor tried to dis-suade him" (*MF* 149). This statement makes sense only if the contrast between the two scribes is meaningful. Semprun does not explain it here, but the reader of *L'écriture ou la vie* knows that his contentious scribe saved his life by writing *Stukkateur* instead of *Student*. By implication, the indifference of François' scribe, his lack of concern for a fellow human being, somehow led to François' death. The contrast is emphasized in yet another episode, recounted earlier: Semprun, sent out on backbreaking duty carrying stones, was helped by an anonymous Russian comrade who took the heaviest stones from him; François, on similar duty, had no such luck, and his physical decline dates from that moment.

And that, of course, is the fascination of François L.: he is Semprun as *Muselmann*, Semprun as he might have been with just a little less luck. François is a student of the humanities, speaks German, knows many poems by heart, and plans to write a book about Buchenwald if he survives. Looking at him, Semprun might well say: "There but for the luck of the draw go I. The necessary dead man, 'le mort qu'il faut,' could have been myself." The question of survival, already important in *L'écriture ou la vie*, here occupies a central place. Albeit implicit, the question that hovers over the narrative (and maybe over all camp memoirs) is clear: "Why did I survive while others died?" Semprun's repeated story of the registration card suggests that survival, while it may be a matter of pure luck, is also the result of solidarity, a sense of fraternity among prisoners even if they do not know each other's names.

But survival carries another nagging question as well, which comes to the fore in this book: Are those who survived guilty, in some way? And if not, do they still have an obligation to the dead? Semprun already approached these questions in *L'écriture ou la vie*, in discussing the suicides of Primo Levi and Paul Celan. Here he confronts them explicitly, in the very beginning of the book. His first mention is ironic, sarcastic even:

Il semble, en effet, et cela n'a pas cessé de me surprendre, qu'il faut afficher quelque honte, une conscience coupable, du moins, si l'on aspire à être présentable, digne de foi. Un survivant digne de ce nom, méritant, qu'on puisse inviter aux colloques sur la question.

Certes, le meilleur témoin, le seul vrai témoin, en réalité, d'après les spécialistes, c'est celui qui n'a pas survécu, celui qui est allé jusqu'au bout de l'expérience, et qui en est mort. Mais ni

les historiens ni les sociologues ne sont encore parvenus à ré-
soudre cette contradiction: comment inviter les vrais témoins,
c'est à dire les morts, à leurs colloques? Comment les faire parler?

Voilà une question, en tout cas, que le temps qui passe réglera
de lui-même: il n'y aura bientôt plus de témoins gênants, à
l'encombrante mémoire. (*MF* 16)

It appears, in effect, and it does not cease to surprise me, that
one must manifest a certain shame, a guilty conscience, at least,
if one aspires to be presentable, reliable. A survivor worthy of the
name, deserving to be invited to conferences on the question.

Certainly, the best witness, the only true witness, in fact, according to the specialists, is one who did not survive, who went
to the very end of the experience and who died of it. But neither
historians nor sociologists have yet succeeded in resolving this
contradiction: how to invite the true witnesses, that is to say the
dead, to their conferences? How to make them talk?

That is a question, in any case, that the passage of time will
resolve by itself: soon there will no longer be any bothersome
witnesses, with their cumbersome memory.

We might speculate that this whole story of the *Doppelgänger* is
Semprun's reply—ironic, defiant, but also serious—to those theorists
(he may have been thinking of Agamben) who claim that only the
dead were the true witnesses. The reply is ironic, because if François
L. is largely invented, as Semprun hints may be the case, then Semprun's own status as witness is put into question, in positivist terms at
least; and it is defiant, because whatever liberties he may take with
positive facts, Semprun reminds us that he is incontrovertibly a survivor and a witness, even if a willfully "bothersome" one, a "témoin
gênant." Finally, however, it is serious, because Semprun suggests that
the *Muselmann* was not some sublimely different creature, but simply
a prisoner like the others who did not have the luck of some others.
There is therefore no reason to anoint and privilege this figure, especially if it is true that even those who survived did not so much
escape from death as "come back" from it. This could be, as well,
Semprun's refusal of suicide, and his refusal to privilege the survivor
who kills himself (Celan, Améry, Levi).

But there are at least two other reasons to speak here of seriousness.

First, as suggested by the paragraph I quoted, Semprun is very much aware of his own and other witnesses' mortality. François was the double who died, while he survived; but now, more than fifty years later, he knows that soon it will be his turn. Toward the end of the book, he recalls François' muffled last words, a Latin quotation that Semprun identified only decades later: "Post mortem nihil est ipsaque mors nihil" (164) ["There is nothing after death, and death itself is nothing"]. Is this perhaps a comforting message from the *Muselmann* to the aged survivor?

The other reason to speak of seriousness is that the figure of François, who is presented as the very first addressee of Semprun's oft-repeated story about the entry into Buchenwald, also appears as the reason why Semprun writes. The dying François says to him, when he sees him in the infirmary: "No, not you" (157). Semprun's reply is an apostrophe, an address to the dead: "No, not I, François, I am not going to die. Not this night, in any case, I promise you. I will survive this night, I will try to survive many other nights, in order to remember. . . . I will try to survive in order to remember you" (*MF* 157). The survivor witness, while he cannot speak *for* (in place of) the dead, can speak *about* them—indeed, it his obligation to do so. That is why the task of witnessing is, for the survivor-writer, both impossible and inexhaustible. "One cannot say it, but one will never have said it all."

Returning now, very briefly, to the theoretical concerns with which I began, I would say—or say again—that continuous revision is the literary performance of the working through of trauma, a performance that Semprun's Buchenwald memoirs enact brilliantly.

Do Facts Matter in Holocaust Memoirs?

WILKOMIRSKI/WIESEL

$\mathcal{T}$HE FRENCH POET André Breton once wrote: "Life is other than what one writes."[1] He did not mean that writing is a lie, but rather, that writing is always one step behind or ahead of or next to the facts of lived experience—all the more so when that experience took place decades ago. This chapter follows up on some of the theoretical implications of Breton's remark. What happens to the gap between facts and writing when the latter is concerned with issues of great collective significance such as the Holocaust? The two examples I will discuss—Binjamin Wilkomirski's *Fragments* (1996) and Elie Wiesel's *Tous les fleuves vont à la mer* (1994)—both raise, albeit in very different ways, questions about memory and its relation to historical truth. Having been published as literary memoirs, they also raise questions about genre. In what *kind* of writing do facts matter most, and why?

"Memory" and "memoir" are almost the same word in English and are the same word, *mémoire*, in French. But memory is a mental faculty, while memoir is a text. Although memoirs have no specific formal characteristics (other than those of autobiographical writing in general, which comes in many varieties), they all have at least one thing in common: a memoir relates "experiences that the writer has lived through."[2] Unlike a full-scale autobiography, a memoir can be confined to a single event or a single moment in a life. It need not be the work of an important person, nor does it have to be well written (although that helps). Its primary claim to our attention is not literariness but factuality. In the novelist Anna Quindlen's words, "What really happened—that is the allure of memoir." She adds almost immediately, however: "Fact is different from truth, and truth is different from insight. . . . [W]ith few exceptions, . . . fiction tells the truth far better than personal experience does."[3]

It may seem that Quindlen is suggesting fiction has no relation to personal experience, but her argument is just the opposite: Personal experience, when written, veers almost inevitably toward fiction. The necessity for details that give the "feel of life" to narrated experience leads toward invention—which is why, as a former journalist who respects facts too much to invent them, Quindlen quips that she "will never write a memoir." In a more serious vein, she concludes: "I'm suspicious of memory itself. . . . Memory is such a shapeshifter of a thing, so influenced by old photographs and old letters, self-image and self-doubt." Individual memories may merge with family mythologies, eventually taking on the feel of lived recollection. Quindlen's essay reminds us, in a pithy way, that the bedrock of factuality on which memoir rests (or is assumed to rest) is as fragile as memory itself.

Does that mean there are no significant differences between memoir and novel, between recollection and invention? No. Differences exist, and literary theorists have been trying to pinpoint them ever since Plato and Aristotle. Among contemporary theorists, Paul Ricoeur and Dorrit Cohn have provided the most systematic arguments for maintaining a strict division between the "nonreferential" nature of fictional discourse and the referentiality of historical discourse, which is necessarily constrained by the facts and by what can be known about them. While I agree that referentiality is an essential criterion, I am less positive than Cohn and Ricoeur about the *textual* specificity of fiction. According to Cohn, fictional narrative is "ruled by formal patterns that are ruled out in all other orders of discourse."[4] I think the situation is less clear-cut, especially as concerns the status of the literary memoir. As we saw in the discussion of Jorge Semprun's Buchenwald memoirs, a literary memoir can lay claim both to referentiality and to its transgression; conversely (and Cohn acknowledges this), a novel can imitate, formally, any kind of speech act, including the act of imperfectly recollecting a personal past. We have a brilliant demonstration of this in W. G. Sebald's acclaimed novels, *The Emigrants* and *Austerlitz*. The narrator of *The Emigrants* recalls fragments of his own past and seeks out the stories of dead relatives and acquaintances as they are recalled, incompletely and imperfectly, by those who knew them; similarly, the narrator of *Austerlitz* reconstructs the story of the title character, who himself attempts to discover a traumatic past that he has largely forgotten. Sebald includes photographs of persons in these books, a fascinating insertion of "the real" into a novel—but these photographs, apparently of real people long ago, highlight rather than efface the ontological difference between their historical subjects (who are unidentified, and possibly unidentifiable) and the fictional characters whose stories they ostensibly illustrate.

If novels can look and feel textually like memoirs, the converse is also true and more paradoxical: literary memoirs can look like novels, yet lay claim to a bedrock of historical fact. Jorge Semprun, whose work I discussed in the preceding chapter, has explored this paradox in his autobiographical books about Buchenwald. In a less self-conscious mode, one finds another confirmation of it in Frank McCourt's bestseller *Angela's Ashes*, one of the most successful memoirs of the last two decades. Not only is McCourt's prose stylized, deploying a full range of rhetorical figures from anaphora to ellipsis to metaphor to onomatopeia, but he also presents us with detailed dialogues that took place before his and even before his mother's birth! No reader can be unaware of the literary artifice and patterning, the imaginative projections, in a word, of the novelistic technique in this work; yet *Angela's Ashes* has been internationally received as a work recounting events that really happened during the author's impoverished childhood in New York and Limerick. McCourt has recounted in interviews that travel tours were being organized to visit the sites in Limerick immortalized in his memoir.[5] This bears out the referential appeal of his book—but just to complicate matters, in St. Petersburg, tourists can visit both the house where Dostoevsky wrote *Crime and Punishment* and, in the same neighborhood, the house where his fictional creation Raskolnikov killed the old pawnbroker.

Textual traits, in sum, do not necessarily provide a criterion for distinguishing memoirs from novels written in the first person—the two genres look alike. Some narratologists, following the lead of Philippe Lejeune's classic work on autobiography, *Le pacte autobiogra-phique*, propose a single decisive textual criterion: if the proper name of the narrator-protagonist is identical with that of the author on the book's cover, the work is autobiography, not fiction. But many works do not tell us the narrator's name, and some contemporary writers have taken pleasure in playing with the criterion itself—whence the genre that Serge Doubrovsky has dubbed "autofiction," where the narrator-hero's name is identical to the author's, and the events re-counted are also largely factual, but the work is presented as a novel. (We will encounter this genre again in Chapter 8.) Despite these plea-surable skirmishes on the boundaries, however, the first question that a reader is likely to ask about a written narrative is: "Is it fiction or nonfiction"? And the way the work is read will largely be determined by the answer to that question. Here as in some other domains, one finds parallels between genre and gender; despite psychological and biological demonstrations of the difficulty in drawing absolute lines between the sexes, the first question we still ask about a newborn child is "boy or girl?" There exists a *conventional, institutional* boundary be-tween a work offered as memoir and a work offered as novel—and it is in terms of reading conventions rather than in terms of textual traits that works in the two genres are best distinguished.

Meir Sternberg, discussing the difference between fictional and his-torical narrative, puts it succinctly: "What kind of contract binds [writer and audience] together? What does the writer stand committed to? What is the audience supposed to assume?"[6] In Sternberg's view (one he shares with many other theorists, including Cohn and Ri-coeur), the most important distinction between the two modes is that historical writing makes truth claims, whereas fictional writing is in-dependent of such claims.[7] This distinction is conventional, not tex-tual—many novels begin with a statement like "I'm going to tell you my true story," yet are unproblematically received as fiction. By con-ventional, I mean the set of implicit and explicit understandings that frame the publication and reception of any work, starting with the contract between author and publisher, proceeding with critical re-ception, and ending with the placing of the work on bookshelves of libraries and bookstores—and, in the case of a lucky few, in the col-umns of the *New York Times* bestseller list.

Memoirs resemble historical narratives insofar as they make truth claims—more exactly, claims to referentiality and verifiability—that put them on the other side of a boundary from novels. Interestingly, this conventional boundary becomes most apparent when it is violated. There was such a violation, albeit a minor one, in the contradictory accounts given by Semprun of his entry into the camp at Buchenwald, which I analyzed in Chapter 6. The contradiction made it impossible to determine which account was the factual one, but it did not invalidate Semprun's claim about the historical truth of his presence in Buchenwald. A much more radical violation of the fiction/nonfiction boundary exists in cases of fraud or hoax. Fraud or hoax does not refer to memoirs that "do not tell the whole truth"—few memoirs do. It refers, rather, to the work as a whole and its relation to the writer: is he or she the person whose experiences are recounted in the book? Interestingly, the violation is felt as violation only in relation to memoir, not to novel. No one cares, particularly—except perhaps the author's friends and family, who may figure in it—if a work billed as a novel turns out to be straight autobiography. But if a memoir is shown to be fraudulent, because the person who claims to be recounting his or her experiences could not possibly have had those experiences or anything like them, then shock waves are created. All the more so if the experiences recounted are traumatic, whether in the framework of an individual life (as in memoirs of sexual abuse) or in the framework of collective experience (as in memoirs about war or genocide). Jerzy Kosinski's famous novel, *The Painted Bird* (1965), offers a curious variation on this rule. When it was published, the author and the publisher let it be known that the novel was autobiographical, Kosinski's own story as a young boy during the Holocaust; that assumption influenced many reviewers, including Elie Wiesel, who gave it a rave review in the *New York Times Book Review*.[8] Later, it turned out that Kosinski's life story was very different from that of his brutally mistreated protanogist, and that led to a certain discredit for the author. Since the book was called a novel, readers should in principle not have been shocked by the discovery that it was mostly invented, but for many readers, the earlier assumption that it was "really" autobiographical had placed the work in a different category as far as reading conventions were concerned. Hence, despite the generic label, they felt they had been duped.

Delusion or Fraud: The Wilkomirski Case

This brings me to the by-now widely discussed case of Binjamin Wilkomirski and his book, *Fragments: Memories of a Wartime Childhood.* Received with nearly universally hyperbolic praise when it first appeared in Germany in 1995, and shortly thereafter in English and many other languages, *Fragments* presents itself as a memoir, specifically a Holocaust memoir written by a Jew who lived through horrendous experiences in extermination camps in Poland as a very young child. The memoir won several awards in the United States and abroad; its author, a Swiss musician and instrument maker whose first book this was, appeared in numerous official venues and was the subject of documentaries and interviews as a child survivor of the Holocaust. The story he tells in *Fragments* is that, the sole survivor of his family, he was smuggled out of a Krakow orphanage after the war and deposited in a children's home in Switzerland, from where he was adopted by a childless couple. Enjoined by all the adults around him to "forget the past," Wilkomirski explains in an "Afterword" that it took him many years to allow himself to speak or write about his memories. He likens himself to the hundreds of "children without identity" who survived the Holocaust "lacking any certain information about their origins, . . . furnished with false names and often with false papers too."[9]

Fragments can be read as Wilkomirski's attempt to record the "shards of memory" that remained with him from his early childhood, and an attempt as well to show how those early memories continued to inflect his way of being in the world long after he had reached safety in Switzerland. Like *Angela's Ashes*, this is a highly stylized work; the decision to restrict the narrative perspective almost exclusively to the young boy allows for some very powerful effects. For example, when the boy first arrives in the Swiss home, he is left alone in the dining room, apparently just after the other children have had lunch. He is astonished to find that the tables have cloths and white plates, not the grey tin plates on bare wood that he is used to. When he goes closer, he is even more amazed: "The children hadn't eaten everything on their plates! They'd left bits in strips around the edges. These leftovers were all over everywhere, and apparently nobody was guarding them." (21). He rushes to the table and begins to stuff the cheese rinds—for that is what they are—into his mouth and clothes: " 'These stupid kids!' I thought. 'How can anyone be dumb enough to leave food lying around unprotected? They don't seem to have a clue. Maybe they're new here, and they don't know yet that surviving means laying in supplies, finding a good hiding place, defending your food. Never ever leave food unguarded, that's what Jankl always told me.' " (22).

When the workers at the home discover the child with his mouth full of garbage, they are disgusted: "Cheese rinds! He's eating cheese rinds! Monster!" (23).

The clash of rules and world views between what the child had learned in order to survive in the camps and what he was expected to know in the "normal" world afterward structures this memoir and is rendered with what can only be called a masterful artistry. Alternating between the boy's experiences during his first years in Switzerland and the earlier memories they trigger (for example, the view of baskets heaped with fresh bread on the breakfast table triggers his one memory of his mother, who gave him a piece of dry bread on her deathbed in Majdanek), the narrative moves forward and back, producing new experiences and new memories but no new understanding—until the final chapter, when the boy, already a senior in high school, discovers that the war really is over. Watching a documentary about the Nazi camps, he sees the liberation of Mauthausen by Allied troops, and realizes that he is free and that he missed his own liberation.

Fragments is a powerful book, as most of its first readers agreed. While some reviewers mentioned the book's self-conscious artistry, others praised its absence of "artifice" and its "unpretentious recounting of a child's inner life."[10] The child advocate Jonathan Kozol, while aware of the book's "stunning and austerely written" quality, considered it "free from literary artifice of any kind at all."[11] The equation of "lack of artifice" with authenticity—and, conversely, of artifice with inauthenticity—is symptomatic of the factual appeal of memoir. Despite its appeal, however, *Fragments* has been proven beyond doubt to be a fabrication, the work of a man who is not who he says (and may genuinely believe) he is. After more than a year of doubt and controversy following the first accusation of fraud in 1998, the German and American publishers withdrew the book from the market.[12] Their decision was based on the work of a historian, Stefan Maechler, who had been hired by Wilkomirski's literary agent in Zurich to investigate the matter and who eventually published a detailed book about it. According to the facts uncovered by Maechler, Bruno Doesseker—for that was his legal name until he changed it to Wilkomirski—was indeed an adopted child, but not one born in Latvia; rather, he was the illegitimate son of a Swiss woman, Yvonne Grosjean, who, unable to support him, gave him up to foster parents when he was two years old and later agreed to his adoption by the Doessekers. She kept sufficient track of his whereabouts to mention him in her will when she died in 1981, and—in an action quite damaging to his story—Wilkomirski sued for his part of her small estate, which was legally coming to him under Swiss law.[13] Binjamin Wilkomirski is a "found" name, adopted by Bruno Doesseker/Grosjean when he became convinced of his "true identity" as a child survivor of the Holocaust. His powerful memoir is based not on his experiences but on his fantasies and on the memories of others; before writing his book, Wilkomirski/Doesseker/Grosjean had read thousands of testimonies and historical works in his obsessive pursuit of a Holocaust identity.

This story, which reads like a psychological thriller (it has in fact inspired a detective story by the popular novelist Sara Paretsky), has caused much ink to flow and will probably continue to do so for some time.[14] It is fascinating existentially, historically, and in terms of narrative theory. Here I will focus only on two questions, relating to problems of factuality and of genre.

First, should we care whether *Fragments* is a memoir or a fabrication—does it matter, finally, who Wilkomirski is and what the generic status of his book is? I think it does matter, though perhaps not for the reasons that may immediately come to mind. I am not overly worried, for example, about the ammunition this book provided to Holocaust deniers; the deniers had their say quite early, in an article circulated on the Internet very soon after the story broke in 1998, "Des faussaires et des dupes" ["Of frauds and of dupes"] by Serge Thion, a well-known French negationist and author of several negationist pamphlets.[15] Thion uses the familiar negationist device of reasoning by synecdoche: if a single detail in a testimony is false, that renders the whole thing false; if a single testimony is a fake, that renders all testimonies suspect. But we must resist such pernicious reasoning by association. If Wilkomirski invented his memories, it does not follow that Elie Wiesel or Rudolf Vrba (both of whom Thion mentions in his article) invented theirs.

Historians have never relied exclusively on survivor testimonies, and even less on a single testimony, in writing the history of the Holocaust. This may seem obvious, but given the emotional stakes involved, it is worth emphasizing. It does not mean that history has a privileged access to facts whereas memoirs do not, merely that historians rely on multiple sources and confront various kinds of documents in constructing their versions of events. The constructedness of all narratives, including historical narratives, does not—as some people fear—undermine the historical existence of past events. Ernst van Alphen espouses what can be called a postmodernist view of Holocaust writing, including historiography, which emphasizes the continuing reinterpretation and reframing of past events in the present, as well as the inseparability of event from interpretive framework even at the moment it is being experienced; yet he insists, I think rightly, that the *existence* of the Holocaust does not depend on individual constructions: "If we are to make sense of the Holocaust, the ontological question of the reality of the event—did it happen?—must be firmly distinguished from the epistemological question of how we gain access to it."[16] To admit the constructedness of all narratives, including histories and memoirs, is not to renounce the distinction between invention and truth claim. Memoirs, in their own way, make truth claims: "This is what happened, to the best of my recollection." But even if every memoir about the Holocaust were to prove inaccurate in some details, that would still not negate the Holocaust's historical existence.

Positivist historians sometimes fall into the trap of reasoning like the deniers. The psychoanalyst Dori Laub recounts an anecdote about a survivor witness of the attempted Auschwitz uprising on October 7, 1944. The witness, testifying for the Fortunoff Archive of videotestimones at Yale University, recalled her astonishment at the event and mistakenly remembered seeing four chimneys burning when in fact only one chimney had been set on fire. According to Laub, the historians at a conference who watched the videotaped testimony concluded that all of it was unreliable: "Since the memory of the testifying woman turned out to be, in this way, fallible, one could not accept—nor give credence to—her whole account of the events. It was utterly important to remain accurate, lest the revisionists in history discredit everything."[17] The historians were no doubt right to insist on the documented facts about the uprising (which, it should be noted, are based in large part on survivor testimonies, by people who were more closely involved with the uprising).[18] However, the value and the particular truth of this survivor's testimony was not necessarily diminished by the error in factual detail. A psychoanalyst at the conference provided the interpretive frame: "The number [of chimneys set on fire] mattered less than the fact of the occurrence. The event itself [the uprising] was almost inconceivable. The woman testified to an event that broke the all-compelling frame of Auschwitz. . . . That was historical truth."[19] At this point, we might want to differentiate historical truth from factual detail or introduce distinctions between various kinds of historical truth. In either case, the woman's account is not discredited as testimony about the *existence* of the Auschwitz uprising.

To return to our question—does the generic status of *Fragments* matter?—I believe it does, but not because the existence of the Holocaust is at stake. Nor do I think that if *Fragments* were a genuine memoir, that would guarantee the factual accuracy of every memory recounted in the book. A memoir, whether a Holocaust memoir or any other kind, provides only a single mediated perspective on reality, not a direct, immediate apprehension of the "thing itself." Theorists of narrative as well as specialists in Holocaust writing have amply shown that no first-person narrative is "untouched by figuration and by shaping," as Michael-André Bernstein puts it. To believe in "the absolute authority given to first person testimony," Bernstein writes, is to give credence to "one of the most pervasive myths of our era."[20]

I agree with Bernstein on that point. It does not imply, however, that categorical distinctions do not matter. Borderlines, those areas where boundaries begin to blur, fascinate contemporary theorists, but boundary blurrings can exist only because categories do. And of all the categories in our lives, those of fact and fiction, with their various literary equivalents such as memoir or novel, remain—despite our theoretical sophistication about the constructed nature of representation, and even of perception—very strong.

Some contemporary writers (including those, like Semprun, whose subject is their own experience in the Holocaust) play on those categories, mixing and twisting them in various ways, but such self-conscious playing does not do away with conventional designations. On the contrary, it maintains them. The French novelist Alain Robbe-Grillet includes in his autobiography, *Le miroir qui revient* (1984), a character named Henri de Corinthe, who is clearly fictional. The autobiography still functions as autobiography, however, with some novelistic "nuggets" in it; in the two subsequent volumes, Robbe-Grillet made the mixing of genres even more explicit. Another, somewhat different instance is Georges Perec's *W ou le souvenir d'enfance* [*W or The Memory of Childhood*], which consists of two parallel narratives told in alternating chapters: a science-fiction narrative about the island of W, which finally turns out to be an allegory of the Nazi death camps, and a memoir about Perec's childhood in wartime France. Although both narratives have first-person narrators, the fictional "I" and the autobiographical "I" are differentiated: the appearance of Perec's name is a clear textual indicator in the autobiographical sections, while the nonrealist mode of the science-fiction segments indicates fictional discourse. The overall effect of the work depends on this juxtaposition, with the reader constantly shuttling from one world to the other, and wondering what the relation between them is. (I discuss this book in greater detail in Chapter 8.)

Unlike Perec's and Robbe-Grillet's works, Wilkomirski's book does not *play* with categories—it obfuscates them, which is not the same thing. The problem with *Fragments*, as a text, is precisely that it does not recognize, or at any rate does not admit, its own fictionality.

This leads to my second question: Is the solution to the problem simply to relabel the work, move it from "memoir" to "novel"? Or does it, rather, belong in another category, that of the discredited or false memoir? Given the highly crafted nature of this work, one can well argue for keeping it in print under a new label as fiction. Arthur Samuelson, the American publisher at Schocken, told Elena Lappin in early 1999: "It's only a fraud if you call it non-fiction. I would then reissue it, in the fiction category."[21] In November 1999, however, when the book was withdrawn from the market, there was no mention of reissuing it as fiction. Instead, the text soon reappeared as a piece of evidence in the "Wilkomirski Affair," included as the appendix to Stefan Maechler's historical study by that title. This reframing altered the nature of the text; the words are the same, but the work is not. However, it is still not a novel; nor can we call it a novel if we consider

Wilkomirski's own claim to referentiality. In his "Afterword" to *Fragments* (which was included in the original edition of the book because the German publisher had received a letter denouncing it and had asked Wilkomirski for an explanation), Wilkomirski states that the official identity papers he possesses have "nothing to do with either the history of this century or my personal history."[22] In a newspaper interview given in September 1998, replying to the published accusations by Bruno Ganzfried, Wilkomirski suggested that the official documents were forged by Swiss authorities after the war, just as in the case of other "children without identity."[23] The *New York Times* reported in November 1999 that, even when he was confronted by the historian Stefan Maechler's report, which caused the German publisher to withdraw the book, the author "declared defiantly, 'I am Benjamin Wilkomirski.' "[24]

Using the criterion of truth claim, therefore, we must call *Fragments* not a novel but a false—or perhaps better, a deluded—memoir. The question is, what happens to such works once they have been uncovered? Elena Lappin mentions an earlier Holocaust memoir that was subsequently shown to be mostly fiction, Martin Gray's *For Those I Loved:* Gray's book is now cited "only on revisionist websites."[25] It would seem that a false memoir does not, by virtue of its falsity, automatically convert into fiction. More often than not, it converts into oblivion.

Wilkomirski's case bears striking similarities to another *cause célèbre* of the same decade, *The Education of Little Tree* (1990), which was purportedly an autobiography by a Native American and was praised for its authenticity, but which turned out instead to have been the work of a white supremacist. Henry Louis Gates, Jr., reflecting on the *Little Tree* case, cites other examples of fraudulent autobiographies, notably some nineteenth-century slave narratives, which proved to be an embarrassment to their first publishers and promoters. Gates argues that "authenticity" is a category easy to fake, and suggests that the difference between factual and fictional writing may be ultimately impossible to maintain.[26] Even if all that is granted, I believe the generic categories continue to function in most people's reading experience.

But there is a factor we have not sufficiently considered yet: Whatever else it might claim to be, *Fragments* is an artful work, powerful in its effect. Does it deserve to fall into oblivion? Tzvetan Todorov, in an essay aptly titled "Fictions and Truths," tells a story that bears an uncanny resemblance to Wilkomirski's, even though it happened almost three hundred years ago. A hugely popular book published in London in 1704 and immediately translated into French, *Description of the Isle of Formosa in Asia* [*Description de l'île de Formose en Asie*], purportedly an eyewitness account by a native of the island who offered lurid descriptions of its cannibalistic religious practices among other exotica, turned out to be a fake. Like Wilkomirski's book, Psalmanazar's *Description* was challenged even before it was published; members of the Royal Academy suspected him of fraud, but the book was published anyway and enjoyed several years of notoriety. The issue of Psalmanazar's identity was finally laid to rest by the author himself, in his *Memoirs* published in 1764 after his death. "Today we know with certainty that the *Description* is a fraud, that Psalmanazar was never in China and that his real name wasn't even Psalmanazar," writes Todorov, in a sentence that could just as well apply to Wilkomirski.[27] But there is a major difference, which Todorov invokes in concluding his discussion of this work: "As a piece of historical writing, Psalmanazar's *Description* deserves no respect, because it is a fake. As a piece of fiction, it does not command admiration, because it does not present itself as a fiction and because its author lacks eloquence." (141).

Although Todorov lumps them together, self-designation and eloquence are independent categories. Wilkomirski's book, too, "does not present itself as a fiction," but its author does not lack eloquence. What then? Todorov answers this question by invoking a completely different work, written two hundred years before Psalmanazar's fake: Amerigo Vespucci's letters about his voyages to the New World, *Mundus novus* and *Quatuor navigatones*. Todorov shows that these accounts, too, had problems: They were clearly full of fabulation and may not even have been written by Vespucci—but they were artful and compelling, and earned their presumed author (who really did travel in the New World—at least that much is certain) a continent named after him. If they offered few truths about "American reality," they did offer truths, by their very artfulness, about the "European imagination" of the time. (158). Earlier, Todorov proposed a distinction between "vérité-adéquation," or truth corresponding to facts, and "vérité-dévoilement," truth that reveals or unveils—the latter being presumably a function of literary skill. (132).

Might we salvage Wilkomirski's deluded memoir by treating it as a compelling piece of writing that "unveils" truths about the effects of the Holocaust on the contemporary imagination? Trauma, horror, and a sense of absolute victimhood: it appears that the Holocaust has become, in today's Europe and America (and increasingly, elsewhere), the ultimate signifier of such torments even for those who have no personal connection to that past event. Wilkomirski suffered trauma as a young child suddenly separated from his mother, and Stefan Maechler speculates that he transformed memories of his foster homes into memories of suffering under the Nazis.[28] James Young has written persuasively about Sylvia Plath's poetic identification with the "Holocaust Jew" and the ethical and interpretive problems it poses. Plath was criticized, by Irving Howe and other Jewish critics, for her use of the Holocaust as a metaphor for personal suffering; the incommensurability of the two terms was, they argued, a trivialization of that collective event. Young, while recognizing and even sharing that criticism, nevertheless concludes that "to remove the Holocaust from the realm of the imagination . . . is to risk excluding it altogether from public consciousness. . . . Better abused memory in this case, which might then be critically qualified, than no memory at all."[29]

Wilkomirski's book presents an extreme version of this problem, a literalization of Plath's metaphors as well as of her self-identification as a "Holocaust Jew." Being an extreme case, *Fragments* poses certain questions starkly: Where does literature end (or begin) and psychopathology begin (or end)? Where should the line be drawn—should the line be drawn?—between personal memory and imagined or "borrowed" memory? To whom does the memory of the Holocaust belong? The fact that *Fragments* raises these questions, powerfully, may be reason enough for its continued presence in our literary landscape—if not as a memoir (it is not that) and not as a novel (it is not that either, at least not yet), then at least as a "case."

Revision and Insight: Wiesel's self-correction

Fake memoirs can be works of literature and they can be instructive, but they leave a bad taste in the mouth, especially when they concern a subject as fraught with emotion and collective significance as the Holocaust. In short, they are depressing. I want to conclude by considering a passage from a memoir whose status as the autobiographical work of a Holocaust survivor is not in doubt, and which presents a quite different—one might say an exhilarating, rather than depressing—problem of memory and factuality concerning the Holocaust.

In his 1994 memoir, *Tous les fleuves vont à la mer* [*All Rivers Run to the Sea*], Volume 1 of a two-volume work, Elie Wiesel recounts once again some of the events known to readers of his classic Holocaust memoir, *La nuit* (1958) [*Night*, (1960)]. After a detailed account of his childhood and early adolescence (before deportation) that complements the more sketchy presentation in *Night*, Wiesel evokes anew the horrific train journey that took him and his family to Auschwitz, a journey he had already memorably described more than thirty years earlier. One long passage, worth quoting in full, is especially pertinent to the present discussion, and since it concerns a problem of translation, it must be quoted in French first:

> Ce voyage dans le train, mon tout premier témoignage le décrit, mais un point demande clarification—et il est délicat: il s'agit de l'atmosphère érotique qui se serait installée dans le wagon. Dans la version française, je dis: "Libérés de toute censure sociale, les jeunes se laissaient aller ouvertement à leurs instincts et, à la faveur de la nuit, s'accouplaient au milieu de nous, sans se préoccuper de qui que ce fût, seuls dans le monde. Les autres faisaient semblant de ne rien voir." Le mot "s'accouplaient" suscita un froncement de sourcils chez des lecteur puritains, ce qui n'est pas trop grave, et chez d'anciens compagnons du même voyage, ce qui l'est davantage. Alors, je repris la version originale en yiddish. Là, le passage se lit différemment: "En raison de la promiscuité, beaucoup d'instincts s'éveillèrent. Instincts érotiques. Des jeunes garçons et filles ont, sous le couvert de la nuit, succombé à leurs sens excités...." En fait, il s'agissait de contacts timides, d'attouchements hésitants qui ne dépassèrent jamais les limites de la décence. Comment ai-je pu traduire cela en "accouplement"? Je ne sais pas. Si, je le sais. Honte mal placée? Je parlais peut-être de moi-même. Je parlais de mes propres désirs, jusqu'alors refoulés. J'étais allongé près d'une femme. Je sentais la chaleur de son corps. Pour la première fois de ma vie, je pouvais toucher

une femme. Quelques frôlements des bras ou des genoux, sans qu'elle s'en rendît compte. Le reste est du domaine des fantasmes.

Je m'en souviens.[30]

That train journey is described in my very first testimony, but one point requires clarification—and it's a delicate one: it involves the erotic atmosphere that supposedly pervaded the wagon. In the French version, I say: "Freed from all social constraints, the young people gave themselves up openly to their instincts and, under the cover of night, coupled [*s'accouplaient*] in our midst, without paying attention to anyone, alone in the world. The others pretended not to see." The word "coupled" provoked raised eyebrows among puritanical readers, which is not too serious, as well as among old companions who were present on the journey, which is more so. I therefore checked the original version in Yiddish. There, the passage reads differently: "Because of the promiscuity, many instincts were awakened. Erotic instincts. Young boys and girls, under the cover of night, succumbed to their aroused senses. . . ." In fact, these were timid contacts, hesitant caresses that never went beyond the limits of propriety. How could I have translated this into "coupling"? I don't know. Or yes, I do know. A misplaced shame? I was perhaps speaking about myself. I was speaking about my own desires, repressed until then. I was lying next to a woman. I felt the warmth of her body. For the first time in my life, I could touch a woman. A few fluttering strokes on her arms and knees, without her knowing it. The rest belongs to fantasy.

I remember it.

Aside from its complex temporal structure (the narrative shuttles between the present, the past of the event, and several moments in between: the writing of the Yiddish version, the writing of the French version, and the response of readers to the latter), this passage is fascinating because it offers an intricate gloss on the problem of facts and writing, which turns out to be—in more ways than one—a problem of translation. As is by now well known, Wiesel published a much longer version of his first book in Yiddish before the whittled-down French version that has become world-famous. The Yiddish version, considerably different in tone (more truculent and accusatory then the French, as its title indicates: *Un di velt hot geshvign*, [*And the World was Silent*]), as well as in some details in the reporting of events and feelings, appeared in a series of Holocaust testimonies in Argentina in 1956 (two years before *La nuit*), and has not yet been translated into French or English. Naomi Seidman has compared the Yiddish and French versions, and concluded that Wiesel transformed the rage evident in the first book into a more "Christianized" version of victimization in the second.[31] Seidman suggests that Wiesel revised his earlier book in order to please Christian readers, and almost reproaches him for it. Not having read the Yiddish book, I can not comment on the details, but it seems clear that the presumed audience of a work exerts an influence on the writer, whether that influence is consciously felt or not. It is not surprising if, writing for a non-Jewish as well as a Jewish public (and responding, perhaps, to the encouragement of the Catholic novelist François Mauriac, who was instrumental in getting the book published in France), Wiesel emphasized the suffering, traumatized survivor rather than the one enraged by the world's indifference. It is equally possible that, having poured out his rage in the first version, he arrived at a different view of himself in retrospect. In neither case need one assume that deliberate calculation was involved.

The passage I am discussing involves yet another work, and hence another potential audience, including the author himself rereading his earlier books. Impelled by the responses of readers to his account in *La nuit* (especially the readers he most cared about, his surviving companions from the journey to Auschwitz), Wiesel returned to his Yiddish text and translated it for French readers. What exactly did the euphemistically vague Yiddish phrase "succumbed to their aroused senses" refer to? If writing is a kind of translation (imperfect, approximative) of lived experience, then what was the experience, the observed and recalled fact that the Yiddish phrase translated? And how best to render it in French?

Rereading himself, Wiesel realizes that he had mistranslated his Yiddish text in the French version—mistranslated it in both senses, since the French translation eliminated the ambiguity of the Yiddish and also offered an inaccurate rendition of what took place in the wagon "in fact." Colin Davis, in a short essay comparing *La nuit* and the 1994 memoir, concludes that in the latter text "Wiesel is sanitising his own earlier account," and sees in the memoir a "detraumatized textuality" that is not as effective or moving as the traumatic text of *La nuit*.[32] Davis recognizes that it would be "outrageous" to criticize Wiesel for finding, in his later work, "some degree of reconciliation with the past," but he clearly prefers the earlier work, finding the 1994 memoir "bland" in its "consolations."[33]

My own aim here is not to judge the two books, or even to compare them as finished works. In any case, it is difficult to compare a massive autobiography covering many years of active life to a condensed, lyrical account of a single traumatic year. What interests me in the passage I have been discussing is that in trying to understand his error in translation, Wiesel discovers a whole new meaning and offers us a whole new version (yet another translation) of his experience in the wagon. This new version, rather than merely "correcting" the previous one, brings another twist to a complex negotiation between memory and forgetting, with forgetting understood not only as an inevitable component in any self-representation of the past, but in its specifically Freudian sense of repression. What the first versions of the journey (in both Yiddish and French) had repressed was the adolescent boy's reaction to his first contact with the body of a woman. "Succumbing to aroused senses," perhaps even "coupling," are now interpreted as fantasies (still more translations?) projected by the boy, repressed by the adult author of *La nuit*, but remembered and recounted by the author of the memoirs more than thirty years later.

Does this revised version efface or attenuate in any way the horror of that train journey to the Nazi extermination camp? Does it alter the categorical status of *Night* as a Holocaust memoir or of Elie Wiesel as a reliable witness? Obviously not. Rather, the revised memory adds a new layer to both Wiesel's and the reader's interpretations of a life-shattering experience, one that has the virtually endless potential to be reviewed and reinterpreted.

To complicate things even further, the passage in question is missing from the English translation of *Tous les fleuves vont à la mer*, *All Rivers Run to the Sea* (1995). When I noticed this omission (in looking for the passage to quote in English), it shocked me, but I discovered the reason for it by checking a recent edition of *Night*. The English translation of *La nuit* has modified the lurid French verb *s'accoupler* [to couple] to a much softer one: "... young people gave way openly to instinct, taking advantage of the darkness to *flirt* in our midst ..."[34] In *La nuit*, translating his own ambiguous Yiddish text ("succumbed to their aroused senses") into French, Wiesel had chosen—for reasons on which he speculates decades later—an explicitly sexual, transgressive word that eliminated the ambiguity. I surmised that by the time *Night* appeared, he had been taken to task by other witnesses; so, for the sake of exactitude, he corrected the sentence in English: the young people, giving way to their instincts, did not couple, they flirted. This correction functioned as yet another mistranslation, albeit this time with a restrictive rather than an expansive effect; "flirted" lacks both the suggestive ambiguity of the Yiddish phrase and the shocking explicitness of the French verb.

Elie Wiesel recently explained that the first English edition of *Night* (1960) had the correct translation from the French, "coupled." It was only later that, prompted by a desire for exactitude, he asked the American publisher to modify the sentence.[35] The current Bantam paperback edition, first published in 1982, is widely used in middle-school classes on the Holocaust.

Will we ever know (and do we want to?) exactly who touched whom in that wagon and how? Personally, I regret only that the passage from the French memoirs was omitted in *All Rivers Run to the Sea*. Elie Wiesel and his wife Marion, who is his translator, have told me that they, too, now regret the omission.[36] But after thinking about it, I realize it has a certain poetic appropriateness, another in a series of mistranslations that may be emblematic of the process of writing. I am glad that Wiesel never corrected the French text of *La nuit*, since his error (or what he subsequently saw as such) allowed an extraordinarily rich reflection to surface in the memoir written many years later. The lesson to be drawn, finally, may be this: If memory is a many-layered "shapeshifter of a thing," never reaching the bedrock one longs for, then the way around that problem is not to keep silent, nor to confine oneself to fiction, but (to borrow a phrase from James Young) to keep on writing and rewriting. Breton was right, life "is" not what one writes. But one may never get closer to it than that.

ჭ 8

The Edge of Memory: Experimental Writing and the 1.5 Generation

PEREC/FEDERMAN

> The question is not "Why continue?" nor "Why can't I continue?"
> . . . but "how to continue?"
> —*G. Perec*, Je suis né

> One can always invent a little. Particularly if it's not possible to remember.
> —*R. Federman*, Double or Nothing

*T*HE CONCEPT OF THE "second generation" is now well established in Holocaust studies: it refers to the children of Holocaust survivors, born after the war, whose lives are indelibly marked by their parents' traumatic experiences but who do not themselves have personal memories of the war. Helen Epstein's pioneering 1979 book, *Children of the Holocaust*, presented Epstein's own memories of growing up as the child of Czech survivors who emigrated to the United States after the war, as well as presenting similar stories from other sons and daughters of survivors living in the United States and Canada. Despite the wide range of cultural, economic, and linguistic backgrounds, these narratives displayed some striking similarities, notably in the way children experienced their parents' silence about what had happened to them and their families—a silence that nevertheless managed to communicate a great deal. Almost at the same time, Nadine Fresco in France published her influential article "La diaspora des cendres," stressing the same combination of silence and transmission.[1] Since then, attention to the specific experience of the second generation has been encouraged by the appearance of major literary and artistic works by members of that generation—perhaps the best known of these being Art Spiegelman's *Maus: A Survivor's Tale*, which became not only an international bestseller but the object of intense critical scrutiny and commentary almost as soon as the first volume was published in 1986. Spiegelman's radical innovation was not only his choice of the "comix" form to represent a historical tragedy, but also his incorporation of his father's voice and story into his own narrative. The memories of the aged survivor are filtered through the son's representation, placing the emphasis not only on the story that is told but on the context of its telling, its effect and meaning for the one who was "not there" but who is connected to it by familial bonds. The Dutch writer Carl Friedman (a woman) created a different version of this configuration in her 1991 novel *Nightfather*, based on her experiences as a little girl whose survivor father could never cease talking about "the camp" but whose incoherent and fragmentary narratives caused only bewilderment in his captive audience, his children. The French writers Henri Raczymow and Patrick Modiano have explored a similar territory, with the difference that in their works there is no "survivor's tale," only tales of impossible quests for the remains of a world by those born after its destruction.[2]

Marianne Hirsch, herself the daughter of survivors, has proposed the term "postmemory" to designate the relation of the second generation to the experience of their parents—a mediated, second-degree memory that involves both a desire for identification with the survivor/victims and a recognition of distance from their experience.[3] Eva Hoffman, another daughter of survivors, has also insisted (in her 2003 book *After Such Knowledge*) on both the filiation and the ontological difference between the memories of survivors and those who come after.

In this chapter, I want to focus on a different, as yet undertheorized generation that I call "1.5." I mean child survivors of the Holocaust, too young to have had an adult understanding of what was happening to them, and sometimes too young to have any memory of it at all, but old enough to have *been there* during the Nazi persecution of Jews. I call this generation undertheorized because only relatively recently, in historical terms, has the concept of "child survivor of the Holocaust" emerged as a separate category for scholarly attention, just as it is relatively recently that child survivors themselves have integrated it into their consciousness. Some psychologists, including Freud's daughter Anna Freud, started to write about children traumatized by the war as early as 1946, but for a long time, in both popular representations and among psychologists, the term "Holocaust survivor" designated all and only those who had been in concentration camps, whatever their age at the time; children who had survived in hiding, the large majority, were not considered survivors, either by themselves or others. The earliest psychological studies were generally of children who had experienced the most extreme loss, orphans from Eastern Europe resettled in Israel and Western Europe after the war.[4] Widespread use of the term "child survivor," in the psychological literature as well as by organized associations of child survivors, started around the early 1980s and has gained momentum in the past two decades.[5]

It is hazardous to generalize about large groups of people, and that fact is enough to make the concept of generations problematic, since implicit in the concept as historians define it is the notion that "groups of coevals are stamped by some collective experience that permanently distinguishes them from other age groups as they move through time."[6] Members of the same generation presumably have not only shared experiences but also shared attitudes and behaviors. Even though persecution in the Holocaust was a collective experience, it is not at all certain that the historical notion of "generation" applies to Holocaust survivors with their extremely diverse backgrounds, whether they were adults or children at the time—or, for that matter, to *their* children. Nevertheless, some generalizations are possible, if not about attitudes and behavior (though some psychologists have sought commonalities among survivors in these areas as well), then at least as regards shared experience. Thus, one could say that the second generation's most salient shared experience is the feeling of belatedness—perhaps best summed up in Henri Raczymow's rueful statement, "We cannot even say that we were *almost* deported."[7] The 1.5 generation's shared experience, amply documented by historical studies as well as individual testimonies, is that of premature bewilderment and helplessness. Almost without exception, Jewish children in Europe during the war experienced the sudden transformation of their world from at least some degree of stability and security to chaos. Moving from a familiar world to new environments, alone or with strangers, having to learn a new name and new identity, learning never to say who they really were—these were among the everyday experiences of Jewish children during the war who survived. (I am not including here those who were deported, almost of whom perished). The luckiest ones lived through it all with their parents, but most experienced at least temporary separation from family and loved ones; many lost one or both parents and other close family members to deportation and murder. All, whether they were aware of it or not, lost large segments of their extended families, sometimes remaining the only survivor. In one sense, however, all were very lucky; only 11 percent of Jews in Europe who were children in 1939 were still alive at the end of the war.[8]

Of course, it can be said that not only children (and not only Jews) but all those who were persecuted by the Nazis experienced feelings of bewilderment and helplessness, not to say massive trauma, during the war. The specific experience of Jewish children was that they were persecuted because of an identity they could not even fully claim, since disaster hit them before the formation of stable identity that we associate with adulthood, and in some cases before any conscious sense of self. Since the majority survived in some form of hiding, they were obliged to cover over or "forget" their Jewishness, thus complicating an already fragile identity; for children in assimilated Jewish families, who did not have a sense of Jewishness to begin with, this involved the bizarre simultaneity of becoming aware for the first time of an imposed identity and having to deny it at the same time. All children, including the few who survived in ghettos and camps, had to live with the knowledge, however ill understood, that Jewishness was the cause of their misery. This is beautifully brought out in Nobel Prize winner Imre Kertész's autobiographical novel *Sorstalanság* (1975) [*Fatelessness*] (2004), whose adolescent protagonist has no connection at all to the Jewish community or to Jewish religious practice, yet is deported to Auschwitz. Paradoxically, premature bewilderment was accompanied by premature aging, having to act (or dissemble) as an adult while still a child.[9] This was a form of violence experienced specifically by the 1.5 generation.

Exactly who belongs to this generation? Where are the boundaries between childhood and adulthood? Categories, always fuzzy around the edges, vary according to one's perspective: psychoanalysts, cognitive psychologists, and legislators draw different lines around childhood. In the context of child development and personal memory, age eleven is one boundary on which psychoanalysts and cognitive psychologists agree. For the former, it marks the move from "latency" to early adolescence, while for the latter it marks an important stage in logical reasoning: a child of eleven or older has a capacity for abstract thought and a vocabulary to name his or her experience that the younger child lacks. Another, earlier age boundary seems necessary as well, below which there are no conscious memories at all, and very little or no vocabulary of any kind available to the child at the time of trauma. In speaking about child survivors of the Holocaust, we can therefore delineate at least three discrete groups, depending on the age of the child at the time of disruption (which itself varied from country to country, an additional factor of difficulty in delineating this generation): children who were "too young to remember" (infancy to around three years old), children "old enough to remember but too young to understand" (approximately age four through ten), and children "old enough to understand but too young to be responsible" (approximately age eleven through fourteen). Obviously, understanding is a relative term, for even young children are capable of understanding that they are in danger and must behave or not behave in certain ways—but a young child does not have the capacity to contextualize the experience and think about it the way an adult would. Similarly for responsibility: by responsible, I mean having to make choices (and to act on those choices) about their own or their family's actions in response to catastrophe—adulthood being the state where one is both capable of naming one's predicament and responsible for acting on it in some considered way. Many children under fourteen were forced to become responsible in this adult sense, but they were certainly too young to be placed in such a position.

While it is possible to generalize in a broad way about Jewish children's wartime experiences, it is clear that individual personalities and temperaments as well as historical and social contingencies played an enormous role in determining the emotional coloration of any given child's response and ways of coping. Children's postwar situations also varied widely, the most significant factor being no doubt whether they lost a parent in the war. All of this helps to explain the differences in child survivors' later memories and understandings of the role that the Holocaust played in their lives. For some, as they look back on it, surviving persecution was a great adventure; for others, it was a tragedy from which they never recovered.[10] The systematic efforts during the past twenty years to collect detailed video-testimonies by Holocaust survivors in a nonclinical setting (as opposed to the earliest studies and case histories, which were generally the result of psychoanalytic interviews or clinical treatment) have yielded an enormous trove of autobiographical narratives and self-representations, a large number of them by people who were children or adolescents during the war. Written testimonies have also been collected and published.[11] One of the outstanding features of all these testimonies is that they occur many years after the events, directing our attention not only to the wide variety of individual experiences but also to how they are remembered and retrospectively interpreted by the one who lived them. This very rich material can provide the basis for detailed studies of the 1.5 generation by psychologists and social scientists.[12]

In addition to any social or collective commonalities one may discover or wish to emphasize, however, it is as personal, subjective expression that the experiences of survivors of the Holocaust can most memorably be communicated. The meaning of their experience remains, despite the collective nature of the historical event and of its official commemorations, individual rather than collective. The psychoanalyst Nancy Chodorow has put it well: "History, when it matters, always matters emotionally and unconsciously [as well as consciously, I would add] to individuals."[13] That is one reason why the collection of oral or written testimonies—each of which tells a unique story, even if it resembles others in many respects—is so important. But I believe that there is a special place for the literary imagination in the narratives of child survivors, and more generally for the artistic representation of their experience. This statement should hardly come as a surprise to a reader who has followed the arguments of this book, especially in the preceding two chapters. The privileging of the literary—which I defined earlier as "the kind of work on language and thought that produces the most complex understandings of self and world, both on the part of the writer and on that of readers"—goes against views I myself (as well as others) have expressed about the appeal of "raw" testimony and of straightforward referential narrative in accounts of Holocaust experience.[14] That may be because now that we have so many straightforward accounts, which of course must be preserved and archived, we will have to think about what will actually endure and continue to be meaningful to people who are not specialists or who have no personal connection to those events. Call it my professional bias, but I believe that works of literary merit (however one interprets that term) have a greater chance to endure than others.

An impressive number of contemporary writers, writing in a wide array of languages, were children or adolescents during the Holocaust and have dealt with that experience in their works: Aharon Appelfeld, Louis Begley, Serge Doubrovsky, Raymond Federman, Saul Friedländer, Elisabeth Gille, Jean-Claude Grumberg, Imre Kertész, Ruth Kluger, Sarah Kofman, Serge Koster, Georges Perec, Régine Robin, Lore Segal, Elie Wiesel—the list could be extended. Some of these writers are better known than others; some have written only one autobiographical work, others many; some write directly about their experience, others transpose it into fiction. All have given powerful accounts of what it felt like to be a child or adolescent during the Holocaust, encountering loss, displacement, and terror; and also of what it means to try to look back on that experience at a distance. In their works, we see both the child's helplessness and the adult's attempt to render that helplessness, retrospectively, in language. Their works are highly individualized in literary style, yet bear "family resemblances" in tone, genre, and emotional or narrative content that place them in significant dialogue with each other. Themes of unstable identity and psychological splitting, a preoccupation with absence, emptiness, silence, a permanent sense of loneliness and loss, including the loss of memories relating to family and childhood, and, often, an anguished questioning about what it means to be Jewish after the Holocaust dominate many of these works. Equally compelling is their preoccupation, either explicitly stated or implied in their formal choices, with the question of *how* to tell the story.

Raymond Federman, who dates his "birth" to the moment when his whole immediate family was rounded up by French police, leaving him the sole survivor at age fourteen, has observed: "My life began in incoherence and discontinuity, and my work has undoubtedly been marked by this. Perhaps that is why it has been called experimental."[15]

What is the relation between experiment and existence, when existence starts out with a fracture?

Perec's *W ou le souvenir d'enfance;* or, the Paradox of Suspension

Georges Perec's 1975 book *W ou le souvenir d'enfance [W or the Memory of Childhood]* creates a compelling literary representation of childhood trauma; at the same time, it offers a reflection on the limits and paradoxes of remembering and writing about such trauma in adulthood. Perec, one of France's most innovative writers, whose stature has grown exponentially since his premature death in 1982, four days short of his forty-sixth birthday, was born in Paris to Polish immigrants who had arrived in France during the 1920s. He was four years old when his father, who had enlisted as a foreign combatant at the outbreak of World War II, was killed in June 1940 by advancing German troops not far from the capital. A year and a half later, the five-year old boy said goodbye to his mother at the Gare de Lyon railroad station, joining a trainload of children who were being evacuated by the Red Cross. He was on his way to a village in the foothills of the Alps near Grenoble, where two of his aunts and their families had found refuge; he never saw his mother again. She was rounded up by French police in January 1943 and taken to the transit camp at Drancy outside Paris, from where she was shipped to Auschwitz a month later. Georges was brought up in the family of his paternal aunt, Esther Bienenfeld.[16]

When *W or the Memory of Childhood* was published, it took many readers by surprise. Perec, already a well-known writer, whose first novel, *Les choses,* had won a literary prize in 1965, was associated with the group of experimental novelists and poets who went by the name of Oulipo (short for Ouvroir de littérature potentielle ["workshop of potential literature"]). The Oulipo writers were known for their interest in difficult word games (palindromes, anagrams, and puzzles of various kinds) and mathematical games such as the Japanese game of Go, all of which they often used as the basis for their work. Perec, a champion player with words, had accomplished a tour de force in 1969 when he published a full-length novel from which the most commonly used vowel in the French language, the letter E, was absent. The story it tells, in mock detective mode (with transparent allusions to Poe's "The Purloined Letter" and other classics of the genre) centers on mysterious disappearances and mixed-up identities, leaving almost no survivors—it is an astonishingly readable and entertaining tale, despite the contortions of language it necessitated. Not surprisingly, the title of this novel (whose heroes include Anton Voyl and Amaury Conson, plays on the French words for "vowel" and "consonant," ["voyelle" and "consonne") was *La disparition,* "*The Disappearance*."[17] Because of work like this (*La disparition* was followed by a brief text titled *Les revenentes* [*Female Revenants*], whose only vowels were Es!), most readers thought of Perec as a playful, unusually clever writer; and since his name sounds like many typical Breton place and family names ending in "ec" or "ecq" (like Michel Houellebecq), few readers knew of his Polish Jewish family history marked by the Holocaust.

W or the Memory of Childhood did not break with Perec's experimental mode of writing; but in this work, what had appeared as purely formal experimentation in earlier works takes on a profound existential significance. Doubling, splitting, discontinuity, and absence become not only signs of the work's formal ambition but also signs imbued with personal and historical meaning, related to the nature of childhood memory and of traumatic separation and loss experienced in childhood. After the publication of *W,* Perec's earlier works, with their mysterious disappearances, confused identities, and violent crimes, suddenly acquired a horrific autobiographical resonance.[18] He himself pointed the way by dedicating *W or the Memory of Childhood* "to E"— the letter E which had disappeared and then returned, but also "eux" ["them"], his parents, who had disappeared forever and returned only metaphorically, in flashes, in his book.[19] The book, painful in its subject, was also painful to write. Started in 1969, it was not finished until six years later, and most of its writing coincided with an intense analysis that Perec undertook from 1971 to 1975 with the psychoanalyst J. B. Pontalis. The end of the analysis coincided almost exactly with the publication of the book.[20]

W or the Memory of Childhood: doubleness is present, indeed twice present, already on the cover. The capital letter W (which in French is pronounced as "double V") is itself "doubled" by the appositional phrase "the memory of childhood"—but to complicate matters, the conjunction "or" leads to two possible interpretations. According to one, "memory of childhood" is a kind of repetition, synonymous with W, as in some classic titles: *Candide or Optimism, Tartuffe or The Impostor*. But "or" can also indicate difference, an alternative between two divergent entities: in that case, W is not another version of the memory of childhood, but an alternative to it. Perec plays on both these meanings. The book consists of two apparently independent narratives told in alternating chapters. The W series (nineteen chapters set in italic type) tell a story inspired by Jules Verne's tales and other science-fiction adventures, narrated in the first person by a character named Gaspard Winckler; the other chapters, which constitute the memory series (eighteen chapters set in roman type) are also in the first person, but the speaker here is Perec himself and the discourse is not fictional but autobiographical. Yet another doubling, then: two narrators who say "I" and two narrative genres, two modes of discourse—adventure or life story, fiction or autobiography. According to the eminent theorist of autobiography Philippe Lejeune, this "montage" of autobiography and fiction in a single work was totally unknown before Perec invented it. But Lejeune insists that Perec "was not looking for novelty"—rather, he "found it impossible to do otherwise."[21]

How does one write an autobiography when one has "no childhood memories," as Perec states hyperbolically in the opening of the very first memory chapter of the book? One solution is to prop up memory with fiction; another is to make the absence of memory itself the subject of the book. Originally, Perec planned three parallel series for *W or the Memory of Childhood*: the science fiction tale (which was the first to be written, published as a serial in the bimonthly literary magazine *La Quinzaine Littéraire* in 1969); the autobiographical fragments he did remember, including a short piece he wrote about his parents as early as 1959; and a "critical" series that would comment on the other two. The final version reduces this tripartite schema to a double one, with critical comments incorporated into the memory chapters. The result is what Lejeune calls a "critical autobiography," comprising both personal memories and a critique of memory that comments on its own hesitations, incompletions, or errors.

Of course, the problem of remembering one's childhood is not limited to people who are Holocaust survivors or survivors of childhood trauma. As Freud wrote in his essay on screen memories, the "raw material" of early childhood experiences "remains unknown to us in its original form," no matter who we are.[22] Perec, who last saw his mother when he was five years old, was hardly unusual in not being able to remember her; but the circumstances of their separation and of her disappearance, as well as the silence that surrounded them, were not those of a usual childhood. Officially, Cyrla Perec's death was not acknowledged until 1958, when a death certificate was issued listing her place of death erroneously as Drancy. Perec fascinates Lejeune because the writer's self-reflexive questioning coincides with the extreme experience of Jews in the Holocaust. Perec envisaged autobiography, Lejeune notes, as "oblique, multiple, shattered and at the same time endlessly turning around the unspeakable *[l'indicible]*."[23]

Lejeune is certainly right about the inexhaustibility of the subject, as well as about Perec's oblique approaches to it. However, I think we need a moratorium, or even a downright taboo, on the use of the word "unspeakable" in connection with the Holocaust. If a thing is spoken about, however obliquely, then it is not unspeakable—on the contrary, it may be the object about and around which one can never stop speaking. Speaking can take many forms; sometimes, as popular wisdom has it, silence speaks louder than words. In any case, we are concerned here not with speaking but with writing. The problem, as Perec well knew, was not whether "it" could be written, but *how* it could be written. With difficulty, to be sure, but also, as he so brilliantly showed, with invention—and yes, silence, but a silence that speaks, like the famous suspension points between parentheses on the otherwise empty page that separates Parts I and II of *W or the Memory of Childhood*:

(. . .)

Is the ellipsis a form of saying, or of not saying? It is both, a sign that says, "I will not say"—and that has inspired commentators to say a great deal. Warren Motte, one among many, calls it "the key statement of the book."[24]

What do the suspension points say? Critics have pointed out that Perec's games with numbers and letters often hide coded allusions to his parents.[25] The break between Parts I and II occurs after Chapter 11, which is a "W" chapter. Perec's mother was deported in the convoy of February 11, 1943. After the ellipsis, the alternating pattern of odd and even chapters (odd for W, even for autobiography) reverses, in a chiasmus: Chapter 12 resumes the W narrative instead of the autobiography, contrary to what the preceding pattern would lead one to expect. And the W narrative itself shifts radically, for the first-person narrator disappears and we have a series of impersonal descriptions of the island society that become more and more horrific, until at last it is clear that the island of W is a version of a Nazi concentration camp. It is as if the whole book swiveled on its axis or crossed in the middle of an X, or in the middle of a swastika—Perec shows in Chapter 15 that the letter X, itself a variant on the "double V," can be recomposed into the Nazi symbol as well as into a Jewish star. For a young child, the sudden separation from the mother is like "being turned inside out," a psychological state figured by the trope of chiasmus. After the suspension points, almost no mention is made of Perec's mother in this book about his childhood.

But there is more to suspension than this single occurrence; indeed, it is in the figure of suspension that the relation between the experimental and the existential in this work is most tellingly articulated. Suspension points, as the OED tells us, are used "to indicate an omission or an interval in a printed text." However, the rhetorical figure of suspension also implies suspense, an interruption or deferral used to create heightened expectation and surprise. Suspension is thus a paradoxical figure, at once an omission and the promise of more to come. That is exactly how Perec described his science fiction "serial novel" when he first proposed it to the editor of *La Quinzaine Littéraire* in 1969: "a construction of episodes each of which would conclude positively the preceding one and prepare, in mystery and suspension (or suspense) [*dans le mystère et le suspens (ou suspense)*], the one that follows."[26] In the book, "suspension or suspense" is introduced not only between the episodes of the W series, but between the two series themselves. Each one regularly interrupts the other, promising more to come—and promising, as well, to any reader used to "normal" construction, that the relation between the two series will eventually be elucidated.

The characteristic of promises, however, is that they may or may not be kept. The memory chapters of *W or the Memory of Childhood* are full of holes and gaps that are never filled in—indeed, Perec cut out more and more as he progressed, during the six years of writing; and even the W chapters, which promise a story of adventure, sud-

denly abandon both the narrative and the main character and veer
into static (albeit increasingly horrifying) descriptions. As for the relation of the two series, we get something like an elucidation early
on—but it is equivocal, itself full of holes and "suspense." In order
not to create still more holes, I will reproduce Perec's comment here
in its entirety (the spaces are in the text):

> When I was thirteen I made up a story which I told and drew in
> pictures. Later I forgot it. Seven years ago, one evening in Venice,
> I suddenly remembered that this story was called W and that it
> was, in a way, if not the story of my childhood, then at least a
> story of my childhood.
>
> Apart from the title thus wrested back, I had practically no
> memory of W. All I knew of it came to a couple of lines: it was
> about the life of a community concerned exclusively with sport,
> on a tiny island off Tierra del Fuego.
>
> Once again the snares of writing were set. Once again I was
> like a child playing hide-and-seek, who doesn't know what he
> fears or wants more: to stay hidden, or to be found.
>
> Later I came across one of the drawings I had done around the
> age of thirteen. With their help I reinvented W and wrote it,
> publishing it as I wrote, in serial form, in *La Quinzaine littéraire*
> between September 1969 and August 1970.
>
> Today, four years later, I propose to bring to term—by which
> I mean just as much "to mark the end of" as "to give a name
> to"—this gradual unravelling. W is no more like my Olympic
> fantasy than that Olympic fantasy was like my childhood. But
> in the crisscross web they weave as in my reading of them I
> know there is to be found the inscription and description of the
> path I have taken, the passage of my history and the story of my
> passage [*le cheminement de mon histoire et l'histoire de mon chemi-
> nement*].[27]

The "crisscross web they weave": While different in genre and discourse, the tale of W and the autobiographical fragments do crisscross at several points. Gaspard Winckler, the fictional narrator, shares
with the autobiographical "I" an uncertainty about his own history:

"For years I sought out traces of my history, looking up maps and directories . . . I found nothing" (3, *10*). And like the autobiographer, Winckler has the feeling of being the "sole depository" of the tale he tells, since all those he writes about have disappeared. Perec will say, in a later chapter, that his writing is conditioned, in its very possibility, by his parents' disappearance: "I know that what I say is blank, is neutral, is a sign, once and for all, of a once-and-for-all annihilation" (42, *59*). Numerous other details underline similarities between the two stories and the two narrators, suggesting a metaphorical relation between the series. There are also metonymic details that migrate from one series to the other. Bernard Magné calls these recurrent elements "sutures," and has made a detailed list of them.[28] Whether metaphoric or metonymic, such details confirm the image of the "crisscross web" between the two series, but there is another possible relation between them as well, suggested by Perec in the first part of the passage quoted above—not crisscrossing but juxtaposing, not an interconnected web but parallel lines that unfold without any point of contact or similarity. The story of W that he invented at age thirteen was, Perec writes, "a story" (not "the story") of his childhood—but exactly *how* it was that story remains undefined. For one thing, he no longer has any memory of the story he invented at age thirteen; at best, he has "reinvented" it on the basis of drawings from that time— but the W he has reinvented "is no more like my Olympic fantasy than that Olympic fantasy was like my childhood." Whereas the image of the web suggests connection—whether based on proximity or similarity, metonymy or metaphor—and hence a kind of integration, the emphasis here is on *non*connection, or on a connection that remains unknowable. The two series coexist, that is all.

And yet, despite the broken promises, this book transmits a great deal of emotion and even of information. Régine Robin, a subtle commentator of Perec as well as a child survivor and writer herself, has a wonderfully suggestive sentence that is pertinent here—she is referring to her own idea about writing, but it applies just as well to Perec: "the transmission if there is one occurs only in the blanks."[29] Here, then, is another paradox of suspension, one that Perec himself was well aware of. He wrote by way of introduction to *W ou le souvenir d'enfance* (in what is called the "prière d'insérer" in French publishing, an authorial gloss inserted on a separate page in the original edition—

it is on the back cover of the current French paperback edition):
"There are two texts in this book simply alternating; it could appear
that they have nothing in common, but they are nevertheless inextri-
cably intertwined, as if neither one could exist on its own. . . ." Perec
ends his gloss with a complex play on the figure of suspension. After
noting that the W series "begins by telling one story and then suddenly launches into another" (referring to the break between Parts I
and II), he writes, "In that rupture, that break which suspends the
narrative around some unnamed expectation, is the initial place from
which this book emerged, those *suspension points* to which are attached
the broken threads of childhood and the weave of writing [*ces* points
de suspension *auxquels se sont accrochés les fils rompus de l'enfance et la
trame de l'écriture*]."[30] The break suspends, cuts off, yet is also the
"initial place" of writing; and the way Perec uses the verb ("suspends
the narrative *around* some expectation") alludes to another meaning of
"suspend," in French and in English: to hang, to attach "so as to allow
of movement about the point of attachment," says the OED. As if to
emphasize the contradictory meanings of the word and the figure,
Perec repeats it, this time even underlining "suspension points": what
is a standard marker of omission becomes a series of fixed points on
which to hang the broken threads of childhood and his (broken?)
writing. Note that the suspension points do not repair the broken
threads, they merely give them an anchor.

Within the text of *W or the Memory of Childhood*, the word "suspension" occurs twice, at crucial moments. In the last autobiographical
chapter before the break (Chapter 10), Perec recalls the "only
memory" he has of his mother, which was the last time he saw her,
when she accompanied him to the train station. This may actually be
"the" childhood memory alluded to in the book's title, though as usual
we cannot be certain—it is the only childhood episode evoked more
than once.[31] Here, he recalls that she bought him a magazine showing
"Charlot" (Charlie Chaplin) hanging by his suspenders from a parachute; and in his memory, his own arm was in a sling. But he tells us
right away that this was a false memory, for his aunt and cousins have
assured him that his arm was fine, no need for a sling. He then adds
that he may have worn a hernia brace or truss, a "suspensory bandage"
["suspensoir"], and appends a note to say that he did indeed wear one
and was operated for hernia in Grenoble a few months later—this fact

does not change the "fantasy," he says, but simply indicates one of its origins (*W* 81, 77–78).

Why does Perec refer to the memory of this episode as a fantasy? One clue may lie in his specification of the technical name for hernia brace, "suspensoir," linked by both sound and meaning to Charlot's suspenders. Philippe Lejeune has shown that the "Charlot" image could not have appeared on an illustrated book sold in Paris in 1943, under German occupation, and probably dates from after the war.[32] Clearly this part of the memory was imagined, like the arm in a sling, although in this case Perec appends no self-correction. Instead, he provides a gloss on the whole episode as he remembers it:

> A triple trait runs through this memory: parachute, arm in a sling, hernia brace: it involves suspension [*suspension*], support, almost artifical limbs [*prothèses*]. In order to be, you had to be propped [*Pour être, besoin d'étai*]. Sixteen years later, in 1958, when, by chance, military service briefly made a parachutist of me, I was able to read, at the very instant of jumping, the deciphered text of that memory: I was thrown into the void; all the threads were broken; I fell, alone and without support. The parachute opened. The canopy unfurled, a fragile and firm suspension [*suspens*] before the controlled descent [*la chute maîtrisée*]. (55, trans. modified; 77)

The "triple trait," in fact a triple metaphor, that Perec analyzes here implies both terrifying loss (amputation, free fall without support) and the possibility of attenuating it through substitutions, prostheses, props (the sling, the brace, the parachute). The generalization, almost a maxim, "In order to be, you had to be propped," suggests the possibility of losing one's very being, or self, at such a moment of separation. The second half of the passage, which reads the childhood memory through his later memory of an actual parachute jump, introduces both a further gloss and a literary dimension: the childhood memory is a "text" to be "deciphered," like a fantasy elaborated in writing.[33]

If one wanted to be very optimistic, one could suggest that the transformation of a terrifying free fall ("I fell, alone and without support") into a "controlled descent" (the French is even stronger: a "mastered fall") is a function of writing, as if the deployment of writing is what saved Perec from falling apart. Lejeune calls writing Perec's "parachute."[34]

But that, I think, may overstate the case. There is certainly a suggestion, here and elsewhere in the book (as well as throughout Perec's work), that writing is a form of substitution for loss, both reparative and a form of commemoration; but such affirmations are accompanied, sometimes in the same sentence, by the contrary sense that writing can never replace, cover over, or otherwise compensate for the void left by the death of his parents. At most, writing is a trace, the sign of something that once was but that has disappeared: an assertion of the writer's life, yes, but also a reminder of death, of an unjust and definitive absence (42, 59). That is why the figure of suspension is so richly suggestive in this work, spanning the realms of life and of rhetoric and carrying in a single word two totally contradictory meanings: rupture, anchor.

The second time Perec uses the word "suspension" occurs in Chapter 15, where he once again evokes a memory of having his arm in a sling, this time pinned behind his back as the result of a skating accident in the village near Grenoble where he lived during the last year of the war. But he discovers, after a visit to the village many years later, that the memory was false, just like the memory of his arm at the train station: it was a classmate, not he, who had had the accident; he was merely its witness. Perec writes, in two tortuous sentences that must be quoted in the original as well as in translation:

> Comme pour le bras en écharpe de la gare de Lyon, je vois bien ce que pouvaient remplacer ces fractures éminemment réparables qu'une immobilisation temporaire suffisait à réduire, même si la métaphore, aujourd'hui, me semble inopérante pour décrire ce qui précisément avait été cassé et qu'il était sans doute vain d'espérer enfermer dans le simulacre d'un membre fantôme. Plus simplement, ces thérapeutiques imaginaires, ces *points de suspension*, désignaient des douleurs nommables et venaient à point justifier des cajoleries dont les raisons réelles n'étaient données qu'à voix basse (*109–110;* Perec's emphasis).

As in the case of my arm-in-a-sling at the Gare de Lyon, I can see perfectly well what it was that these easily mendable fractures, which could be remedied simply by keeping them still for a stretch, were meant to replace, although today it seems to me that the metaphor will not serve as a way of describing what exactly had been broken—and what it was surely pointless hoping to enclose in the simulacrum of a missing limb. In simpler terms, these imaginary therapies, more supportive than restrictive, these *suspension points*, indicated pains that could be named; they cropped up on cue to justify indulgences whose actual cause was mentioned only in an undertone (80–81, trans. modified).

Through this veritable cascade of metaphors, associations, and substitutions, Perec succeeds in saying that metaphoric substitutions will never adequately represent the fracture they are meant to replace. All they can do is act as suspension points, serving at once as pegs on which to hang "the pains that can be named" and as coverups for the pain that cannot be named. This statement refers, of course, as much to the support provided by writing as to external supports, like the indulgences or "cajoleries" extended to an orphaned child.

Freud, in one of his last, incomplete writings, began to theorize a phenomenon he had already noticed earlier without giving it a name; he called it the splitting of the ego, a process that occurs "under the influence of a psychical trauma."[35] What is at stake in this process is the subject's attitude toward a frightening or painful reality, and the "solution" consists in recognizing the reality and denying it at the same time. Freud remarks that "this way of dealing with reality... almost deserves to be described as artful."[36] The pertinence of this remark to Perec's way of deploying the figure of suspension will become even more evident after we look at Raymond Federman.

Federman's *Double or Nothing*; or, How (not) to Say It

Raymond Federman shares Perec's self-reflexiveness and inventiveness, as well as his background as the son of poor Polish Jewish immigrants living in Paris during the war. Unlike Perec, however, Federman has only recently been integrated into the canon of Holocaust writing. Despite the fact that all of his creative works (close to a dozen novels and several volumes of poetry as well as books of criticism) turn around his own childhood trauma, he was known for many years chiefly as an American avant-garde writer and theorist, and that was how he presented himself as well. Interestingly, it was in Germany in the mid-1980s that he made his first "breakthrough" as both an experimental and post-Holocaust writer, and a popular one: His readership in Germany is still far wider than in the United States, where he remains a relatively hidden treasure.[37] Largely ignored in France until the last few years, even though he had published several works originally in French, he has finally been recognized in his native country. His first novel, *Double or Nothing*, published in 1971, appeared in French translation in 2003 and was widely reviewed in the French press as an innovative work by a French child survivor of the Holocaust. Other translations and new editions of French works have followed, as well as conferences and special issues of journals devoted to his writing. Perhaps in response to the growing international interest in his work, Federman, now in his late seventies, continues to publish at an impressive rate—his most recent book, *The Farm*, an "autofiction" about his survival during the war, has already appeared in French translation (*Retour au fumier*, 2005) and is scheduled for publication in the United States in 2006.[38]

Older than Perec by eight years (born in 1928), Raymond Federman had just turned fourteen when his immediate family—mother, father, and two sisters—were taken away by French police in the infamous "rafle du Vél d'Hiv," the roundup of more than 12,000 Jews (men, women, and children) on July 16–17, 1942, almost all of whom, including the Federmans, ended up in Auschwitz. Raymond was spared because his mother, at the last minute, thrust him into a utilities closet on the landing outside their apartment door; the boy, half-naked, sat all day in the closet and finally ventured out at night, dressed in his father's overcoat. He eventually made his way to the unoccupied zone in the south of France, working as a hired hand on a farm until the end of the war. In 1947, a relative in the United States arranged for him to emigrate.[39] After spending several years in Detroit, where he earned a high school diploma and learned to play the jazz saxophone while supporting himself with a series of odd jobs, Raymond went to New York, worked in a lampshade factory, and was drafted into the Army during the Korean War. In 1954, at age twenty-six, he enrolled on the GI Bill at Columbia University, obtained his BA in comparative literature, and went on to do a doctorate in French at UCLA. He wrote his doctoral dissertation on the early works of Samuel Beckett (published in 1965 under the title *Journey to Chaos*.) In 1971, his autobiographical novel *Double or Nothing* established him as one of the leading experimental writers in the United States, little known by the general public but highly appreciated by specialists interested in the American avant-garde. Meanwhile, like a number of other American postmodernists, he earned a living as a professor; he retired from the University of Buffalo a few years ago, and now lives in California.

Throughout most of the 1970s, Federman himself wrote about his own work exclusively in terms of avant-garde formal experimentation—in 1975, he edited a book titled *Surfiction*, whose lead essay by that same title was a manifesto of the "New Fiction" in America. Like the *nouveaux romanciers* in France, who clearly influenced him, Federman rejected the Sartrean notion of engagement, which called on writers to represent their own historical moment in their works. Fiction, Federman proclaimed, had only itself as both source and object: "It is from itself, from its own substance that the fictitious discourse will proliferate—imitating, repeating, parodying, retracting what it says." And he concluded, in a sentence that appears like a straightforward translation from French formalist theory of those years: "Thus fiction will become the metaphor of its own narrative process."[40]

To a reader today, especially one who knows Federman's personal history, what seems most striking in this "surfiction" manifesto is its omission of any reference to the past or to history. "Most fiction is based on the experiences of the one who writes," Federman acknowledges, but then immediately explains that the experiences he has in mind "are not anterior to, but simultaneous with, the writing process. There cannot be any truth nor any reality exterior to fiction."[41] Following this dictum, we would have to read Federman's novels—including the early novels written at the same time as the manifesto— as totally indifferent to and shut off from history, both personal and collective (history with both a small and a capital "H"). That, in fact, is how Linda Hutcheon categorized Federman's work in her 1988 book *A Poetics of Postmodernism*. Hutcheon sought to show (partly in response to Marxist critiques of postmodernism) that postmodernist fiction was much more turned toward history than its critics recognized, albeit in a form unlike that of the classical historical novel. But she excluded Federman and other surfictionists from her postmodernist canon of "historiographic metafiction," precisely because, in her view, they were not interested in history. She saw Federman's work, along with that of the French New Novelists, as examples of "late modernist extremism," characterized by "hermeticism and autotelic reflexivity."[42] That was not a compliment!

Hutcheon, of course, was simply taking Federman at his word—or rather, at the words he had written more than ten years earlier.[43] By 1988, he had shifted considerably in his theoretical pronouncements. Self-reflexive fiction, the fiction of postmodernism, he stated in a 1988 essay, was a response to the "moral crisis provoked by the Holocaust." And about his own work, he wrote around the same time: "If I was given a gift at all which forced me to write, it was what happened to me, often in spite of myself, during the first twenty-five years of my life. Much of the fiction I have written found its source in those early years."[44] This is a rather different view of the writer's experience from the one advanced in the surfiction manifesto. But already earlier, in a 1980 interview with the critic Larry McCaffery, Federman had invoked personal experience as the source and even as the subject of his fiction. Responding to a question about the "elaborate voices-within-voices narrative structure" of his novels, he explained: "I think that it's true of all fiction writers—but especially those who base their fiction on personal experiences—that they have to invent for themselves a way of distancing themselves from their subject. . . . And yet, paradoxically in my case, the more complex the system of distancing becomes the closer I seem to be getting to my own biography."[45] One could hardly be more explicit about the referential overlap between fiction and autobiography in his works.

It is true that by the early 1980s, even the discourse of the *nouveau roman* had changed its course. Alain Robbe-Grillet proclaimed, in the first volume of his autobiography published in 1984, that the formalist readings of the 1970s, to which he had prescribed, were becoming an established orthodoxy to combat; in any case, he had never written about anything other than himself![46] It was as if a long historical amnesia had come to an end. One cannot help wondering whether this was not related to the increasing movement, in the 1980s, all over Europe but especially in France, toward a reconsideration of World War II in both historiography and in public memory. Robbe-Grillet's autobiography, which treats the war years in some detail (he was twenty years old in 1943 and did obligatory labor service in Germany), was published the same year as the return of Klaus Barbie to France to face trial for crimes against humanity committed forty years earlier. The massive *lieux de mémoire* project directed by Pierre Nora—not limited to World War II, but inaugurating a new historiography of memory that included the war—was launched during those same years, with the first volume appearing in 1984. In the United States, the intellectual climate was also shifting: structuralism and deconstruction had been absorbed, and various forms of "new historicism" were on the rise.

Federman's insight that "the more complex the system of distancing" the closer he gets to his biography has important implications both for the psychology of childhood trauma and for the experimental writing of the 1.5 generation. What are the ways he invents to distance himself from, and at the same time bring himself closer to, his life story? One could write a whole book on that subject, for Federman has made use in his works of the full panoply of distancing devices beloved by metafictionists: multiple narrative voices, self-reflexive commentary, mock dialogues between the "author" and his audience (or his characters), intertextual allusions both to his own works and to his favorite writers (with Beckett and Céline in first place), word plays and punning, especially on his own name (Federman, "featherman," *homme de plume*, writer), and a boisterous humor and playfulness even in—or especially in—treating the most painful subjects. He loves to make lists (as did Perec), collecting, classifying, accumulating, often to burlesque effect.[47] Being bilingual, he inserts French words or whole passages into his English texts, sometimes translating them and other times not. One important novel (*The Voice in the Closet*, 1979) and much of his poetry was written in both languages and published in bilingual editions. English and French are, as he puts it, in "internal (one should almost say infernal) dialogue" in his head and in his texts.[48] In his early novels, which are formally the most innovative, he created veritable verbal collages, using the page as a canvas to produce complex visual as well as linguistic meanings.

For want of a book-length study, I will devote my attention to Federman's first novel, *Double or Nothing*, whose subtitle is a whole program: "a real fictitious discourse." It is worth noting that this novel was published several years before the "surfiction" manifesto that claimed fiction was always only about itself.

Double or Nothing is a brilliant work, combining techniques of concrete poetry with a complex, multilayered narrative. Federman has explained that he began it as a series of handwritten notes for a novel and only gradually discovered that the notes were themselves to be the substance as well as the form he was seeking.[49] He then spent several years transcribing and rearranging them typographically (this was in the days before computers), so that in the end he had a manuscript each of whose pages stood on its own visually; at the same time, they conveyed the picaresque tale, in fractured form, of a young French Jewish immigrant to America who had lost his whole family during the war. Not surprisingly, no mainstream publisher would touch the finished manuscript—it was not viable commercially, he was told, unless he gave up all the fancy typography and fractured narrative and simply told the story. After all, he did have a good story: from wartime misery to freedom in America, a classic American road book by and about a young man on the make, his head full of sexual fantasies and dreams of getting rich quick—double or nothing, a gambler in life as well as in casinos. But "simply telling that story" was what Federman neither wanted nor was able to do. *Double or Nothing* was published by a small press in Chicago, its layout painstakingly arranged on every page, unchanged.[50]

The book has two opening chapters, the first of which is titled "This Is Not a Beginning" and begins this way:

Once upon a time (two or three weeks ago), a rather stubborn and determined middle-aged man decided *to record* (for posterity), exactly as it happened, word by word and step by step, the story of another man (for indeed what is GREAT in man is that he is a bridge and not a goal), a somewhat paranoiac fellow (unmarried, unattached, and quite irresponsible), who had decided to lock himself in a room (a furnished room with a private bath, cooking facilities, a bed, a table, and at least one chair), in New York City, for a year (364 days, to be precise), to write the story of another person—a shy young man about 19 years old—who, after the war (the Second World War), had come to America (the land of opportunities) from France under the sponsorship of his uncle . . .

and so on to the bottom of the page in a single sentence that contains, in summary form, not only the narrative we are about to read but also the whole past history of the young man whose story in America will be told by the "paranoiac fellow" who plans to shut himself in a room for a year to write, eating nothing but noodles (we will soon learn) because of his restricted budget. Although the traditional opening formula, "once upon a time," promises a tale of adventure told by a single narrator in chronological mode, we immediately note the twist: the tale told here will be that of a writing project, involving at least three narrative "persons" whose relationship is ambiguous, and the march of linear time will be replaced by the meanderings of retrospection and prospection.

The many parentheses that pepper these first few lines continue down the page, both prolonging the sentence and impeding its progress. Postponement is the basic principle of this novel, as of many others by Federman. As a figure, it is of course related to digression and to . . . suspension. One difference between Federman and Perec is that Perec's suspensions create mainly gaps, whereas Federman's create excess, as if there was so much to tell that no single line of narrative or thought could be developed without qualifications, additions, corrections, or straying to other stories, other thoughts. The effect in both cases is to make the reading more difficult, as well as to call attention to the act of telling. It can also often be humorous, as in the great exemplars of digressive narrative, Sterne's *Tristram Shandy* and Diderot's *Jacques le Fataliste et son maître*, both of which Federman knows well. In this instance, the humor is in jarring contrast to the past history of the young man, which is evoked briefly on this opening page as part of a letter he wrote to his American relative: "that his parents (both his father and mother) and his two sisters (one older and the other younger than he) had been deported (they were Jewish) to a German concentration camp (Auschwitz probably) and never returned, no doubt having been exterminated deliberately (X-X-X-X) . . ."

Aside from the multiple parentheses, the conceit of a long page consisting of a single sentence, the temporal dislocations evoking past and future, and the three narrative "persons" introduced here (to which is added yet a fourth at the end of the chapter), this first page introduces a typographical sign that Federman will use in all of his subsequent fiction: the four X's that mark the extermination of his family. Like Perec's play with letters and typographical symbols in *W or the Memory of Childhood*, Federman's use of the Xes here points to both saying and not saying. In one sense, the Xes repeat what has already been said ("exterminated deliberately") and are therefore redundant; in another sense, they are conventional signs of erasure, and also function as cover-ups for the names of the parents and the sisters, which are not given either here or elsewhere in this book.[51] Commenting on these Xes in an autobiographical essay some years ago, Federman wrote: "For me these signs represent the necessity and impossibility of expressing the erasure of my family," adding that he wrote all of his work "in order to decipher the darkness into which I was plunged that day [when his mother thrust him in the closet]."[52] More recently, Federman has stated that he sees the writer's task as "the subtle and necessary displacement of the original event (the story) towards its erasure (the absence of story)."[53] The rows of Xes on the opening page of *Double or Nothing* can be seen as accomplishing that displacement: they indicate the event, but only under erasure.

The paradoxical combination of an *excess of communication* (redundancy) and a *lack of communication* ('exing-out,' covering up) recurs throughout *Double or Nothing* (the title already says as much) and throughout Federman's oeuvre, in various forms. I will suggest that this combination—which can also be thought of as the simultaneous expression of affirmation and denial—has a psychological as well as an aesthetic significance in writing by the 1.5 generation. But first, I want to look at a few more examples from *Double or Nothing*, just for the pleasure of it. For as Perec said, and as Federman has also said, the writer's problem is not only to tell the truth, but how to tell it. We have known at least since the bloody tragedies of Aeschylus that if the writer succeeds in telling it well, the result is pleasure, no matter how dark the truth, or how painful.

Given Federman's use of the individual page as a canvas, every page of *Double or Nothing* merits extended commentary. Take, for example, page 39. It begins with a running dialogue between two of the narrative instances mentioned in the opening chapter:

After he lands in New York he'll have to be on his own YES
uncle Arthur NO David will be waiting for him on the pier You're
sure about that NO Uncle Sam James David Yes David is better
That's what I said before

The "noodler," planning what he will invent once he has rented his
room and started his year of noodles, is here interrupted by another
voice approving or disapproving his choice of names for the American
relative: YES, NO, David is better. This could also be the internal
dialogue of a single person—we are told at several moments in the
book that there is "no difference" between the various narrative voices,
nor even, finally, between the person of the "noodler" who is the
inventor and the young protagonist who is his invention. The protagonist's name keeps changing as well, as the inventor wonders what to
call him; on this page he is Jacques, but elsewhere he is called Jack,
Solomon, Richard, Raymond, Dick, Boris, Dominique, "doesn't
matter, it's the same guy."[54] The instability of the proper name points
to the fictionality of the text, the freedom of the one who invents; but
in the context of this book, one cannot help but associate the instability of proper names with a whole collective history. Jews who passed
for Christian during the war had to adopt new names, and the anxiety
surrounding this change in identity is a recurrent theme in memoirs
and novels by those who were children at the time. In many immigrant
families, the change of name was accompanied by a change in language, Yiddish being the forbidden tongue, the "language of death,"
as Régine Robin calls it in her autobiographical story "Gratok."[55]
Having to renounce the language spoken at home was tantamount to
renouncing family and filiation, sometimes with tragic results—Sarah
Kofman's beautiful memoir, *Rue Ordener, Rue Labat*, gives a devastating
account of a young child's response to such a splitting of identity and
allegiance. Most Jews resumed their original name after the war, but
a significant number changed their name officially to their wartime
aliases or adopted other new names devoid of Jewish resonance. As
Nicole Lapierre points out in her historical study of changes in name,
a permanent change of name is one more obstacle to the sense of
continuity and the transmission of family history.[56]

Federman did not change his name, but the emphasis he places on the vacillations of the protagonist's name in *Double or Nothing* shows his awareness of the problem.[57] Further down on page 39, the protagonist's ever-shifting name is linked both to Jewishness and to a loss of language, in a series of lines that create a striking visual disruption:

                                        Jacques doesn't speak a damn
word of Yiddish of course French Jews don't speak it any more A dead tongue
for them A least not the new generation
                    the left over generation
                        the reduced generation Those who didn't end up as lampshades
(I don't have to go into that but it's there in the background and will alwa
ys be there Can't avoid it even if you want to THE CAMPS
                                    &
                            THE LAMPS
                                    H
                                    A
                                    D
                                    E
                                    S

The disruption begins with the series of phrases in apposition ("the new generation, the left over generation, the reduced generation") and ends with the calligram in underlined capital letters, the words forming a lamp. Although structurally the first three phrases are equivalent (reinforced by the perfect alignment of the word "generation" on the three lines), the series is a descending spiral of meanings defining the 1.5 generation: from "new," which sounds hopeful, to "left over," which cancels the hopeful note and introduces the notion of abandonment, to "reduced," which emphasizes the absence of those who were killed, and finally to the tragicomic remark about lampshades. This is followed by a qualification, within hand-drawn parentheses, "I don't have to go into that," which is immediately qualified in turn: "but it's been there in the background and will alwa/ys be there Can't avoid it even if you want to."[58]

What we have here so far is an elaborate structure of saying and unsaying or qualifying what one has just said. Roland Barthes, in one of his marvelous short essays, calls this kind of speech "le bredouil-lement," a stammering or sputtering. "Bredouillement" is the opposite of "bruissement," the smooth humming of language like a well-oiled machine.[59] When a speaker or a machine sputters, it is a sign that something is not quite right: the speaker wants to correct or qualify or cancel what he has said, but can do it only by saying more. Barthes calls this "une très singulière annulation par ajout" ["a very curious cancellation by addition"] and notes that this kind of speech signals a double failure: it is hard to understand, yet one ends up by under-standing it in the end. But what one understands is precisely that something is not right. "The sputtering (of the motor or of the sub-ject) is, in sum, a fear: I fear that I may not be able to go on."[60] It is not a coincidence, I think, that the "sputtering" on this page of *Double of Nothing* occurs, visually as well as verbally, at the moment when the word CAMPS appears, the first time after the opening page of the book. At that point, the horizontal movement of reading breaks down completely, and we have large white spaces surrounding the iconic/calligrammatic representation of a lamp with a shade, formed by words that denote the same meaning. The icon, or calligram, repeats and therefore reinforces the verbal meaning, but it also disrupts the reading and makes the text harder to follow—all the more so as the concluding half of the parenthesis is horizontal, allowing for another version of the lamp calligram that requires one to invert the page. The white spaces signal emptiness, a disruption or arrest of speech, but they can also be thought of as reinforcing the meanings of reduction and abandonment associated with "the new generation," the phrase after which the first blank space on the page occurs. A Beckettian paradox, then: nothingness *is*.

Or else, "le bredouillement" speaks its own important truth. Perec, in one of his unpublished notebooks, wrote, "apprendre à bredouiller" ["learn to stammer"]. Régine Robin, who quotes this phrase, notes that for Perec, stammering or stumbling ["le trébuchement"] was a whole "program."[61] One could say the same about Federman and others as well. Aharon Appelfeld, in his laconic (and very moving) memoir about his childhood in and after the Holocaust, writes, "A fluent stream of words awakens suspicion within me. I prefer stuttering, for in stuttering I hear the friction and the disquiet. . . ." Only by "stuttering" does the writer, Appelfeld claims, "offer something from inside."[62]

I propose to call the paradoxical figure of affirmation and denial, of saying and not saying, by its rhetorical name: preterition. The emblematic form of preterition is a sentence of the type "I will not speak about X," where X is named and designated precisely as the thing that will not be said. Usually, no detailed description or narrative development about X occurs in such a sentence (though it is possible, often with comic effect), but the subject that is not to be spoken of is at least mentioned. This is exactly what happens in *Double or Nothing* every time the word "camps" and other words associated with it occur on the page.

The most radical figure of preterition is doubtless the sentence: "I must forget about X." That is exactly the sentence we find at almost the very end of the book (p. 181), again in the context of Jewish identity and of the protagonist's protean name:

> (I   don't   like   Dominique.   I've   never   liked   Dominique)
> Too   effeminate   not Jewish   enough   *(you can't avoid the facts)*   But
> we must forget about that about the Jews the Camps and about the   LAMPS
>   H
>   A
>   D
>   E
>   S
>   (never again*)*

You can't avoid the facts, but we must forget about that: preterition, the self-contradictory figure of approach and avoidance, affirmation and negation, amnesia and anamnesis, is, I propose, an emblematic figure for both Perec's and Federman's writing about childhood trauma and about the early experience of loss and abandonment. "I will not say, I must forget, I have forgotten, I have no childhood memories . . ." followed by childhood memories, or, as in *Double or Nothing*, by single words ("lampshades") freighted with memory and fantasy. Perec's suspension points, at once a silence and an anchor for writing, are a kind of preterition: how to say it while not saying, or while saying in pieces.

As for Federman, his whole oeuvre is a series of variations on the crucial event that is everywhere present yet nowhere recounted in straightforward fashion in his books. Being the self-conscious writer that he is, he himself has provided some of the best commentaries on his own elusiveness. In his 1982 novel *The Twofold Vibration*, the two sidekicks of the "author," Namredef and Moinous (obvious alter egos for Federman, whose name appears once, on p. 124), say about the "old man" whose story is the main subject of the book (and who is yet another alter ego), "Whenever he spoke of his past, [it was] always offhandedly, casually, and we were never sure if he was serious or merely teasing us."[63] Many pages later, the old man reads them the manuscript of his new novel (which readers may recognize as Federman's *The Voice in the Closet*), and there ensues a debate about "that story" he is always telling, "about the little boy in the closet." The old man says, "never mind the story, what do you think of the writing, . . . the form, that's what concerns me." Namredef and Moinous respond that the writing is "heavy going, hard to follow," and finally express their frustration: "Ah shit, that's all you're interested in, form, form and semantic games, but what about the content, yes what about the story of the little boy in the closet, what about the Jews, the camps, the gas chambers, the final solution, why the hell don't you come out with it." To which the old man replies:

> It's all there you schmucks, inside the words, . . . if you read the text carefully then you'll see appear before you on the shattered white space the people drawn by the black words, flattened and disseminated on the surface of the paper inside the black ink-blood, that was the challenge, never to speak the reality of the event but to render it concrete into the blackness of the words.[64]

We note the usual humor in the situation (three tired and drunk guys in a hotel room, all of them the same person incidentally, debating literature and reality in language peppered with obscenities)—but also the seriousness.

Of course, this is not the last we hear about the question of how to say it. One of the most delightful metacommentaries by Federman occurs in his 1997 novel *La fourrure de ma tante Rachel* [*Aunt Rachel's Fur*; 2001], and itself takes the form of preterition: "No, don't insist,

I am not going to tell you what happened before I landed on that farm, after I jumped off a freight train which was probably taking me to my final solution, no I'm not going to go into that again," says the narrator.[65] In fact, he has never "gone into it," either in this novel or in others.[66] Further on the same page, he ducks the question again by way of a metacommentary on "the noodle novel," *Double or Nothing:*

> I won't go into too many details about the fucking animals, I already told parts of the farm story in the noodle novel when I was doing some flashback, all you have to do is visit the noodle novel when we're finished here and you'll see for yourself how I suffered in my youth, in that novel I tell everything, the war, the occupation, the yellow star, La Grande Rafle, the collaboration, the deportation, the trains, the camps, the extermination, La Libération, and finally, finally America and jazz, and all the loneliness. . . ."[67]

But this is obviously a feint, for he no more "tells" about the war, the occupation, the yellow star and all the rest in "the noodle novel" then he does here; in fact he tells of it even less! In *Double or Nothing*, as in this sentence, what we get is simply a series of words so rich in associations that merely alluding to them creates an emotional effect. Approach-avoidance, statement and denial, memory and forgetting.

Experiment and Existence: A Few Conclusions

As I said earlier, it is hazardous to generalize about any group, including child survivors of the Holocaust, and child survivors who are innovative writers are no exception. Yet, what would be the point of analyzing recurrent figures in the work of a Perec or a Federman if we did not then speculate, however tentatively, about the more general psychological and aesthetic implications of their writerly choices? The paradoxical combination of "saying while not saying" that characterizes the figure of preterition—with its attendant figures of suspension, postponement, digression, juxtaposition, and metacommentary—is, I have suggested, emblematic of experimental writing about childhood trauma, in particular the experience of childhood loss. Returning now to an idea I broached but then suspended some pages back, I would speculate that the psychological correlative of preterition is what Freud called the splitting of the ego, the simultaneous recognition and denial of a painful reality.

It is unfortunate, in today's perspective, that the painful reality Freud himself adduced in discussing this phenomenon was the "fact" of female castration as discovered by the little boy. Both in the essay on "Splitting of the Ego in the Defensive Process" (1938) and in the earlier essay "Fetishism" (1927), Freud links his discussion of the ego's relation to reality to the boy's fear of castration, a fear that is confirmed by his "sight of the female genitals."[68] As many contemporary commentators have noted, "the reality of female castration" is Freud's own blind spot, the sign of his masculine bias.[69] But there is more to his theory of fetishism than an outdated (albeit ever fascinating, to judge by the number of critical responses to it) reflection on sexual difference. Interpolated toward the end of the "Fetishism" essay is a long passage that most commentators ignore and that has nothing to do with female genitals, but everything to do with the psychological response to traumatic childhood loss.

Freud introduces this digression as "another point of interest" linked to earlier speculations on his part (in two essays dating from 1924) regarding the difference between neurosis and psychosis. He mentions that he recently learned that two of his patients, young men, had lost their fathers at a young age, and "each—one when he was two years old and the other when he was ten—had failed to take cognizance of the death of his beloved father . . . and yet neither of them had developed a psychosis."[70] Freud explains that according to his earlier theory, what distinguishes neurosis from psychosis is the ego's acknowledgment of a painful reality: neurotics recognize reality, while psychotics deny it. By that theory, the boys' refusal to acknowledge their fathers' death should have led to psychosis, but it did not. Freud therefore concludes that their reaction was more complex than he had thought: "It was only one current in their mental life that had not recognized their father's death; there was another current which took full account of the fact. The attitude which fitted in with the wish and the attitude which fitted in with reality existed side by side."[71] The "oscillation" (Freud's own term, though he uses it as a verb: "oscillated between two assumptions") between recognition and denial of the father's death is structurally identical, according to his analysis, to the "oscillation" of the fetishist who both acknowledges and denies the "reality" of female castration. Today, we reject the major premise of this argument ("the unwelcome fact of women's castration"[72]); but the psychological structure it describes remains, I think, rich in possibilities.

The splitting of the ego, as Freud analyzes it in the essay on fetishism, functions as a defense mechanism by allowing the subject both to recognize and to deny a traumatic loss. Such splitting is neurotic, but not psychotic. The psychoanalyst Octave Mannoni has pointed out that "I know it, but still . . ." ["Je sais bien, mais quand même . . ."] is the fetishist sentence par excellence.[73] The fetishist "knows" that the fetish is only a substitute for the lost object, but still he derives satisfaction from it. In fact, the "lost" object—the mother's penis—never existed, but the little boy's fantasy about it did, according to Freud's theory. Also according to the theory, fetishism is strictly a male perversion, bound up with the male fear of castration. But as Freud's own analysis suggests, fetishism as a structure of simultaneous denial and affirmation of reality, resulting in the "compromise solution" of a symbolic substitution for a lost object, has a more general applicability. The two little boys really did lose their fathers, not only in fantasy, and there is no reason to assume that their complex response to the father's death ("I know it, but still") could not have occurred in a little girl.

Sarah Kofman, in an extended commentary on both Freud's text and on Jacques Derrida's *Glas* (1974)—yet another work by a wartime child that consists of a montage of two heterogeneous discourses, the one philosophical, the other literary—spoke about a "generalized fetishism" that corresponds to the "mixing of genres" and the "undecidable oscillation" between them.[74] In this generalized fetishism, Freud's own obsessive emphasis on castration and on the maleness of the phenomenon disappears. What remains—in any case, what I want to emphasize—is Freud's remark that "this way of dealing with reality . . . almost deserves to be called artful."[75] Writers and artists are traffickers in substitution, as well as in the simultaneous affirmation and denial of reality: "I say 'a flower,' and there emerges the absence of all bouquets," Mallarmé famously wrote.

We might say, then, that preterition is the rhetorical figure that corresponds to recognition/denial of traumatic childhood loss; it is a compromise formation, allowing the subject of loss to move forward, to invent, to continue, however haltingly—or as Barthes would say, sputteringly.

As for the aesthetic implications of preterition, I hope to have shown that while it is always the same basic structure of affirmation and denial, it can lead to ever new verbal and visual inventions. In one sense, preterition simply keeps repeating that it is impossible to say what must be said, that there will never be a language adequate to express the enormity of the event. The affirmation of this impossibility can itself become a cliché, but it can also be the motor for new ways of saying. Maurice Blanchot, in his meditation on writing and disaster, quotes Schlegel's remark that "to have a system" and "not to have a system" are equally lethal for philosophical thought—"whence the necessity of maintaining, while abandoning, both of those demands at the same time." Blanchot adds that what is true for philosophy is also true for writing; "one can become a writer only by never being a writer; the minute you are one, you are no longer one."[76]

To keep repeating the same thing, but always as if for the first time, in other words, differently: in his essay titled "The Necessity and Impossibility of Being a Jewish Writer," Raymond Federman writes:

> It is this impossibility of saying the same old thing the same old way which must become a necessity, and thus enable the writer to reach us again, to move us again, and force us, perhaps, to understand what we have not been capable of understanding for more than fifty years. It is NOT through content but form, NOT with numbers or statistics but fiction and poetry that we will eventually come to terms with the Holocaust and its consequences.[77]

But this eloquent defense of the aesthetic imagination raises a whole new question, or even two: Should we accord a special privilege, in the matter of "imagining the Holocaust," to writers who were actually alive at the time and experienced the losses and the terror for which they try to find an adequate language (however blurry their memories may be)? Conversely, what is the relation of the experimental 1.5-generation writers to the broader movement of postmodernism? There are, after all, many others writers, both older and younger, who apparently have no relation to the Holocaust and do not write about it, but whose writing is also fragmented and also manifests the figures of suspension and preterition.

The second question is easier to answer, so I will begin with it. Obviously, no writing occurs in a vacuum, and experimental writers like Perec and Federman are part of a modernist and postmodernist tradition of literary experimentation; their works could not exist without those of Proust, Joyce, Faulkner, and Beckett—nor are their works the only ones about which this can be said. While modernist and postmodernist experimentation are surely linked to the upheavals of the twentieth century, they are not necessarily linked to individual life stories—or else, they are linked to the lives of all those who lived in the century, not only to the specific trauma of child survivors of the Holocaust. This fact does not, however, diminish the interest of the particular conjunction of life experience and writing that is manifested in the works I have been discussing.

The first question is harder. Sara Horowitz, in a perceptive essay, speaks of writers who are child survivors as occupying a transitional place, between the adult survivor writer, whose "actual experiences, . . . whether represented or transfigured in the work itself, validate the writing and anchor it in a specific historical reality," and those second-generation writers who attempt to re-create, exclusively through their imagination, a reality they never experienced and could not, ontologically, have experienced. Self-conscious writers who are child survivors, Horowitz claims (she mentions Begley and Ida Fink, though Fink was really a young woman and not a child during the war) "knowingly unsettle the issues of authenticity, reliability, and memory that are most problematic for second generation writers." The sentence she quotes by Begley, "Our man has no childhood that he can bear to remember; he has had to invent one," has also been uttered, in almost exactly the same words, by Perec, Federman, and other self-conscious 1.5-generation writers like Régine Robin.[78] The question still persists, however, whether their survivor status gives them a privileged access to the subjects they wrestle with.

Not surprisingly, my answer would be yes and no. No, because there have been beautiful books written about the Holocaust and even about the experience of the 1.5 generation, not only by second generation writers like Raczymow and Modiano whose family history is implicated in the event but also by other writers who "were not there" and who have no personal or family ties to Jewish suffering. Anne Michaels's *Fugitive Pieces* (1996) and W. G. Sebald's *Austerlitz* (2001) are prize-winning examples of the power of imagination to construct the inner world of a child survivor who lost his whole family. Michaels (born in 1958 in Toronto) and Sebald (born in 1944 in a small town in Bavaria) imagine adult protagonists who seek to come to terms with their barely remembered childhood memories. Like Perec, Federman, and Robin, Michaels and Sebald are part of a literary tradition that will—at least, one hopes—continue to evolve long after the death of the last Holocaust survivor. Individual talent is not necessarily a consequence of childhood suffering (and even less so of a particular, historically situated suffering), though it may be related to it.

There is also a "yes" to the question of the survivor's privileged status, however, and that "yes" has to do precisely with the "having been there." What I wrote in Chapter 2 about Paul Ricoeur's view of history is relevant here as well: The ontological status of something that "once was" distinguishes the historical past from an imagined or fictional past. Similarly, the ontological status of the survivor must be distinguished from that of a person who, by imaginative projection, imagines what it is like to be one. This does not mean that the survivor's version of the past is "truer" or even more factually accurate, let alone more powerful artistically than that of a later writer of talent; it simply means that the survivor, by virtue of "having been there," testifies to the historical status of the event, *even if* he or she has no reliable memories of it, as is the case with many members of the 1.5 generation. Federman, in his humorous way, has suggested something like this: "Federman in his person *bespeaks the authority of his experience but not its sentiment.* Sentiment is secondary, external, an after the fact category. Let others weep. Federman salutes."[79] The sentiment is the product of writing and telling and can be shared by all, including those authors and readers who were not there. The "authority of the experience," however, belongs only to one who was there—which, I repeat, does not mean that everything the survivor remembers is factually true, or even that the survivor has an "authoritative" understanding of his or her experience. The only true authority of the survivor is "in his [or her] person." Like ashes after a fire, the survivor is a sign pointing to, or representing, something that "once was." The semiotician Charles Peirce called such signs, which have a physical proximity to the objects they represent, indices. The survivor is an index.

But an index does not speak; it must be interpreted. The nice thing about being a person as well as an index is that you can interpret your own indexical status, but others can interpret it as well—whence the deep resonance of the final paragraph in Raymond Federman's reflection on the necessity and impossibility of being a Jewish writer:

> And so when the historians close their books, when the statisticians stop counting, the memorialists and witnesses can no longer remember, then the poet, the novelist, the artist comes and surveys the devastated landscape left by the fire—the ashes. He rummages through the debris in search of a design. For if the essence, the meaning, or the meaninglessness of the Holocaust will survive our sordid history, it will be in works of art.[80]

Here, the artist and the witness are two different people, with the artist given privilege, since the witness can forget (and will certainly disappear). But when the witness who experienced and the artist who interprets are one and the same person, and when the artist is a self-conscious, post-Beckettian, postmodern, post-Holocaust artist, then the conjunction of experiment and existence yields (among others) the structures of approach and avoidance, of event and erasure, that I have sought to analyze in these pages.

✨ 9

Amnesia and Amnesty:
Reflections on Forgetting
and Forgiving

$\mathcal{I}$NEVITABLY, a reflection on memory leads to forgetting. Forgetting is memory's ultimate edge, both defining it and putting it into question. The French ethnographer Marc Augé, in his short but profound book *Les formes de l'oubli* [*Forms of Forgetting*] begins with the insight that "forgetting is an integral part of memory itself."[1] Augé proposes a striking visual image to describe this relation: "Memories are shaped by forgetting, like the contours of the shore by the sea" (29). The paradox that is suggested by this image, and then explicitly stated by Augé, is that forgetting is the active agent in the formation of memories. Like the sea sculpting the land it surrounds, forgetting gives memories their shape and relief. Augé plays nicely with the two words for memory in French, "la mémoire" and "le souvenir," the one designating the faculty of remembering while the other refers to a specific thing remembered: "Forgetting, in sum, is the dynamic force of the faculty of memory [*la mémoire*], and memories [*le souvenir*] are its product." (30). But we should no doubt add "meaningful memories," for what forgetting accomplishes is the highlighting of some past impressions and experiences and the elimination—or at least, the bracketing—of others. This is beautifully brought out, by counterexample, in Borges's invention of Funes the Memorious, that strange human creature who is unable to forget anything at all: "In the overly replete world of Funes there were nothing but details, almost contiguous details."[2] A world without differences or—what amounts to the same thing—of nothing but differences, where every detail stands on its own and has the same value as every other, is a world without meaning, whether it is an individual world like that of Funes (who, incidentally, dies very young, ground down by memories) or the social world as a whole. In a sociological perspective, as Karl Mannheim remarked, it is the succession of generations that effects "the necessary social purpose of enabling us to forget. If society is to continue, social remembering is just as important as forgetting and action starting from scratch."[3] Similarly, Ernest Renan, reflecting on what constitutes a nation, wrote, "The essence of a nation is that all the individuals in it should have many things in common, and also that all should have forgotten many things."[4] And Nietzsche, in *The Use and Abuse of History*, made the point that no action is possible in the present without some forgetting of the past.

Forgetting, then, is not only part and parcel of the very working of individual and collective memory; it is also salutary, an actively benign faculty. Augé calls his book a "praise of forgetting," *éloge de l'oubli*—by which, he explains, he does not mean to denigrate memory, but merely to give forgetting its due. If there is a "duty to remember," there is also, just as importantly, a "duty to forget."

Forgive and forget? There is the question; and there, I would add, is a weak link in Augé's reasoning, for he does not sufficiently recognize, or struggle with, the difficulty of certain kinds of forgetting—precisely those that are linked to, or dependent on, forgiving. Of course he does not ignore the Holocaust or other mass atrocities that produce unforgettable memories, along with virtually insoluble questions about forgiving. But he rushes over them, noting only that in order to go on with their lives, the survivors of horror must "give forgetting its due" (120). No one can argue with that statement, but it seems somehow too easy. Surely, victims of horrific crimes will encounter some difficulties in carrying out such a program, especially when millions of other victims were also involved. And as I discussed in Chapter 4, injunctions to forget ring very hollow when they are pronounced in certain contexts—for example, by perpetrators of the crimes in question.

The linguistic coincidence, or perhaps the linguistic unconscious, that places forgetting and forgiving in close proximity—whether phonetically and semantically as in English or German, or by semantic association alone as in many other languages—points to the problems, and the dilemmas, that need to be explored. Is forgiving a necessary prerequisite, or accompaniment, to forgetting an offense or a crime, individually or as a group? Are some actions unforgivable, and hence unforgettable, at least by those who suffered as a result? And even if forgiveness is possible, should forgetting be resisted in the name of historical memory? Such questions have preoccupied some of our most distinguished contemporary thinkers. Paul Ricoeur, for example, ends his magisterial study of memory and history *La mémoire, l'histoire, l'oubli* (published in 2000) by reflecting on "l'oubli et le pardon," forgetting and forgiving, which he sees as constituting, together and separately, the "horizon" of his whole undertaking. Not by chance, it is also in these final chapters that Ricoeur reflects on the relation between another linguistic pair, amnesia and amnesty. In one sense, this is simply a rewriting of the first pair in juridical and collective, rather than ethical and individual, terms, but the substitution of "amnesia" for "forgetting" introduces a negative note. To forget is human, but amnesia is an illness—or worse still, an alibi. The questions can then be formulated as follows: If forgetting is salutary as well as inevitable, both individually and collectively, under what conditions does it become a reprehensible amnesia? And if forgiveness is among the highest human accomplishments (Ricoeur places it in the same family as love, joy, and wisdom), under what conditions does it fall into a "caricature of pardon,"[5] a botched amnesty?

Clearly, these are not questions with simple answers. To help focus the discussion, I will consider historical examples mainly from France. The theoretical issues, however, are broad and generalizable.

Amnesty, As Solution and as Problem

In ordinary usage, "amnesty" is usually taken to mean a collective pardon. That is how Ricoeur tends to use it as well. In terms of jurisprudence, however, amnesty has specific characteristics that distinguish it from pardon. A pardon is an executive privilege and is granted on a case-by-case basis, each time to a single individual who has been convicted of a crime. An amnesty, by contrast, always refers to a collectivity: it is a collective decision—in modern times, it is voted by the legislature—and is granted to a class of individuals, more or less broadly defined. (It can even be trivial; in France, whenever a new President comes into office, he is expected to ask the National Assembly to vote an amnesty for minor misdemeanors such as traffic violations). The most significant difference is that a pardon is by definition granted *after* judgment and sentencing, and does not efface the sentence but merely "lifts" it or lightens it. Amnesty, on the other hand, can occur before, during, or after the completion of legal procedures, halting those in course, preventing those that have not yet occurred, and literally wiping out those that have already been completed. A pardon is an official forgiveness, while amnesty is an official forgetting. Amnesty not only prevents or undoes legal action but wipes out the very memory of offense. In France (though not in most other countries where amnesty is practiced, I am told by legal experts), it is a crime to allude to someone's past activities if those activities fall under a law of amnesty; an amnesty also shuts down archives that contain traces of those activities. Technically, even historians and journalists can be prosecuted if they refer to an amnestied person's previous offenses. Some have been sued for libel (and occasionally condemned), not because what they said was false but because they said it at all.[6]

The most problematic aspect of amnesty, and the one that makes it so unpopular these days, is its official injunction to forget. Ricoeur calls it an "amnésie commandée,"[7] a prescribed amnesia; as such, it has been attacked as both unethical and ineffective. Already Emile Zola thundered against amnesty in 1900, shortly after the crisis of the Dreyfus Affair, when the government asked and obtained an amnesty applicable to all those, whether dreyfusards or anti-dreyfusards, who had violated laws during the height of the crisis. Zola, who had been condemned (as he had fully expected) in 1898 for publishing *J'Accuse*, had an appeal in process and was furious to be deprived of his new day in court. Like other dreyfusards who opposed the amnesty, he was also upset that many Army officers who had perjured themselves in getting Dreyfus convicted could not be brought to justice after the law was passed. "Aren't you aware that it is a curious procedure to bury the embarrassing questions, with the childish idea that you are suppressing them?" Zola asked in an open letter to France's senators.[8] He thereby showed a rather good understanding of the concept of "return of the repressed" before Freud had put it into currency.

As the fierce debates that surrounded the amnesty of 1900 showed, amnesty is always political—this is a fact, not a term of opprobrium. In some cases, amnesty can give rise to ongoing problems, or be considered as the problem itself. I will discuss one such case in a moment, whose effects, it has been argued, are still being felt—I refer to the amnesties voted in France in the 1950s for collaborators under the German occupation. But first, it will be useful to take a step back and recall that at its origins, amnesty as official forgetting was seen and felt to be a solution rather than a problem—and indeed, it can still be seen that way from a certain angle of vision. The original amnesty, which gave the procedure its name, occurred in Athens in 403 B.C. and has been studied in depth by Nicole Loraux in her book *La cité divisée*. As she shows, that first amnesty was a political act of civic reconciliation, marking the end of a civil war in which the "30 Tyrants" were vanquished and democracy was reinstated in Athens. The amnesty—which excluded the tyrants and some of their supporters but included all others who had participated in the conflict—contained two provisions. One was a decree that stated, "It is forbidden to remember/recall the misfortunes [that have just ended]": *me mnesikakein*. The other was an oath that individuals had to pronounce: "I will not remember/recall the misfortunes [that were directed against me]": *ou mnenasikakeso*.[9] On the one hand, a collective interdiction to remember; on the other, an individual oath promising to forget wrongs one suffered, all with the aim of reestablishing civic harmony.[10] Easier said than done, one might add. Loraux cites Aristotle's anecdote that in 403 B.C. a recalcitrant citizen who refused the interdiction to remember was promptly tried and put to death in order to serve as an example; after that, Aristotle noted, "no one recalled the misfortunes."[11] (At least, we may suppose, not in public.)

It is noteworthy that there was neither a request for, nor a granting of, pardon involved in the Athenian amnesty. Stéphane Gacon, the author of a recent historical study of amnesty, emphasizes just this point. He argues that, in its ideal form as a political solution, amnesty occurs among equals: those who are amnestied are recognized as brothers (or, when relevant, sisters) by those in power who grant the amnesty.[12] This recalls Johan Huizinga's analysis of classical warfare, which always took place between equals who recognized each other as such.[13] Gacon, who studies in detail the major French amnesties voted over a roughly hundred-year period, from the Paris Commune to the Algerian War, calls this ideal form "l'amnistie républicaine." In this form of amnesty, he notes, "the citizens [of the Republic, represented by the National Assembly] restore their freedom and civil rights to men and women who found themselves, by reason of their political activities, in contradiction with the majority. . . . The citizens grant amnesty to other citizens with the primary aim of reestablishing a national unity broken by civil conflict."[14] Thus, in 1880, after years of discussion and debate, the newly solidified Third Republic issued a general amnesty for those who had participated in the Commune of 1871. This delay is part of the logic of republican amnesty, which assumes that even appropriate punishment must have an end, as long as only a political difference among citizens is involved. Furthermore, the amnesty of 1880 appears to have marked a genuine passing of generations: many of those who voted the amnesty had not been personally implicated in the events of 1871, and the vote no longer faced fierce opposition. Officially and in fact, this chapter of national history could be considered closed. While the Commune continued to be commemorated by the Socialists, who had been in favor of the amnesty all along (the Commune still remains a significant "site of memory" for the Left), it stopped being a subject of national debate or preoccupation.

The same cannot be said, as we know, for the years of German occupation in France. The amnesties of collaborators in the 1950s, which were supposed to close that chapter of French history, did not have the desired effect. What, then, went wrong? This question is worth exploring in some detail. First, we must recall that France was the only country in Western Europe that officially collaborated with the Nazis. In Norway, to cite just one contrast, the King and the Parliament went into exile and the Germans had to appoint a highly unpopular "puppet" government. The Vichy regime, legally voted into power after the fall of France, saw itself not as (or not only as) the legitimate government of a conquered nation but also as a "full partner" of the Germans in the running of the country—and, presumably, in the running of Europe after a German victory. Furthermore, Pétain's government proclaimed itself as leading a "national revolution," sweeping away decades of left-wing "decadence" and restoring France to its traditional values: family, work, fatherland. After the Liberation, there was a return to parliamentary democracy, and many collaborators were tried and given sentences ranging from "national indignity" (deprivation of civil rights for a fixed number of years) to capital punishment.[15] But as always happens in such cases (Italy after Mussolini, Argentina and Chile after the generals, Eastern Europe after communism), the reestablished democracy could not afford to throw out, let alone bring to trial, everyone who had worked in the administration or the judiciary, or been otherwise implicated with Vichy. Even in Germany, where a much more radical change occurred after the war, not everyone who had been implicated in Nazism could be brought to justice.

In France, many of the worst offenders—the most highly placed members of the government, the most avidly collaborationist writers and publishers, those who had worked for the German police or for their French equivalent, the murderous *Milice*, as well as many others—were tried in the years immediately following the war. However, at the very same time as these trials were going on (1945–1949), a campaign began for amnesty, led by the right-wing parties which had resurfaced along with the democracy. These parties shared many of Vichy's views about French society, even if they were happy to see the Nazis conquered. As early as 1947, a first, very partial amnesty (for minor crimes like black marketeering) was voted that freed more than half of those in prison for collaboration; two sweeping amnesties followed, in 1951 and 1953, which emptied the prisons of all but a few of the most serious offenders and restored thousands of people to full civil rights. This did not occur without violent protest by the Communist Party and by many former members of the Resistance, who asked whether their sacrifices and suffering (tens of thousands of *résistants* had been deported for their activities, and many thousands were murdered) were now to be forgotten. But by the early 1950s the Cold War was in full swing, and advocates of amnesty used anticommunism as one argument for "national reconciliation."

Henry Rousso, in his book *The Vichy Syndrome*, argued that the renewal of left-right divisions immediately after the war hampered the national "work of mourning" and that the amnesties put a premature stop to it—whence Rousso's well-known thesis that the 1950s inaugurated a period of "repression" as far as memory of Vichy and the Occupation was concerned. Rousso's use of Freudian concepts in discussing national historical phenomena has been widely criticized, but if these concepts are taken in a broadly metaphorical sense, they can be illuminating. Take mourning, for example. Strictly speaking, it does not appear to be the appropriate Freudian reference, for Freud defines mourning as the gradual process by which an individual comes to terms with the loss of a beloved object or ideal and transfers attention to a different one. Aside from the difficulty of transposing an individual psychological response to the collective level, it is not clear what the lost object would have been, for the nation, in postwar France. It could not have been Vichy, since most people did not mourn its passing, and even if some did, very few admitted it. Was the lost object the nation's honor? That may appear plausible, but a country cannot consider its honor lost forever, to be replaced by something else. If, however, we consider Freud's idea that mourning is a gradual and continuous process of reality testing (it is the recognition of the reality of loss that leads to the end of mourning), then we might conclude, in accordance with Rousso's argument, that what the postwar amnesties cut short was the gradually evolving understanding of France's complex history during the war. The "lost object" that was incompletely mourned, in other words, was not Vichy, nor the Occupation, but their *history*.

Rousso has noted in a more recent article that "the amnesty laws of 1951–53 prevented [historians] for a long time from writing freely about the period, since in principle it was forbidden to cite the names of persons condemned after the Liberation and then amnestied."[16] Invoking yet another Freudian concept, we might say that the postwar amnesties prevented a genuine working through of a painful history. Instead, they prescribed forgetting, turning the page on the past—a forced amnesia, which corresponds approximately to what Rousso calls the "repressed memory" of the Vichy years.

Again, the Freudian reference is not strictly correct, since repression is an unconscious forgetting, whereas the Gaullist "hijacking of memory" (as Rousso calls it) in favor of the Resistance during the 1950s and 1960s appears to have been quite conscious. Forgetting works in strange ways, however, collectively as individually: the "return of the repressed" in the early 1970s would not have been felt as such a shock if people had not actually forgotten (never mind whether consciously or unconsciously) the facts about Vichy and the Occupation that surfaced, or more exactly resurfaced, during those years.

Chief among those facts was that not all Frenchmen and women had supported, let alone participated in, the Resistance and that the systematic persecution of Jews was not accomplished exclusively by the Nazis but was greatly facilitated, and occasionally even anticipated, by the Vichy government.

Actually, both of these facts were known and acknowledged after the war, without truly entering into public discourse. Vichy's anti-Semitic policies and actions were invoked by the prosecution in the major purge trials, including those of Pétain, Laval, and René Bousquet, the head of the police at the time of the infamous Vél d'Hiv roundup of Jews in Paris in July 1942.[17] But at the time of the trials, the chief accusation was that of "intelligence with the enemy," considered to be the gravest offense. Thus, curiously from today's perspective, the idea that the French police acted on its own in the roundups of Jews, especially of foreign Jews, was considered a mitigating circumstance; as was the idea that France had its own brand of anti-Semitism and did not need to follow German models. This latter argument was used in the unsuccessful defense of Robert Brasillach, who was condemned to death and executed not because he published articles that amounted to calls for murder (of Jews), but because his enthusiastic support of the Nazis was judged to be high treason.[18]

The specificity (and gravity) of collaboration in crimes against humanity was not a concept that operated in France at the time of the postwar trials, although the concept of crime against humanity had already been formulated at Nurnberg. Furthermore, as I have suggested, the general amnesia about Vichy and collaboration that followed the all-too-rapid amnesties did not allow for gradual discovery or revision of views, even by historians. Some historians in the mid-1950s subscribed to the now totally discredited theory that Pétain too had resisted the Germans—he being the "shield" while De Gaulle was the "sword." All this may explain why the appearance of Marcel Ophuls's 1971 film *The Sorrow and the Pity*, which reminded the French about Vichy anti-Semitism and collaboration, and about choices other than Resistance by most French people during the Occupation, was received with outrage by so many. Similarly, Robert Paxton's 1972 book *Vichy France: Old Guard and New Order*, which documents and dispassionately analyzes Vichy's antirepublicanism as well as its anti-Semitism, and which is now lauded by French histo-

rians as a classic with its author venerated in the profession, was received in 1973 (when it was translated into French) with much less
enthusiasm—to put it mildly. Nevertheless, these reminders of
historical reality—along with other important factors such as the
events of May 1968, de Gaulle's departure from the Presidency and
his death, the coming of age of "Jewish memory" in France, as well
as the rise of Holocaust negationism, countered by intensified Holocaust commemoration all over the world—put an end to the period
of repression and inaugurated what Rousso calls the period of obsession, which is still going on and which has itself become the object of
criticism in recent years.

To return, then, to the question of what went wrong with the amnesties of the 1950s: clearly, they demonstrate the difficulty, if not the
downright impossibility, of prescribed forgetting on a national scale,
concerning events whose interpretation commands no national consensus. But since amnesty is by definition invoked only for such events
(otherwise, there would be nothing to "forget"), the amnesties of the
1950s also demonstrate the difficulties of amnesty as such in contemporary times. The deeper the political and ideological divisions that
characterized the event and its aftermath, the more difficult it is to
forget an offense by the opposing side, especially if the forgetting itself
becomes a contested object of legislation.

According to the argument of repressed memory, it is the very attempt to effect a forced forgetting that eventually leads to the return
of the repressed—in this case, to the obsession with memory of World
War II. While this explanation is too neat and schematic, it does suggest an interesting dialectical pattern of *discourse about* memory and
forgetting where painful historical events are concerned. "Never
forget" is an injunction familiar to all students of the Holocaust. In
France, starting around 1980, the phrase "devoir de mémoire" ["duty
to remember"] became a slogan about not only the Holocaust but any
number of other events that had not been sufficiently reckoned with,
from torture in Algeria to the evil deeds of Stalinism.[19] In recent years,
however, the "duty to remember" has itself provoked a critical coun-
terdiscourse. If amnesty can be criticized as an abuse of forgetting,
critics of the "duty to remember" have pointed to the dangers of an
"abuse of memory."[20] Thus the argument of a book like Augé's *Les
formes de l'oubli*, which concludes with the provocative injunction of a

"duty to forget" in order not to repeat the past. Augé seems to want to stand on its head Santayana's well-known dictum (to which Freud also subscribed) that those who forget the past are doomed to repeat it. On the contrary, Augé insists, it is forgetting that makes movement toward the future and beginning anew *[recommencement]* possible.

Why, then, is the injunction to forget problematic? More exactly, under what circumstances is it—or does it become—problematic, or even reprehensible? One such circumstance is juridical. The juridical concept of statute of limitations (in French, *prescription*), which has been compared to the "natural" forgetting of an offense through the passage of time (as opposed to the imposed forgetting of an amnesty), does not apply to crimes against humanity. Such crimes are juridically unforgettable; they can be pursued to the end of time. (Interestingly, as we saw in Chapter 3, the adoption in France of a law declaring crimes against humanity *imprescriptibles* occurred during the height of the period of repressed memory of Vichy, in 1964).

Another circumstance is ethical: the moral authority of an injunction to forget depends on who is pronouncing the injunction. It is one thing if a disinterested party declares the value of moving forward, of not letting the past paralyze one; it is quite another thing if the perpetrator does so. The defenders of the former Chilean dictator Pinochet, and Pinochet himself, have urged forgetting: "It is best to remain silent and to forget. It is the only thing to do," declared Pinochet to a British newspaper in November 1998, on the twenty-second anniversary of his coup d'état, after he had been arrested in London.[21] Understandably, some listeners were not convinced—and as I discussed in Chapter 4, it was equally unconvincing when Klaus Barbie declared, on the eve of his extradition to France to stand trial for crimes against humanity, that he had forgotten his wartime past as a Nazi interrogator: "I have forgotten. If they haven't forgotten, it's their concern." "They" were his former victims, or their families, who showed up in droves to testify at his trial. They had not forgotten. The injunction to forget a crime becomes absurd as well as reprehensible when it is uttered by—or on behalf of—the perpetrator. This was also the argument developed by the philosopher Vladimir Jankélévitch, in an impassioned essay written around the time when the law about the statute of limitations was being debated in France. According to Jankélévitch—a respected professor at the Sorbonne, a con-

temporary of Sartre and author of many books, who as a Jew had been
revoked from his teaching post under Vichy and had survived in hiding
as a member of the Resistance—it was obscene to speak about a statute
of limitations for "the most monstrous crime in history." Only those
who had not suffered during the war could be ready, twenty years
later, to "forgive and forget."[22]

Here we can see the originality of the amnesty procedure practiced
by contemporary truth commissions, of which the South African
Truth and Reconciliation Commission is the best known. According
to the legislation that set up the Commission, the granting of amnesty
to perpetrators of human rights violations during the period of apart-
heid was conditional, the condition being that the person applying for
amnesty provided "full and honest accounts of their behavior."[23] The
Commission could reject the application in the case of particularly
heinous crimes or those not politically motivated (for example, cases
of personal vendetta). When amnesty was granted, however—and this
was the novelty of the truth commission—its proclaimed aim was to
lead, at least in the short run, not to forgetting but to disclosure. The
stated goals of the Commission, as of truth commissions in general,
legal scholar Martha Minow notes, were "to gain public acknowledgment for the harms and accounts as full as possible of what happened."[24] Thus, "the conditional amnesty process does not foreclose
truth-seeking, but instead promotes it."[25]

That, at least, is how truth commissions work in principle, rede-
fining the very concept of amnesty. The underlying premise is that in
order to produce genuine reconciliation and, eventually, genuine forgetting of violations on a national scale, as amnesty is meant to do,
there must first be an airing of memories and their public acknowledgment by perpetrators as well as victims. In practice, truth commissions, including the one in South Africa, do not always lead to
ideal results. Bitterness may remain among victims, who are prevented
by the amnesty from seeking more traditional forms of justice, such
as a criminal trial of the perpetrator; and perpetrators may fail to
acknowledge the wrongfulness of their acts. But still, the linking of
amnesty to disclosure rather than to an artificial forgetting is a novel
idea, one that seems like a step in the right direction.[26]

It is worth emphasizing that forgiveness is not prescribed in this
new version of amnesty and may be neither asked for by the perpe-

trator nor offered by the victim or the victim's family. That leaves open the questions with which we began: are some past histories and memories, whether individual or collective, too painful, too troubling, too *present* to let go of, to finish mourning for, to forget? And to forgive?

Forgiving?

The idea of moving forward or beginning anew, which most theorists—including Augé and Mannheim, along with many others—link to forgetting, is also central to reflections on forgiving. Hannah Arendt, in a short text that has been a starting point for many of today's thinkers on this subject (and it is striking how many major thinkers, notably in France, have felt compelled to reflect on forgiveness in the last few years), introduces the concept of forgiveness when she discusses the irreversibility of human actions in time. Since one is never able to control the proliferating consequences of one's actions, nor to reverse an action once it has occurred, forgiveness by another (presumably, one who has been affected by the action) is the closest approximation to such a reversal: "The possible redemption from the predicament of irreversibility—of being unable to undo what one has done though one did not, and could not, have known what he was doing—is the faculty of forgiving."[27] Arendt emphasizes the value that forgiveness has for both of the parties involved. Forgiveness, she writes, "is the exact opposite of vengeance. . . . [It] is the only reaction which does not merely re-act but acts anew and unexpectedly, unconditioned by the act which provoked it and therefore freeing from its consequences both the one who forgives and the one who is forgiven."[28]

Commentators have criticized various aspects of Arendt's view of forgiveness, even while recognizing its impact and importance. Martha Minow, for example, writing about contemporary responses to mass atrocities, titles her book *Between Vengeance and Forgiveness* in order to underline the fact that intermediate possibilities exist between those two poles. She quotes one theorist: "Boundless vindictive rage is not the only alternative to unmerited forgiveness."[29] But in fact, one of the problems with Arendt's view is that it does not allow for unmerited forgiveness. In her definition, only acts that are "trespasses" committed without full knowledge of what one was doing, and which one would like to undo if one could (in ordinary parlance, for which one is sorry, though she does not use that word) qualify for forgiveness— or, it would seem, for punishment. Punishment, she writes, is not the opposite of, but the alternative to, forgiveness, and both are opposed to vengeance: "They attempt to put an end to something that without interference could go on endlessly."[30] Offenses that qualify as an "extremity of crime and willed evil" or that fall under the rubric of what she calls (following Kant) "radical evil"—she alludes to the Nazi atrocities as an example—can be neither punished nor forgiven, because "they transcend the realm of human affairs and the potentialities of human power, both of which they radically destroy wherever they make their appearance."[31] She modified this rather startling assertion in later writings, notably in her book on the Eichmann trial, in which she called for international tribunals to punish crimes against humanity.[35]

In a sense, then, in her reflection on forgiveness Arendt avoids the really hard cases. In her scheme, the "trespasser" wishes he or she could undo the offense, and the one who forgives allows that wish to come true, symbolically if not in reality. Perhaps not surprisingly, she ends her essay by talking about love and about its political equivalent, respect. What love is in the individual sphere, "respect is in the larger domain of human affairs," and it explains why nobody can forgive himself: "Here, as in action and speech generally, we are dependent upon others."[33]

Julia Kristeva, who has written a book on Arendt, takes up her idea that forgiveness requires the presence of an other, but—in a radical shift away from Arendt, who insists on placing forgiveness into a theory of politics—Kristeva limits it to the private realm alone, as an ethical or existential event rather than a political one.[34] Arendt's own discussion of forgiveness may allow for such a shift, since she states that forgiveness is "an eminently personal affair, in which what was done is forgiven for the sake of *who* did it." But she adds, parenthetically, that while it is personal, forgiveness is "not necessarily individual or private."[35] And she explicitly assigns forgiveness a role in politics, mentioning the Roman principle of sparing the vanquished and the right of heads of state to commute the death sentence as examples.[36]

For Kristeva, by contrast, the ideal situation of forgiveness occurs in the psychoanalytic cure, with the analyst functioning not as one who "absolves" but as one who offers "meaning" and thereby allows the analysand to pardon him or herself—that is, to "be reborn," to "begin anew." Kristeva shares with Arendt the notion that in order for forgiveness to occur a change of heart must have taken place: "Forgiveness is a question of hearing the request of the subject who desires forgiveness and, once this request has been heard, of allowing renewal, rebirth."[37] Without the request, which is a veritable repentance [*repentir*]—in psychoanalytic terms, we might say an active desire for self-examination and change—"there is no forgiveness to offer."[38] Furthermore, since forgiveness is purely inter- (or intra-) personal, it is irrelevant in the political sphere. There, one must operate not with models of forgiveness, according to Kristeva, but with models of judgment and punishment.

Despite her indebtedness to Arendt, Kristeva's conception of forgiveness is thus very different from hers. Sigrid Weigel, one of the commentators who responded to Kristeva's views (in the issue of *PMLA* in which her text appeared) characterized them as diametrically opposed to Arendt's, "turning the scene of forgiveness into a quasi-religious situation," whereas for Arendt it was essentially in the public realm.[39] Weigel's characterization of Arendt may be too categorical, for Arendt allows for forgiveness in the private realm as well as in the public one. Weigel is right to point out, however, that in Kristeva's scheme forgiveness is a purely private matter, with religious overtones. What Arendt suggests, instead, is that it is precisely in the public realm that forgiveness, as a gesture of forgetting old wrongs and starting anew, is most important to think about.

Like Kristeva, Jacques Derrida—to whom Kristeva was in part responding in the interview I have quoted—also places forgiveness, at least in a philosophical perspective, outside the realm of the political and of the juridical. But he does so for very different reasons. Whereas Kristeva believes in the necessity of just punishment and considers forgiveness irrelevant to the public sphere, Derrida wants to push the idea of forgiveness to its "mad" or "impossible" version (in his words), even in the public sphere—more exactly, even *against* the public sphere, as in the expression "pushing against," carrying an idea to its ultimate, often paradoxical consequences. Concerning forgiveness, he launches a paradox that defies both ordinary and juridical notions:

"Forgiveness forgives only the unforgivable . . . there is forgiveness, if there is any, only where there is the unforgivable."[40] So conceived, forgiveness is "heterogeneous to the order of politics"[41] and is at the same indissociable from it; that is the claim Derrida makes here. He derides the recent "geopolitics of forgiveness," in which governments ask to be forgiven for past collective offenses and offer collective reparations, even in cultures (like Japan's) that are totally foreign to the "Abrahamic" (Jewish, Christian, Islamic) notions of repentance and absolution. He also rejects the widely shared notion (expounded by Arendt and Kristeva, as well as by Vladimir Jankélévitch, whom Derrida quotes) that forgiveness must be requested in order to be given. "What would a forgiveness be that forgave only the forgivable?"[42]— or, he adds, that was granted only to one who repents? Such a person would no longer be the one who committed the offense, having repented of it. "Pure" forgiving has nothing to do with "the order of conditions." And yet, Derrida insists, it is inseparable from that order: "These two poles, the *unconditional* and the *conditional*, are absolutely heterogeneous, and must remain irreducible to each other. They are nonetheless indissociable: if one wants, and one must want, forgiveness to become effective, concrete, historical; if one wants it to arrive, to happen by changing things, it is necessary that this purity engage itself in a series of conditions of all kinds (psychosociological, political, etc.). It is between these two poles, irreconcilable but indissociable, that decisions and responsibilities are to be taken."

This idea is so important that he immediately restates it: "Yet despite all the confusions which reduce forgiveness to amnesty or to amnesia . . . , to the work of mourning or to some political therapy of reconciliation, in short to some historical ecology, it must never be forgotten, nevertheless, that all of that refers to a certain idea of pure and unconditional forgiveness, without which this discourse would not have the least meaning."[43] Later, he says he is " 'torn' between a 'hyperbolic' ethical vision of forgiveness, pure forgiveness, and the reality of a society at work in pragmatic processes of reconciliation."[44] True to himself, he also revels in—or at least, insists on maintaining—this paradox, this aporia. Whence his idea that "pure" forgiveness, which alone deserves that name, is at once mad, impossible, and absolutely necessary.

A similar paradox, expressed in more transparently religious terms, characterizes some of Ricoeur's views on forgiveness, concluding his book on memory, history, and forgetting. Citing Derrida, Ricoeur agrees that forgiveness in its most mysterious and "highest" expression, that of charity, forgives even the unforgivable and is unconditional.[45] He too uses the words "folie," and "impossible" to characterize this kind of forgiveness—and he also evokes "joy," "wisdom," and "love," words that Derrida eschews. Elsewhere in his discussion, however, Ricoeur asserts that forgiveness must be preceded by the recognition of a fault on the part of the wrongdoer. He thus aligns himself with Arendt in that respect, as well as in his association of forgiveness with love. But, perhaps again moved by a religious impulse, he criticizes Arendt for restricting her discussion of forgiveness to the political level. For him, forgiveness implies the ability to separate the agent from his act—which ultimately means allowing for the possibility that the guilty one [*le coupable*] is "capable of something other than his crimes and his faults." In fact, Arendt, too, states that forgiveness concerns a *person*, not only an action. But Ricoeur's view is redemptive. For him, forgiveness proclaims to the sinner, "You are more worthy than your actions."[46]

In the end, though, Ricoeur may be reaching for too many things at once. He envisions an "eschatology," expressed as a wish that personal memory should aspire to (or tend toward) a state of happiness. "The coming of a memory is always an event: 'It is he! It is she!' " That kind of recognition produces "la mémoire heureuse," happy memory, devoutly to be wished for. History, by contrast, should tend not toward happiness but toward critical evaluation and a sense of justice.

And what about forgetting? Curiously, in these very last pages Ricoeur returns to the question of amnesty, which he had earlier condemned as a "forced amnesia" and as a "parody of forgiveness."[47] Evoking now not its negative aspects but its original conciliatory function, he speaks of the "spiritual stakes of amnesty: to silence the non-forgetting of memory" for the sake of political unity. For the sake of that unity, the philosopher will refrain from condemning the "successive amnesties that the French Republic has been so fond of," but will underline their exclusively "utilitarian, therapeutic" function (an interestingly nonpsychoanalytic use of the word "therapeutic"). Furthermore, and at the same time, the philosopher will listen to the voice of "unforgetful memory" [*l'inoublieuse mémoire*], excluded from the field of power by the "prosaically political" concerns of "forgetful memory" [*l'oublieuse mémoire*]. At the price of this double allegiance—to "forgetful memory" for the sake of public harmony, and to "unforgetful memory" for the sake of philosophical truth—amnesty can finally be maintained separately from amnesia.[48] And amnesia, presumably, can be replaced by a less negative kind of forgetting.

Forgetting without amnesia, forgiving without effacing the debt one owes to the dead. These are uncomfortable positions to struggle with, for both individuals and societies that have experienced—as all too many individuals and societies have in the past century—acts of collective violence and hatred. Martha Minow, in her thoughtful book, notes that no response is ever fully adequate in the face of such acts, yet silence—that is, indifference—is also unacceptable.[49] Like others before her, she refuses "tidiness" and "the temptations of closure"[50]—a wise choice which I shall follow, by not concluding; merely stopping, here.

Notes
Works Cited
Index

Notes

Introduction

1. Winter, "The Generation of Memory: Reflections on the 'Memory Boom' in Contemporary Historical Studies," p. 69.

2. Huyssen, *Present Pasts: Urban Palimpsests and the Politics of Memory*, p. 14.

3. Levy and Sznaider, "Memory Unbound: The Holocaust and the Formation of Cosmopolitan Memory," p. 88.

4. Bauman, *Modernity and the Holocaust*, p. 12.

5. Winter and Sivan, eds., *War and Remembrance in the Twentieth Century*, p. 4.

6. Ricoeur, *La mémoire, l'histoire, l'oubli*, p. 367.

7. "Myths of the Nations. 1945—Arena of Memories," Deutsches Historisches Museum, Berlin, October 2, 2004–February 27, 2005. The exhibit was accompanied by a two-volume work containing essays by major historians of memory, discussing memories of the war in twenty-five countries in Europe, and Israel: Monika Flacke, ed., *Mythen der Nationen: 1945—Arena der Erinnerungen*.

8. Sontag, *Regarding the Pain of Others*, pp. 85–86.

9. Halbwachs, *Les cadres sociaux de la mémoire*.

10. Stein, *Wars I Have Seen*, p. 3.

11. Winter and Sivan, eds., *War and Remembrance in the Twentieth Century*, p. 6.

12. Rév, *Retroactive Justice*, p. 9.

13. Adorno, "What Does 'Coming to Terms with the Past' Mean"?

14. Maier, "A Surfeit of Memory? Reflections on History, Melancholy and Denial," pp. 150–151. Originally delivered as a conference paper at Yale University, October 1992.

15. Gedi and Elam, "Collective Memory—What Is It?" p. 40.

16. Novick, *The Holocaust in American Life*, Introduction and Chapter 11.

17. Rousso, *Le syndrome de Vichy: de 1944 à nos jours;* Conan and Rousso, *Vichy:*

Un passé qui ne passe pas; Rousso, *La hantise du passé: Entretiens avec Philippe Petit.*
All three exist in English translation.

18. The argument about Judaeo-centrism is made most explicitly in Conan and
Rousso, *Vichy: Un passé qui ne passe pas*, pp. 269–274.

19. Klein, "On the Emergence of *Memory* in Historical Discourse," p. 130.

20. Rousso, *La hantise du passé*, pp. 122ff.

21. Robin, *La mémoire saturée*, p. 341 and *passim*.

22. Claude Lanzmann, "The Obscenity of Understanding: An Evening with
Claude Lanzmann," and "Hier Ist Kein Warum."

23. Dominick LaCapra, *History and Memory After Auschwitz*, Chapter 4.

24. Lanzmann, "Représenter l'irreprésentable," p. 8.

25. For informative accounts of the debates over the Berlin memorial, see
James Young, *At Memory's Edge: After-images of the Holocaust in Contemporary Art
and Architecture* and Caroline Wiedmer, *The Claims of Memory: Representations of
the Holocaust in Contemporary Germany and France.*

26. Wieviorka, *L'ère du témoin.*

27. "Cultural Citizenship: Varieties of Belonging," conference held at Harvard
University, February 19 and 20, 2004.

28. Judt, "The Past is Another Country: Myth and Memory in Postwar Europe."

1. *"Choosing Our Past"*

1. See P. Nora, "La nation-mémoire," and "Comment écrire l'histoire de
France?" in *Les lieux de mémoire*, quarto ed., vol. 2, p. 2212 and pp. 2229–2230.
Unless otherwise indicated, all translations from the French, here and elsewhere
in this book, are my own.

2. Quoted in Rousso, *Le syndrome de Vichy, de 1944 à nos jours* p. 30; the speech
appears in its entirety in Charles de Gaulle, *Discours et messages, t. 1, Pendant la
guerre, juin 1940–janvier 1946*, pp. 439–440. In the twin museums in Paris devoted
to General Leclerc and Jean Moulin, heroes of the Liberation and of the Resistance, the film of de Gaulle's speech is projected continuously on a large wall. I
have analyzed the speech in detail in my essay for the CD-Rom *La Résistance en
Ile-de-France*, "Discours de Charles de Gaulle du 25 Août 1944."

3. Rousso, *Le Syndrome de Vichy*, pp. 30–32.

4. For a good brief historical summary of the liberation of Paris, see Julian
Jackson, *France: The Dark Years*, pp. 561–67.

5. For Beauvoir's presumed authorship, see Deirdre Bair, *Simone de Beauvoir:
A Life*, p. 322. These articles were never republished during Sartre's lifetime, but
were reprinted in the daily *Le Monde* for the fortieth anniversary of the Liberation,
August 20–27, 1984.

6. *Combat*, August 29, 1944; *Le monde*, August 22, 1984.

7. *Combat*, August 30, 1944; *Le monde*, August 23, 1984.

8. "La délivrance est à nos portes" ["Deliverance is at our door"], *Combat*,
September 2, 1944; *Le Monde*, August 26–27, 1984.

9. For a detailed account of the history of the CNE, see Gisèle Sapiro, *La
guerre des écrivains, 1940–1953*, Chapter 7. Sartre, vetoed at first by some of the
communist members, was admitted to the group in January 1943.

10. For a detailed analysis of reactions to Sartre's two wartime plays, *No Exit* (1944) and *The Flies* (1943), see Ingrid Galster, *Le théâtre de Jean-Paul Sartre devant ses premiers critiques.*

11. For an excellent history of the Editions de Minuit during these years, see Anne Simonin, *Les Editions de Minuit: 1942–1955: Le devoir d'insoumission.* Simonin lists fifty-one French writers who contributed (all under pseudonyms) to this clandestine press between 1942 and 1944 (p. 151 and appendix catalog pp. 56–57). Simonin reports that, according to the testimony of the press's organizer, Jean Lescure, Sartre refused to contribute (p. 188n).

12. This essay, like the other two I will discuss, was reprinted in *Situations, III* (1949). Sartre made some changes in the texts; in this paragraph, a minor but not insignificant change is that "cette condition," referring to the condition of saying "no," becomes "notre condition," [our condition] more universal (*Situations, III,* p. 12).

13. Sartre "La République du silence," *Situations, III,* p. 14. This was one of the very few changes he made in this text.

14. G. Joseph, *Une si douce Occupation: Simone de Beauvoir, Jean-Paul Sartre, 1940–1944,* pp. 365–366. Joseph's too-obvious animus against Sartre and Beauvoir often acts against his arguments.

15. A. Boschetti, *Sartre et "Les Temps Modernes: Une entreprise intellectuelle,* p. 148.

16. *La France Libre,* December 1944, p. 9; reprinted in *Situations, III,* p. 16. In further page references, given in parentheses, *F* will refer to *La France Libre* and *S* to *Situations, III.* As I have noted, some passages are modified or omitted altogether in the later version.

17. Philippe Burrin, *La France à l'heure allemande: 1940–1944.*

18. Robert Paxton, *Vichy France: Old Guard and New Order, 1940–1944,* Chapter 2.

19. I have analyzed, somewhat critically, Sartre's portrayal of the Jew in "The Jew in Sartre's *Réflexions sur la question juive:* An Exercise in Historical Reading," and in "Rereading Rereading: Further Reflections on Sartre's *Réflexions.*"

20. Unsigned article, "Un industriel américain déclare . . . ," *Combat,* January 7–8, 1945, p. 1.

21. Sartre, "Qu'est-ce qu'un collaborateur? I: Aspect social de la collaboration," *République française,* August 1945, p. 5; reprinted, with numerous changes, in *Situations, III,* p. 46.

22. Burrin, *La France à l'heure allemande,* Appendix, table 1.

23. p. 6 (my emphasis; the italicized sentences are omitted in *Situations, III).*

24. For an outline of Brasillach's career before and during the war, see Kaplan, *The Collaborator: The Trial and Execution of Robert Brasillach,* Chapters 1 and 2. Kaplan briefly discusses Sartre's "Qu'est-ce qu'un collaborateur?" in her *Reproductions of Banality: Fascism, Literature, and French Intellectual Life,* pp. 14–15.

25. Sartre, "Qu'est-ce qu'un collaborateur? II: Aspect psychologique du collaborationisme," *La République Française,* September 1945, p. 15.

26. Sartre (unsigned), "Drieu la Rochelle ou la haine de soi," *Les Lettres françaises,* clandestine ed., no. 6, April 1943; see Contat and Rybalka, *Les écrits de Sartre,* p. 93.

27. Kaplan, *The Collaborator,* p. 157.

28. Pierre Vidal-Naquet recounted this in the paper he delivered at the Conference on "*Anti-Semite and Jew*, Fifty Years Later" at New York University, April 24, 1998; published as "Remembrances of a 1946 Reader."

29. *The Atlantic Monthly*, December 1944, p. 39.

30. This fact is strikingly borne out by the English subtitles of the documentary film *Sartre par lui-même*, where Sartre is shown recording his text for the radio. As he reads the section that evokes the silence of *résistants* who were arrested and tortured, clearly designating them in the third person ("ils"), the subtitles translate all the pronouns as "we"! Thus, Sartre seems to be speaking here about himself and other French people as part of that small minority. It is as if the English translation followed the desire for unanimity evident in this text to its logical and grammatical consequences, beyond what Sartre's own scrupulousness could allow him to say. (I thank Dorothy Kaufmann for having drawn my attention to this revealing error).

31. Sartre, "Victoire du Gaullisme," p. 2.

32. Sartre, "New Writing in France," p. 84.

33. Sartre, "New Writing in France," p. 85 (editor's note).

34. Liebling and Sheffer, eds., *La République du Silence: The Story of the French Resistance*, p. 442; Liebling, *The Republic of Silence*, p. 494.

35. John Gerassi, *Jean-Paul Sartre: Hated Conscience of His Century*, p. 187. Others who have evaluated Sartre's political positions after the war have had much less admiring judgments. See, for example, Judt, *Past Imperfect: French Intellectuals, 1944–1956*.

36. Burrin, "Vichy," in *Les lieux de mémoire*, p. 2482.

37. Conan and Rousso, *Vichy: Un passé qui ne passe pas*.

2. Narrative Desire

1. Rousso, *Le syndrome de Vichy, de 1944 à nos jours*; in subsequent works, Rousso has deplored the "obsession" with Vichy. See Conant and Rousso, *Vichy: Un passé qui ne passé pas*, and Rousso, *La hantise du passé*.

2. For a good overview of the Papon trial in the context of the other trials for crimes against humanity, see Golsan, ed., *The Papon Affair: Memory and Justice on Trial*, and also Chalandon and Nivelle, *Crimes contre l'humanité: Barbie, Touvier, Bousquet, Papon*. I discuss the Barbie trial and its significance in Chapter 4.

3. Serge Klarsfeld began publishing his books about the persecution of Jews under Vichy during the years when efforts were being made to extradite Barbie, starting with *Le mémorial de la déportation des Juifs de France* in 1977. Klarsfeld, whose father was deported and killed at Auschwitz, is a founder of the association Fils et Filles de Déportés Juifs de France (Sons and Daughters of Jewish Deportees from France), which has been active in promoting the memory of the Holocaust in France. His book about the deportation of Jewish children from Izieu, in which Barbie played a major role, appeared shortly after the latter's extradition to France; see Klarsfeld, *Les enfants d'Izieu: Une tragédie juive*.

4. To complicate matters, the French Supreme Court of Appeals declared in December 1995 that certain crimes against the Resistance could also be considered as crimes against humanity. For more on this, see Chapter 4, pp. 81–82.

5. The most authoritative book on Moulin's life (and afterlife) is the massive

1999 biography by Daniel Cordier, a former *résistant* who acted as Moulin's secretary in Lyon; a self-taught but highly respected historian, Cordier has devoted his work exclusively to the study of Moulin's life and influence. See *Jean Moulin: La République des catacombes*. An excellent collective volume that studies multiple aspects of Moulin's life and politics is *Jean Moulin face à l'histoire*, ed. Jean-Pierre Azéma.

6. Vergès's first major media appearance where he accused members of the Resistance of betraying Moulin was on November 12, 1983, on French television. This produced an enormous outcry in the press in the days that followed—see, for example, Théolleyre, "La provocation de l'avocat de Klaus Barbie," and Derogy, "Affaire Barbie: Les masques de Vergès," in *L'Express*.

7. "Transfert des cendres de Jean Moulin au Panthéon: discours prononcé à Paris le 19 décembre 1964," in Malraux, *La politique, la culture*, pp. 295–305. For more on the Malraux-Moulin connection, see Chapter 3.

8. Frenay first made this accusation in his memoir *La nuit finira*, and repeated it in a book devoted entirely to Moulin, *L'énigme Jean Moulin*.

9. All of those imprisoned, except Raymond Aubrac, were transferred to Paris shortly thereafter. One man (Henri Aubry, of Combat) was released in Paris, while the others were deported. For detailed studies of Caluire and its aftermath, see Cordier, *Jean Moulin*, Chapters 17–18; Veillon and Azéma, "Le point sur Caluire;" and Veillon and Alary, "Caluire: Un objet d'histoire entre mythe et polémique."

10. Barbie, who was working for U.S. intelligence in Germany (the United States refused to extradite him to France), gave three depositions in 1948 to the French police commissioner Louis Bibes; he affirmed that René Hardy had given away Caluire. Hardy himself reproduced the full text of Barbie's depositions in his 1984 book of self-justification, *Derniers mots*. For a concise account of the two Hardy trials, see Cordier, *Jean Moulin*, Chapter 24.

11. A few excerpts from this film, *Que la vérité est amère*, directed by Claude Bal, are included in Marcel Ophuls's documentary film, *Hotel Terminus: The Life and Times of Klaus Barbie*, which I discuss in Chapter 4. For a detailed account of Barbie's appearances in the French press from 1972 to 1984, see Henri Noguères, *La vérité aura le dernier mot*. As its title suggests, Noguères' book is intended as a refutation of Hardy's *Derniers mots*.

12. See, for example, articles by Jean Darriulat in the daily *Le Matin*, May 5–6 and May 7, 1984; these and many other articles can be found in the *dossier de presse* on the Resistance, Institut des Sciences Politiques, Paris.

13. In 1990, the Court of Appeals upheld an earlier condemnation of Vergès and Bal for libel against the Aubracs. See *Le Monde*, "Publication Judiciaire," February 23, 1990, p. 12.

14. Lucie Aubrac, *Ils partiront dans l'ivresse*, p. 11; in English, *Outwitting the Gestapo*, p. 7. Years before writing this memoir, Lucie Aubrac had given interviews where she recounted versions of her story (see Ania Francos, *Il était des femmes dans la Résistance*, pp. 251–254); and as early as 1945 she had published a study of the Resistance which emphasized all of its heroic aspects and in which she told some elements of her and Raymond's story without giving their names; see L. Aubrac, *La Résistance. Naissance et organisation*. A few years after "l'Affaire Aubrac," she published a short book on the Resistance that is sold in various museums

devoted to World War II in France, along with her 1984 memoir; see L. Aubrac, *La Résistance expliquée à mes petits-enfants.*

15. These testimonies, by Eugène Brédillot and Serge Ravanel, were dropped from later editions of the book. Ravanel's statement regarding what the Germans knew about Aubrac's identity was partly incorrect.

16. Raymond Aubrac, *Où la mémoire s'attarde*, Chapter 2.

17. Rioux, "Review of *Où la mémoire s'attarde*," *Le Monde des livres*, September 6, 1996, p. XI.

18. See, for example, Conan, "Aubrac: Le passé revisité" and Grassin, "Review of *Lucie Aubrac*" in *L'Express*; Wieviorka, "Les secrets de l'affaire Jean Moulin" and Lefort and Séguret, "Les Mystères Aubrac" in *Libération;* Frodon and Greilshamer, "Review of *Lucie Aubrac*" in *Le Monde;* and Muratori-Phillippe, "Affaire Aubrac: Les ombres d'une légende" in *Le Figaro.*

19. Paul Quinio, " 'Lucie Aubrac' hébergée dans les écoles." Regarding the box-office success of the film, see Laurence Alfonsi, "La réception du film *Lucie Aubrac*," p. 42. For a thoughtful discussion of the film and the "affair," see Leah D. Hewitt, "Identity Wars in 'L'Affaire (Lucie) Aubrac': History, Fiction, Film."

20. Vernant, "La mémoire et les historiens."

21. Halbwachs, *Les cadres sociaux de la mémoire.*

22. White, *Metahistory* and *Tropics of Discourse.*

23. Chauvy, "Les trois mystères Aubrac."

24. Muratori-Philippe, "Affaire Aubrac: Les ombres d'une légende." Many of the negative reviews of the film mentioned Chauvy's forthcoming book, opposing it to the "legend" shown in the film.

25. Gérard Chauvy, *Aubrac: Lyon 1943;* the preface is by René Fallas.

26. Chauvy, *Aubrac: Lyon, 1943*, pp. 382, 385, 401.

27. At a press conference on October 8, 1991, Raymond Aubrac asked that a commission of historians investigate "l'affaire de Caluire." (Reported in *Le Monde*, "Suite aux accusations de Klaus Barbie: M. Raymond Aubrac demande la création d'une commission d'historiens sur 'L'Affaire de Caluire,' " October 10, 1991).

28. While condemning Chauvy's method, historians nevertheless consider some of the documents he furnished to be important, as I discuss below.

29. The judgment against Chauvy and the publisher Albin Michel was handed down on April 2, 1998, the same day as the condemnation of Maurice Papon for complicity in crimes against humanity; see Weill, "L'historien Gérard Chauvy condamné pour diffamation envers les Aubrac." The judgment was upheld on appeal.

30. The script has been published: Jean-Luc Godard, *Éloge de l'amour*, p. 117.

31. Vidal-Naquet, *Le trait empoisonné: Réflexions sur l'affaire Jean Moulin*, pp. 41–58.

32. Wieviorka, "Les secrets de l'affaire Jean Moulin" (review of Jacques Baynac, *Les secrets de l'affaire Jean Moulin*), *Le Monde*, Nov. 18, 1998; a few years earlier, another book had portrayed Moulin as a Soviet agent: Wolton, *Le grand recrutement.*

33. The most detailed defense of the Aubracs in the press, refuting Chauvy's story point by point, was by the journalist Gilles Perrault: "Barbie, son Tartuffe, et les Aubrac," *Le Monde*, May 23, 1997. Chauvy responded to Perrault in "Ré-

sponse à Gilles Perrault," June 22/23, 1997. A few months later, the historian François Delpla published a booklength refutation of Chavvy: *Aubrac: Les faits et la calomnie*. Among those who expressed some doubts, even while maintaining their support for the Aubracs, was Moulin's biographer Daniel Cordier, interviewed in *Libération*, April 8, 1997. The Aubracs answered questions in a long interview with Henri Amouroux, author of a multivolume history of the Resistance, in *Le Figaro Magazine*, April 12, 1997. All of these publications occurred before the famous "roundtable" at *Libération*, which I will discuss below.

34. These debates were triggered by the publication of the collective volume *Le livre noir du communisme: Crimes, terreur, et répression*, whose editor, Stéphane Courtois, claimed in his introduction that communism was the "equal" of Nazism. But already months earlier, a strong debate was launched by Karel Bartošek's book about Arthur London, *Les aveux des archives*, claiming that London—imprisoned in Prague during the Slansky trial, and later author of the bestselling book *The Confession*—had remained in the clutches of the Party he was denouncing. Bartošek's book mentions Raymond Aubrac, who worked with the Czech government as a consultant in the 1950s; Bartošek suggests that Aubrac had acted as an "agent"; See Conan, "Prague ou la mémoire blessée," *L'Express*, November 7, 1996. The links between "l'affaire Aubrac" and "l'affaire London" are explored in some detail in several articles in the weekly magazine *Politis*, July 3, 1997.

35. *Libération*, special supplement, "Les Aubrac et les historiens," July 9, 1997, p. II.

36. In November 1991, Raymond Aubrac contacted Robert Frank (who was then head of the Institut d'Histoire du Temps Présent) to repeat his request, and wrote to him again on April 14, 1992. Frank said he would look into the idea, but it never materialized. (Correspondence in Henry Rousso's personal archives—I thank him for letting me consult these documents).

37. "Les Aubrac et les historiens," *Libération*, July 9, 1997. In what follows, I will refer to page numbers of this transcript in parentheses in the text; the special supplement was numbered in capital roman numerals.

38. *Justice*, no. 2 (2000), special section "Points de vues: les Aubrac et les historiens," with critical articles by Lucien Karpik and Daniel Soulez-Larivière and responses by Agulhom, Azéma and Bédarida, Rousso, Vernant.

39. Prost, "Les historiens et les Aubrac: une question de trop," *Le Monde*, July 12, 1997, p. 13; for a similarly critical view by two historians, see Claire Andrieu and Diane de Bellescize, "Les Aubrac, jouets de l'histoire à l'estomac," *Le Monde*, July 17, 1997, p. 12.

40. *Libération* titled the dossier as a whole "Les Aubrac et les historiens," with two pages of introduction signed by the two journalists. The transcript proper is divided into five "chapters," each with a title: 1: "Préliminaires pour un débat, l'histoire et ses acteurs"; 2: "Mars–mai 1943, la première arrestation de Raymond Aubrac"; 3: "Caluire, guet-apens à la villa du Dr. Dugoujon"; 4: "Juillet–septembre 1943, le rapport du commissaire Porte"; and 5: "Le 21 octobre 1943, hypothèses pour une évasion." The last section of the transcript is titled "Epilogue: Des zones d'ombre subsistent."

41. Ricoeur, *La mémoire, l'histoire, l'oubli*, p. 203; further page references will be given parenthetically in the text.

42. The most significant of these details is the date she gives for Raymond's release from prison after his first arrest, May 14, when in fact he was released on May 10. Chauvy, following the "testament de Barbie," uses this discrepancy to suggest that Aubrac was held for "debriefings" by Barbie until the 14th. Lucie Aubrac has explained that, urged by her editor, she chose May 14 because that was an important anniversary in her and Raymond's life as a couple. Her editor, Serge Guillebaud, has seconded this account; see his "Calomnie d'outre-tombe," *Le Nouvel Observateur,* October 24–30, 1991.

43. Rousso, *La hantise du passé,* pp. 50–84.

44. Rousso, *La hantise du passé,* p. 126.

45. Azéma, "Il n'y a pas d'affaire Aubrac," *L'Histoire,* no. 211, June 1997, p. 85. After the court judgment which condemned Chauvy for libel against the Aubracs, Azéma debated the Aubracs' lawyer Georges Kiejman, again affirming the primacy of historical fact over the respect due to persons. See Azéma and Kiejman, "L'histoire au tribunal."

46. Cordier, *Jean Moulin,* p. 801.

47. Although the March arrest was by French police, not by the Germans, Raymond and those arrested with him had one interrogation by Barbie.

48. Document reproduced in Appendix of Chauvy, *Aubrac: Lyon, 1943,* p. 323.

49. "A chaque appel de mon nom pour être confronté à Barbie, . . . je redoutais que mon véritable rôle ait été découvert, mon identité percée à jour. Tout eût alors été perdu." Aubrac, *Où la mémoire s'attarde,* p. 124.

50. Aubrac "Ma part de vérité," p. 79.

51. The Barbie trial was videotaped (the first such event in French judicial history), but was not allowed to be shown on television until November 2000, when the cable channel *Histoire* screened approximately two-thirds of the footage, over consecutive days in two-hour segments, with commentaries by historians and jurists. Raymond Aubrac's testimony (June 15, 1987) was among those shown; I saw it when the series was rebroadcast in July 2001.

52. Aubrac, *Ils partirant dans l'ivresse,* p. 87.

53. Raymond Aubrac, "Ce que cette table-ronde m'a appris," *Libération,* July 10, 1997, p. 30. See also the interview in June 1997, "Ma part de vérité."

54. Lucie Aubrac's account is somewhat ambiguous, falling more into the category of "omission" discussed above. However, the testimony by Serge Ravanel that she included in the 1984 edition states unambiguously that "the Germans did not know his real identity, Raymond Samuel, the fact that he was Jewish, and that his name in the Resistance was Aubrac" (*Ils partiront dans l'ivresse,* original edition, p. 256). As I mentioned earlier, the two concluding testimonies were presented as "presentable in court," a sign of the circumstances of the book's composition. They were both dropped in later editions.

55. "La Marche du siècle," France 3, January 22, 1997 (Inathèque de France, reference number DL: DL T 19970122FR3 008.001/002). As far as I have been able to tell, no one has mentioned this program in any of the discussions of the Aubrac Affair.

56. Klarsfeld, "A Propos de Raymond Aubrac," *Le Monde,* July 25, 1997.

57. Azéma, "Affaire Aubrac: Les faits sont têtus," *Libération,* August 28, 1997.

3. Commemorating the Illustrious Dead

1. *Sur les pas de Jean Moulin*, film directed by Alex Boutin. The complete text of Malraux's eulogy is in Malraux, *La politique, la culture: Discours, articles, entretiens (1925–1975)*, pp. 295–305. I discuss Moulin in the context of the Resistance in Chapters 2 and 4.

2. See the issues of these papers, November 25–26, 1996.

3. Douzou, "La résistance française en quête d'un héros éponyme," p. 438.

4. See, for example, Ben-Amos, *Funerals, Politics, and Memory in Modern France, 1789–1996;* Bonnet, "Les morts illustres"; and Ozouf, "L'Ecole normale des morts."

5. On the Club Jean Moulin, see Andrieu, *Pour l'amour de la République, le Club Jean Moulin: 1958–1970.*

6. Rousso, *Le syndrome de Vichy*, pp. 101–116.

7. For this and other biographical information about Moulin, see Cordier's monumental biography, *Jean Moulin: La république des catacombes.*

8. Douzou, "La Résistance française en quête d'vu héros éponyme," p. 432.

9. This manuscript is among the papers of Laure Moulin at the Bibliothèque Nationale, NaFr 17869.

10. Bonnet, "Les morts illustres," p. 1843.

11. See the article in *Le Monde*, "L'Assemblée déclare imprescriptibles les crimes contre l'humanité," December 18, 1964.

12. See *Le Monde*, "Le projet d'amnistie est approuvé par 269 députés," December 19, 1964. For a discussion of the series of amnesties regarding the Algerian war, see Gacon, *L'Amnistie: De la Commune à la guerre d'Algérie*, pp. 255–319.

13. Aussaresses, *Services spéciaux: Algérie, 1955–1957.*

14. Bonnet, "Les morts illustres," p. 1848. Hugo was buried in the Panthéon immediately after his death; in most other cases, including Malraux's and Moulin's, the "pantheonization" occurs some years after the first burial.

15. Péan, *Une jeunesse française.*

16. See Ben-Amos, *Funerals, Politics, and Memory in Modern France*, pp. 364–365.

17. The photo appears in the booklet accompanying a 1999 exhibition at the Musée Jean Moulin: *Jean Moulin 1899–1943*, p. 24.

18. Schumann, "L'antidestin qui franchit le seuil du Panthéon," *La Croix*, November 26, 1996. The text is accompanied by a photo of a young student carrying a huge portrait of Malraux at the time of the Spanish Civil War.

19. Baecque, "Un héros, Malraux?" *Libération*, November 24, 2001.

20. Todd, *André Malraux*, pp. 373–377.

21. Malraux, *Antimémoires*, pp. 167–201.

22. Malraux, *Antimémoires*, p. 477.

23. Malraux, *Antimémoires*, p. 481.

24. In all of Malraux's novels, only one woman has a full name (May Gisors in *La condition humaine*), and no female character makes any major statement among Malraux's talkative heroes. For a detailed analysis, see Suleiman, "Malraux's Women: A Revision."

25. Friang, *Un autre Malraux*, pp. 63–67.

26. Delbo, *Aucun de nous ne reviendra*.
27. Malraux, *Antimémoires*, p. 507.

4. History, Memory, and Moral Judgment after the Holocaust

1. Adorno, "What Does Coming to Terms with the Past Mean?" p. 115. Further references to this essay are given in the text. The German version is in Adorno, *Erziehung zur Mündigkeit*, pp. 10–28.

2. Postone, "After the Holocaust: History and Identity in West Germany," p. 238.

3. See Rabinbach, "Beyond Bitburg: The Place of the 'Jewish Question' in German History after 1945," pp. 192–194. For a detailed and nuanced account of Adenauer's and other West German politicians' positions in the 1950s, which presents similar conclusions, see Herf, *Divided Memory: The Nazi Past in the Two Germanys*, Chapter 8. The situation changed dramatically in the 1960s, especially after the student movement of 1968. The renewed interest in memory of World War II in France occurred around the same time.

4. Herf, *Divided Memory*, Chapter 5.

5. This was only an impression of mine, based on conversations and informal polling of audiences as I lectured on the film. The impression is confirmed by an article by the film's producer, John S. Friedman, who notes that despite its critical success, the film had very limited distribution and did not earn back its production costs. See Friedman, " 'Hotel Terminus': Le point de vue d'un producteur," p. 39.

6. My account here is based in part on Erna Paris's *Unhealed Wounds: France and the Klaus Barbie Affair*, Chapters 2–6. Paris's book appeared two years before the actual trial, but is informative and reliable about Barbie's earlier career and about the efforts to extradite him. Another account of Barbie's activities, especially detailed and suspenseful about his years in Bolivia and Peru, is provided by Linklater, Hilton, and Ascherson, *The Nazi Legacy: Klaus Barbie and the International Fascist Connection*.

7. Rousso devotes a whole chapter to the Barbie case, including an excellent explanation of the legal issues involved, and alludes to Barbie often throughout the book; the 1990 edition has even more on the trial. For a virtually day-by-day account of the trial, based on dispatches by the daily *Libération*, see Chalandon and Nivelle, *Crimes contre l'humanité: Barbie Touvier Bousquet Papon*, pp. 13–164.

8. Paxton, *Vichy France: Old Guard and New Order*; Marcel Ophuls, *Le Chagrin et la pitié* (screenplay); the film was released in 1971.

9. An early and passionate intellectual response to negationism in France was Pierre Vidal-Naquet's *Les assassins de la mémoire*, written at the time of the Barbie case; in English: *Assassins of Memory*. For a detailed historical account, see Igounet, *Histoire du négationnisme en France*.

10. The best-known memoir provoked by the Barbie trial is Lucie Aubrac's *Ils partiront dans l'ivresse*, which I discussed in Chapter 2. See also Lesèvre, *Face à Barbie: Souvenirs-cauchemars de Montluc à Ravensbrück*. The trial was the first French trial to be filmed. In the fall of 2000, the cable channel *Histoire* obtained legal permission to broadcast seventy hours, slightly less than half of the trial,

accompanied by commentaries by historians. The public impact of these broadcasts (repeated in June–July 2001) has yet to be evaluated.

11. Finkielkraut, *Remembering in Vain: The Klaus Barbie Trial and Crimes against Humanity*, p. 32.

12. Since there is no published screenplay for this film, my quotations in what follows are based on multiple viewings of the two-part video. Considering Ophuls's importance as a filmmaker, it is surprising how little serious critical attention his work has received. The best sources, so far, for detailed commentary on Ophuls's work are the interviews and articles he has given to French and American film journals (see notes 20, 21, 26, 42). One scholarly journal did devote a special issue to Ophuls's work: *Images documentaires*, no. 18/19, 1994.

13. The role of photographs as figures for memory, especially in relation to the Holocaust, has been amply studied and theorized about lately. See especially Hirsch, *Family Frames: Photography, Narrative, and Postmemory*, and Barbie Zelizer, *Remembering to Forget: Holocaust Memory through the Camera's Eye*. Ophuls uses still photos—of Barbie at various times and in various settings, and of his victims during the war—throughout *Hotel Terminus*.

14. I am grateful to Dr. Marion Kant, a musicologist and, with me, a Fellow at the Center for Advanced Judaic Studies at the University of Pennsylvania in spring 2001, for her help in identifying the German folk songs Ophuls uses in the film.

15. For a detailed account of Schneider-Merck's relations with Barbie, see Linklater et al., *The Nazi Legacy*, Chapters 11–12. As his revenge for being defrauded, Schneider-Merck played a significant role in the identification of Altmann as Barbie. Ophuls made important use of *The Nazi Legacy* in choosing interviewees and constructing his film.

16. Reported by Porter, *Through Parisian Eyes: Reflections on Contemporary French Arts and Culture*, pp. 10–11.

17. Marion Kant informs me that German-Jewish exiles (including her father) sang this song in an emigrants' choir in London in the 1930s and early 1940s.

18. See Klarsfeld, *Les enfants d'Izieu: Une tragédie juive.*

19. Ophuls's use of music in his films (one recalls Maurice Chevalier's songs in *The Sorrow and the Pity*), and particularly in *Hotel Terminus*, would deserve a separate study. The sentimental folk songs, all sung by the Vienna Boys' Choir, function as veritable leitmotifs; in addition to the two already mentioned, there are two traditional "wanderers' songs": *Muss i' denn, muss i' denn*, which was taken up by Elvis Presley in the 1960s, and *Das Wandern ist des Müllers Lust*. For a study of the role of music in memory-films about the Holocaust, see Pautrot, "Music and Memory in Film and Fiction: Listening to *Nuit, Lacombe Lucien, Night and Fog*, and *Night Rounds*." For a study of Ophuls's use of film clips from Hollywood musicals in a later film, *November Days* (1990), see Alter, "Marcel Ophuls' *November Days*: German Reunification as 'Musical Comedy.' " Ophuls uses a few musical clips, notably the soundtrack from a Fred Astaire film, in *Hotel Terminus* as well.

20. Porton and Ellickson, "The Troubles He's Seen: An Interview with Marcel Ophuls," p. 11.

21. Jeancolas, "Entretien avec Marcel Ophuls sur *Hotel* Terminus," p. 29. In-

terestingly, Ophuls says that it is the editing that "almost killed" him, although he was physically attacked on a beach in Rio on his way back from Bolivia. He blacked out during the attack, and had to be operated on in Paris. Even now, he still has some "troubles de mémoire" (Jeancolas, "Entretien," p. 26).

22. For a thorough discussion of the various modes of documentary film, see Nichols, *Representing Reality: Issues and Concepts in Documentary*, pp. 32–75; on the interactive mode, see pp. 44–56.

23. Marcel Ophuls, "Faut-il fusiller Speer au lieu de le filmer?" ["Should we shoot Speer instead of filming him?"], p. 115.

24. Hampl, "Memory's Movies."

25. Nichols, *Representing Reality*, p. 51.

26. See Ciment, "Joy to the World: An Interview with Marcel Ophuls;" the allusions to Lanzmann are on pp. 41, 42.

27. Ciment, "Joy to the World," p. 42.

28. Golsan, *Vichy's Afterlife: History and Counterhistory in Postwar France*, p. 87. I do not agree with Golsan's argument that by widening his scope to include Germany, the United States, and South America, Ophuls "revises" *The Sorrow and the Pity* and gets "sidetracked" in this film, away from the question of "Klaus Barbie, his wartime crimes in Lyon, and France's efforts to come to terms with these crimes" (p. 77). In my reading, the wide scope is precisely the point of the film, not a "sidetracking." Rather than letting France off the hook, as Golsan implies, the wider perspective shows that other countries, too, were implicated, if not directly then indirectly, by protecting Nazis after the war. In my view, Ophuls does not "revise" *The Sorrow and the Pity* with this film; rather, he extends and enlarges his inquiry.

29. Jeancolas, "Entretien avec Marcel Ophuls," p. 27.

30. A particularly trenchant critique (which nonetheless recognized the importance of the film) appeared in the MIT student paper, *The Tech:* Thakur, "*Hotel Terminus* Is Sidetracked by Director Ophuls' Pent-up Feelings."

31. Thakur, "*Hotel Terminus* Is Sidetracked," pp. 27–28. One can contrast this with the famous scene in Lanzmann's *Shoah*, where Lanzmann stages a haircut by Abraham Bomba, who cut women's hair in the gas chamber in Treblinka. For a critique of this *mise en scéne*, see LaCapra, *History and Memory after Auschwitz*, p. 96.

32. Personal telephone conversation, June 7, 2001. Ophuls confirmed on this occasion that his first words to Muller were indeed the aggressive question about the little girl. When I asked whether he expected that the question would get the door slammed in his face, he said he thought there was a 50–50 chance, but at least he would have something to show. Thus, although technically not a *mise en scène*, the scene appears retroactively as one.

33. Porton and Ellickson, "The Troubles He's Seen," p. 9.

34. Ophuls, "The Sorrow and the Laughter," p. 115.

35. Ophuls, "The Sorrow and the Laughter," p. 115.

36. Porton and Ellickson, "The Troubles He's Seen," p. 9. Ophuls says here that the "big change" in this direction came with his 1990 film *November Days*, about the fall of the Berlin Wall, but it actually dates from *Hotel Terminus*.

37. Nichols, *Representing Reality*, p. 56.

38. For a good account of the historians' debate, see Rabinbach, "Beyond Bit-

burg," pp. 206–214. For an overview of recent German debates about Nazism in Germany, see Régine Robin, "La honte nationale comme malédiction: Autour de l'affaire 'Walser-Bubis,' " pp. 45–69.

39. Jay Cantor, "Death and the Image," p. 39.

40. See Jeancolas, "Entretien avec Marcel Ophuls," p. 25.

41. Jeancolas, "Entretien avec Marcel Ophuls," p. 126.

42. See, for example, Ciment, "Un cinéaste sur la piste de Klaus Barbie," p. 160.

43. Ophuls, "The Sorrow and the Laughter," p. 112.

44. Jeancolas, "Entretien avec Marcel Ophuls," p. 26.

45. Jeancolas, "Entretien avec Marcel Ophuls," p. 26.

46. Philip Gourevitch, *We Wish to Inform You that Tomorrow We Will Be Killed with Our Families: Stories from Rwanda*; Adam Hochschild, *King's Leopold's Ghost*.

47. Ophuls, "The Sorrow and the Laughter," p. 115.

5. Anamnesis: Remembering Jewish Identity in Central Europe after Communism

1. Kaufman's *A Hole in the Heart of the World: Being Jewish in Eastern Europe After World War II* presents the stories of five families in postwar Poland, Czechoslovakia, Hungary, and East and West Germany. For a discussion focused on Hungary, see Sanders, "The Holocaust in Contemporary Hungarian Literature."

2. Cited by Kovács, "Jewish Groups and Identity Strategies in Post-Communist Hungary," pp. 215–216.

3. On France, see Lapierre, *Changer de nom*, Chapter 4. On Hungary, see Fejtö, *Juifs et Hongrois*, p. 355 (among others).

4. Judt, "The Past is Another Country: Myth and Memory in Postwar in Europe," p. 312.

5. Suleiman and Forgács, "Introduction," in *Contemporary Jewish Writing in Hungary: An Anthology*, especially xxxvi–lxii.

6. *Sunshine*, released in Canada in 1999 and in Europe and the United States in spring 2000, was produced by the Canadian-Hungarian producer Robert Lantos. The screenplay is by Szabó and Israel Horovitz, based on an original story by Szabó; the film's stars are Ralph Fiennes, William Hurt, Rosemary Harris, and Jennifer Ehle. Szabó's best-known films in the West are *Mephisto* (1981), which won the Oscar for best foreign film, and *Being Julia* (2004), starring Annette Bening.

7. Quoted in Randy Gener, "Fiennes, Ehle, Harris Play Across Generations in Sunshine Film," article posted on the Theatre.com Web site on June 8, 2000; I thank Christoph Hüvös for sending it to me; www.theatre.com/news/public/newsbrief.asp?newsid_710.

8. Two excellent recent histories of the Jews in Hungary, within the larger context of Hungarian and European history, are Fejtö's *Hongrois et Juifs* and Patai's *The Jews of Hungary: History, Culture, Psychology*. The standard work on Hungarian Jews and the Holocaust is Braham's *The Politics of Genocide: The Holocaust in Hungary*.

9. Kovács, "Jews and Politics in Hungary," p. 50.

10. Deák, "Strangers at Home," p. 31.

11. See Karády, "Some Social Aspects of Jewish Assimilation in Socialist Hungary, 1945–1956."

12. For a general overview of Szabó's work up to the early 1990s, see Paul, "Szabó." A more in-depth study of the early films, including a long interview with Szabó, is in Italian: De Marchi, *István Szabó*.

13. "Itt vigyázni kell" ["Here we must be careful"], interview with Dóra Mülner, *Népszabadság*, February 8, 2000. (All translations from the Hungarian are my own.)

14. See reviews by French in *The Observer*, April 30, 2000; Carr in *Boston Globe*, June 23, 2000, and Scott in *New York Times*, June 9, 2000. While generally favorable, they all criticized the film's schematicism, especially in characterization.

15. György, "Sorsválasztók" ["Those who chose their fate" or "Those who chose Sors"].

16. Schöpflin, "Review of the movie *Sunshine*, by István Szabó," posted on the Web site of the Centre for the Study of Democracy, University College London: http://www.ucl.ac.uk/cds/gsbr1.htm.

17. Szabó, "Itt vigyázni kell."

18. The reference to the Spinario sculpture may also be an allusion to German Romantic aesthetic theory, notably to Kleist's essay "On the Marionette Theater," whose subject is the relation between "natural" grace and studied artifice. (I thank Irene Kacandes for pointing me to Kleist's use of the Spinario).

19. A detailed study of the archival footage Szabó uses—exactly which images, and when—could be illuminating. Here is an approximate list:

World War I: soldiers and carriages at outbreak of war and at its end.
1919: revolutionary crowds in Budapest (Szabó inserts Fiennes/Ignatz into one shot); later that year, foreign soldiers on horseback in Budapest after the fall of the Kun regime.
1936: Berlin Olympics, showing Hitler, Nazi banners, opening of the Games (from Leni Riefenstahl's famous documentary *Olympia*.
1944–45: A row of Jews wearing yellow stars, marching on a street in Budapest; January 1945, dead horses on the street, a man cutting into one for meat; blown-up bridges over the Danube.
1953: Death of Stalin, crowds marching in Budapest.
1956: Revolutionary crowds, toppling of Stalin statue by a crowd (insert of Fiennes/Ivan); entry of Soviet tanks into Budapest.

20. Szabó confirmed this reading at a symposium on the film at Columbia University on September 23, 2000, and even pointed out that the house where the protagonists live is identical in the two films.

21. Hirsch, "István Szabó: Problems in the Narration of Holocaust Memory," pp. 9–11.

22. De Marchi, *István Szabó*, pp. 2–28; Paul, "Szabó."

23. Rév, *Retroactive Justice: Prehistory of Post-Communism*, p. 9.

24. Rév, *Retroactive Justice*, p. 75.

25. Szabó, "Itt vigyázni kell."

26. Sid Adelman, "Sunshine's Story Based on Director's Life . . . Sort Of."

27. Suleiman and Forgács, "Introduction," in *Contemporary Jewish Writing in Hungary*, p. li.

28. The minister, László Kövér, made his remark in a speech in June 1999; the explanation appeared in the daily *Magyar Hírlap* on August 16. For one sharp response, see Miklós Szabó, "A fogadott prókátor üzeni: A zsidók ne merjenek félni" ["A Message from the Official Spokesman: the Jews had better not be afraid"], *Magyar Hírlap*, September 1, 1999.

29. Rév, *Retroactive Justice*, pp. 282, 288, 290.

30. See Suleiman, *Budapest Diary: In Search of the Motherbook*, pp. 124–26.

31. This Center provoked lively and sometime acrimonious debate among Jewish intellectuals and community leaders—some criticized the government for not doing enough, others for making it "too Jewish" by incorporating a former synagogue into the architectural complex, still others for other reasons. But on the whole, the creation of the Center was an important step toward official recognition of Hungary's responsibility in the Holocaust.

32. Kovács, "Jewish Groups and Identity Strategies," pp. 227, 238–239.

33. Anna Földes, "Sors út" ["The way of fate" or "Sors's way"].

34. György, "Sorsválasztók."

35. See Emery George, "Introduction" to Miklós Radnóti, *The Complete Poetry*, p. 26.

36. Ungvári, "Választott sors?" ["Chosen fate?" or "Did Sors choose?" or "Chosen Sors?"]. The responses to Péter György's article were numerous and varied and appeared in the journal over several months, indicating just how deep an impact Szabó's film had in Hungarian (or at least, in Budapestian) intellectual circles.

37. Haraszti suggests, as I have, that Valerie is the true mouthpiece of the film's values—not as a woman, but as an artist and an individualist. See Haraszti, "Hívasson esztétát!" ["Call an art critic!"].

6. Revision: Historical Trauma and Literary Testimony

1. For a useful history of trauma theory, see Leys, *Trauma: A Genealogy*.

2. LaCapra, "Trauma, Absence, Loss," p. 722.

3. Agamben, *Remnants of Auschwitz*, p. 17.

4. Sartre, *"What is Literature?" and Other Essays*, p. 175; translation modified.

5. Margalit, *The Ethics of Memory*, chap. 5.

6. Schachter, *The Seven Sins of Memory (How the Mind Forgets and Remembers)*; Loftus, *Eyewitness Testimony*, with a new preface by the author; and McNally, *Remembering Trauma*. Many other works by experimental cognitive psychologists could be cited in this domain.

7. Langer, *The Holocaust and the Literary Imagination*, p. 285.

8. Davis, "Understanding the Concentration Camps: Elie Wiesel's *La Nuit* and Jorge Semprun's *Quel beau dimanche!*", p. 295.

9. Ezrahi, *By Words Alone*, p. 169.

10. Lejeune, *Le pacte autobiographique*, Chapter 1.

11. Semprun, "Rencontre avec Jorge Semprun."

12. Semprun, *L'écriture ou la vie*, p. 23; *Literature or Life*, p. 13. Here and elsewhere, I have modified the published English translation somewhat. Hereafter, this work will be abbreviated as *EV*; page references will be given first to the French version, then to the English.

13. Van der Kolk and Van der Hart, "The Intrusive Past," p. 163.

14. LaCapra, "Trauma, Absence, Loss," pp. 716–717.

15. Ezrahi, "Representing Auschwitz," p. 122.

16. Semprun, *Adieu, vive clarté*, p. 195.

17. Semprun, *Quel beau dimanche!*, p. 93; *What a Beautiful Sunday!*, p. 100. Here and elsewhere, I have modified the translation somewhat. Hereafter, this work will be abbreviated as *QB* or *WB* (for the English version). Double page references are to the French version followed by the English version.

18. See Maspero, *Les abeilles & la guêpe*, Chapter 1. See also the chapter on Buchenwald in Halbwachs's biography by Annette Becker, *Maurice Halbwachs, un intellectuel en guerres mondiales, 1914–1945*.

19. Proust, *A la recherche du temps perdu*, vol. IV, p. 269.

20. Semprun and Wiesel, *Se taire est impossible*, p. 18.

21. Semprun, *Le mort qu'il faut*. p. 43; hereafter, this work will be abbreviated as *MF* and page references will be given in parenthesis; my translations.

7. Do Facts Matter in Holocaust Memoirs?

1. Breton, *Nadja*, trans. Richard Howard, p. 71; French, p. 82.

2. This is the main definition given in *The American Heritage Dictionary of the English Language*.

3. Quindlen, "How Dark? How Stormy? I Can't Recall," p. 35.

4. Cohn, *The Distinction of Fiction*, p. xvii. In Chapter 1, Cohn provides a concise and thorough overview of the various meanings attributed to the term "fiction." Ricoeur's more-ample discussion of the differences between fictional and historical narrative is in volumes 2 and 3 of his *Temps et récit*.

5. One interview where McCourt describes the Limerick tours appeared in a Swiss paper, *Sonntagszeitung*, September 9, 1998.

6. Sternberg, *The Poetics of Biblical Narrative*, p. 26.

7. Christopher Ricks, going one step further, argues that even in novels, factual accuracy about historical events, places, or people is important to the reading experience; see Ricks, "Literature and the Matter of Fact," University Lecture, Boston University, 1990. Here one might want to invoke Sternberg's distinction between truth-claim and truth-value, the latter referring to factual *accuracy* while the former refers only to the author's "commitment" to the facts. For Ricks, factual inaccuracies mar the reader's experience even of a novel, especially a realist novel—assuming, of course, that the reader catches the inaccuracy. In a somewhat similar vein, Lawrence Langer has argued that Holocaust fiction must stay close to historical fact, for ethical reasons as well; see Langer, "Fictional Facts and Factual Fictions: History in Holocaust Literature."

8. Sloan, *Jerzy Kosinski: A Biography*, p. 223; Sloan has an extended discussion of the novel's reception, as well as of Kosinski's contradictory statements about it.

9. Wilkomirski, *Fragments*, p. 154; further page references will be given in parentheses.

10. Heschel, "Review of Wilkomirski," p. 73. Among those who mentioned the book's self-conscious artistry was Robert Hanks, in the British paper *The Independent*, December 8, 1996, p. 31.

11. Kozol, "Children of the Camps," p. 25.

12. Carjaval, "Disputed Holocaust Memoir Withdrawn"; and an unsigned article in the *New York Times*, "Publisher Drops Holocaust Book," November 3, 1999. The book's publishers were the Suhrkamp Verlag in Germany and Schocken Books in the United States. The first published accusation against Wilkomirski appeared in August 1998 in the Swiss weekly *Weltwoche*, in an article by the journalist Bruno Ganzfried (Ganzfried, "Die Geliehene Holocaust-Biographie") based on documents as well as interviews with people who had known Wilkomirski as a child. After replies by Wilkomirski and others, Ganzfried wrote two more articles ("Fakten Gegen Erinnerung" and "Bruchstücke Und Scherbenhaufen,") in the same newspaper, repeating his charges, which Wilkomirski continued vehemently to deny. He was supported in this, at first, by his publishers and by some specialists who work with child survivors of the Holocaust. Others, however—including the distinguished historian of the Holocaust Raoul Hilberg and the literary scholar Lawrence Langer—claimed that from the start they had doubted the work's authenticity; see Lappin, "The Man with Two Heads," p. 48, and Eskin, *A Life in Pieces*, pp. 80–85.

13. Maechler, *The Wilkomirski Affair*, pp. 232–234; Wilkomirski claimed that Yvonne Grosjean had left him the money, but Maechler shows that he actually sued for it as her biological son—this is one reason why it is hard to decide whether Wilkomirski is delusional or merely a charlatan.

14. Aside from many articles in the European and American press, the most thorough and engaging accounts of the Wilkomirski/Doesseker story to date are Lappin, "The Man with Two Heads"; Gourevitch, "The Memory Thief"; Maechler, *The Wilkomirski Affair*; and Eskin, *A Life in Pieces*. Eskin's account is also personal, since his mother's family happens to come from Riga and the family's original name was Wilkomirski. The novel by Sara Paretsky (featuring her private eye V. I. Warshawski), clearly modeled on the Wilkomirski case, is titled *Total Recall* (2001).

15. The sender of this Internet article (message dated October 10, 1998) gives its name as "Le Temps Irréparable," with the e-mail address of tempus@flash.net.

16. Van Alphen, *Caught by History*, p. 64.

17. Laub, "Bearing Witness, or the Vicissitudes of Listening," p. 60.

18. For a detailed historical account of the attempted uprising, see Gilbert, *The Holocaust*, Chapter 38. For indications of other sources besides survivor testimonies, see Czech, *Auschwitz Chronicle 1939–1945*.

19. Laub, "Bearing Witness," p. 60.

20. Bernstein, *Foregone Conclusions*, p. 47.

21. Lappin, "Man with Two Heads," p. 49.

22. Wilkomirski, *Fragments*, p. 154.

23. Wilkomirski, "Niemand Muss Mir Glauben Schenken," *Tages Anzeiger*, September 1, 1998, p. 51.

24. *New York Times*, "Publisher Drops Holocaust Book," p. B2. Since then, DNA tests have proven that Wilkomirski is the biological son of Yvonne Grosjean and Rudolf Zehnder, who was still alive at the time of the "affair."

25. Lappin, "Man with Two Heads," p. 49.

26. Gates, " 'Authenticity,' or The Lesson of Little Tree."

27. Todorov, "Fictions et vérités," in *Les morales de l'histoire*, p. 140; further page references will be given in parentheses.

28. Maechler, *Wilkomirski Affair*, p. 245.

29. Young, *Writing and Rewriting the Holocaust*, p. 133.

30. Wiesel, *Tous les fleuves vont à la mer: Mémoires*, I, p. 108; followed by my translation.

31. Seidman, "Elie Wiesel and the Scandal of Jewish Rage."

32. Davis, "Reviewing Memory: Wiesel, Testimony and Self-Reading," pp. 127–128. Davis cites the passage I am considering, along with other examples. We evidently discovered the passage independently: I first spoke about it at a conference, "The Claims of Memory," October 25–27, 1998, at Boston University, honoring Elie Wiesel's seventieth birthday.

33. Davis, "Reviewing Memory," pp. 129–130.

34. Elie Wiesel, *Night*, Bantam edition, 1982, p. 21.

35. Wiesel offered this explanation in response to my paper (an earlier version of this essay) delivered at the conference celebrating his seventieth birthday.

36. Personal conversation, January 23, 1999.

8. The Edge of Memory: Experimental Writing and the 1.5 Generation

1. *Nouvelle Revue de Psychanalyse*, Autumn 1981; trans. as "Remembering the Unknown," 1984.

2. Raczymow, *Contes d'exil et d'oubli* and *Un cri sans voix* (translated as *Writing the Book of Esther*). Almost every one of Modiano's novels treats this problem, but his masterpiece is, I think, *Dora Bruder* (1997), a combination of autobiography, invention, and historical research and speculation about the life and death of a young girl who was deported from France in 1942. Although Modiano does not mention it in the book, he was aided in his historical research by Serge Klarsfeld, the eminent specialist on the deportation of French Jews. (Personal communication and documentation from Serge Klarsfeld, July 2004).

3. See Hirsch, *Family Frames*, as well as "Marked by Memory" and "Surviving Images." Hirsch's definition of postmemory has evolved since she first proposed the term. Originally, it designated the memory "inherited" by children of survivors, but subsequently Hirsch expanded it to include all those born after the war who have a deep interest in the experiences of the survivor generation—what Geoffrey Hartman calls "witnesses by adoption" (Hartman, *The Longest Shadow*). While the broader definition is attractive in its inclusiveness, it is more open to criticism because it does not make clear the distinction between individual memory, public memory, and history. The narrower definition has the advantage of recognizing that an individual's first memories are formed and transmitted in the context of the family.

4. See the extensive bibliography in Keilson, *Sequential Traumatization in Children*. My Harvard colleague (and fellow Radcliffe Institute Fellow in 2005–06), Mary C. Waters, informs me, as this book is going to press, that the term "1.5 generation" is currently used by many sociologists who study immigrant families. It was first proposed in 1991 by Ruben Rumbaut, who defined the "1.5 generation" as children who arrived in the United States between the ages of 5 and 12, and "who are marginal to both the old and the new worlds, and are fully part of neither of them" (quoted in Zhou and Bankston, *Growing Up American*, p. 52). The "in-between" status of this immigrant generation corresponds to my own

definition of the 1.5 generation of the Holocaust. I thank Mary Waters for this information, which proves the fruitfulness of cross-disciplinary conversations.

5. Among psychoanalysts in the United States, attention to child survivors arose in the process of treatment of "second-generation" patients whose parents were child survivors; see Bergmann and Jucovy, *Generations of the Holocaust*, 84–94. A major figure among psychoanalysts studying child survivors was Judith Kestenberg (1910–1999), who was also one of the founders, in 1974, of the Group for the Psychoanalytic Study of the Effects of the Holocaust on the Second Generation (Bergmann and Jucovy, 36). Much of her later work was devoted specifically to child survivors; see, for example, Kestenberg and Brenner, *The Last Witness*, and Kestenberg and Kahn, *Children Surviving Persecution*. Groups of child survivors started meeting in Los Angeles and various cities on the East Coast in the early 1980s and eventually formed the National Association of Jewish Child Holocaust Survivors (NAHOS), which sponsored its first conference in 1987 and has sponsored annual conferences since then; another major organization is the Hidden Child Foundation, which grew out of an international conference held in New York in 1991 and has branches worldwide.

6. Spitzer, "The Historical Problem of Generations," p. 1385. For an extended discussion of this problem as regards child survivors, see my essay, "The 1.5 Generation: Thinking About Child Survivors and the Holocaust." A few excerpts from that essay are integrated into the first part of this chapter.

7. Raczymow, "Memory Shot Through with Holes," p. 104.

8. Dwork, *Children with a Star: Jewish Youth in Nazi Europe*, p. xxiii. Dwork studies both child survivors and children who perished.

9. See Kestenberg and Brenner, *The Last Witness*, Chapter 7.

10. Among those who look back on their time of persecution as an adventure is the financier George Soros, who was fourteen when the Holocaust reached Hungary. In the foreword to his father's memoir, *Maskerado*, Soros writes, "It is a sacrilegious thing to say, but those ten months [from March 1944 to to January 1945, when the Russians entered Budapest] were the happiest times of my life" (p. x). The fact that he lived through the adventure with his father and older brother no doubt helped, as did the confident middle-class lifestyle of the family before and after the war.

11. The Fortunoff Video Archive of Holocaust Testimonies at Yale University marked its twentieth anniversary in 2002 and now has more than 4100 testimonies, carefully indexed; the Survivors of the Shoah Visual History Foundation, founded in 1994, has collected 50,000 testimonies in fifty-seven countries in thirty-two languages. One of the first published collections was Claudine Vegh's *Je ne lui ai pas dit au revoir* [*I Didn't Say Goodbye*], featuring the stories of seventeen French child survivors who had lost at least one parent in the Holocaust. Martin Gilbert's study, *The Boys*, is based largely on written accounts that were either published in newsletters of the '45 Aid Society (the association of the group of child survivors who arrived in Windermere, England, after the war) or were sent to the author in the early 1990s; all were presumably written many years after the war. Other recent collections feature texts written by child survivors, in some cases transcripts of taped interviews approved by the interviewee; see Marks, *The Hidden Children*; Sliwowska, *The Last Eyewitnesses* (translated from Polish); and Bailly, *Traqués, cachés, vivants: Des enfants juifs en France (1940–1945)*. In addition, many

child survivors have written individual booklength accounts of their wartime experiences, usually the only book they have published.

12. A few studies by psychologists have already appeared, attempting to draw general conclusions from the stories of child survivors: Kestenberg and Brenner, *The Last Witness;* Frydman, *Le traumatisme de l'enfant caché;* Cyrulnik, *Un merveilleux malheur;* Sudefeld, ed., *Light from the Ashes: Social Science Careers of Young Holocaust Refugees and Survivors.* Frydman, a hidden child in Belgium who lost his father in the Holocaust, offers his personal account of survival and postwar adjustment, then tries to draw some general conclusions. Cyrulnik, also a child survivor, incorporates his case studies of child Holocaust survivors into a theory of "resilience" that tries to account for how children react to a wide range of traumas. Sudefeld's volume is the least systematic, consisting of written autobiographies, including his own—but there is a theoretical underpinning, as suggested by the book's subtitle. Sudefeld notes in the introduction that "until very recently," he and many others had "never made the connection" between their Holocaust experiences and their later professional pursuits (p. vii).

13. Chodorow, "Born into a World at War: Listening for Affect and Personal Meaning."

14. Suleiman, *Risking Who One Is,* Chapter 11; and "Monuments in a Foreign Tongue: On Reading Holocaust Memoirs by Emigrants." The best known argument in favor of "raw" testimony and against literary elaboration is by Lawrence Langer—see his *Holocaust Testimonies: The Ruins of Memory.*

15. Federman, "A Version of My Life—The Early Years," p. 118.

16. For these and other biographical details about Perec, see David Bellos, *Georges Perec: A Life in Words.* I have discussed *W or the Memory of Childhood* in some detail, but rather differently, in *Risking Who One Is* and in "The 1.5 Generation: Perec's *W or the Memory of Childhood.*"

17. The English translation, appropriately, is devoid of E's: *A Void.*

18. Claude Burgelin, one of Perec's most sensitive readers, argued in his 1988 book that all of Perec's works could be read as disguised forms of autobiography; see Burgelin, *Georges Perec.* Catherine Clément, a novelist and philosopher who was also a hidden child during the war, titled her contribution to a volume of essays on Perec in 1979, "Auschwitz ou la disparition."

19. Some critics have suggested that E could also refer to Perec's aunt Esther Bienenfeld, whom he interviewed extensively in 1967 for a genealogical project about his paternal family that never came to completion. On this project, titled L'Arbre, see Régine Robin, *Le deuil de l'origine,* pp. 195–227.

20. Perec had been in analysis twice before for briefer periods: in 1949 with the child psychologist Françoise Dolto, and in 1956–1957 with another analyst. Claude Burgelin has written a fascinating account of Perec's relation to Pontalis, as reflected especially in complex allusions to the analyst in Perec's last novel, *La vie mode d'emploi.* Pontalis, on his side, published several articles about Perec (disguised under a transparent pseudonym) very soon after the analysis, a procedure whose ethical implications Burgelin rightly questions. See Burgelin, *Les parties de dominos chez Monsieur Lefèvre,* especially Chapter 3. Perec wrote an essay about his analysis, which he said gave him "access to my story and my voice;" see "Les lieux d'une ruse," in *Penser, classer,* p. 71.

21. Lejeune, *La mémoire et l'oblique,* p. 39.

22. Freud, "Screen Memories," p. 322.

23. Lejeune, "Introduction" to Perec, *Je suis né*, p. 8.

24. Motte, "Georges Perec and the Broken Book," p. 246.

25. See, for example, Bernard Magné, "Les sutures dans *W ou le souvenir d'enfance*."

26. Perec, "Lettre à Maurice Nadeau," in *Je suis né*, pp. 63–64.

27. Perec, *W or the Memory of Childhood*, trans. David Bellos, pp. 6–7; *W ou le souvenir d'enfance*, p. 14. In subsequent quotations, page numbers of both the English and French versions will be given in parentheses, with the French pages in italics.

28. Magné, "Les sutures dans *W ou le souvenir d'enfance*."

29. Robin, "Manhattan Bistro," in *L'immense fatigue des pierres*, p. 179.

30. Perec, *W ou le souvenir d'enfance* (Paris: Gallimard, "L'Imaginaire"), 2002, back cover; Perec's italics.

31. Perec mentions this episode twice in Chapter 8 and alludes to it again in Chapter 15. In Chapter 8, he calls it "the only memory" he has of his mother; later in the chapter, he reprints in bold face the earliest text he wrote about his parents, dating from 1959, where this episode is mentioned again. In a 1979 interview, "Le travail de la mémoire" (in *Je suis né*, p. 83) Perec said, about *W or the Memory of Childhood*: "All that autobiographical work was organized around a single memory ["souvenir unique"] that, for me, was deeply hidden, deeply buried and in a certain sense denied." Clearly, the goodbye to his mother gained power retrospectively, when he realized that it was the last time he had seen her.

32. Lejeune, *La mémoire et l'oblique*, p. 82. Lejeune notes that a picture of Charlot as parachutist appears on the cover of an illustrated book titled *Charlot détective*, published in 1935 and republished after the war.

33. In January 1959, at a literary meeting, Perec gave a lengthy impromptu monologue (which was recorded), recalling his first parachute jump; it was subsequently published under the title "Le saut en parachute." In this text he interprets the parachute jump as a sign of "confidence in life," since it involves throwing oneself into the void with the expectation that the parachute will open and "one will be supported"; see *Je suis né*, pp. 41, 42.

34. Lejeune, *La mémoire et l'oblique*, p. 115.

35. Freud, "Splitting of the Ego in the Defensive Process," p. 275.

36. Freud, "Splitting of the Ego," p. 275.

37. On the reception of Federman's works in Germany (in addition to translations, his works have been adapted for the stage and for radio plays), see Thomas Irmer, "Federman in Germany," in *Federman from A to X-X-X-X*, ed. McCaffery, Hartl, and Rice, pp. 126–134. This wonderful collection of texts and photos by Federman fans, with many contributions by Federman himself, was "totally ignored" in the United States and never reviewed, according to an e-mail from the author in August 2004. Catherine Viollet, one of the rare French scholars who wrote about Federman in the early 1990s, complained that he was unknown in France even though he writes in French and English—she herself discovered him while spending a year in Germany; see Viollet, "Raymond Federman: La voix plurielle," p. 193.

38. I thank Raymond Federman for sending me the manuscript of this book in 2004. "Autofiction" is a genre category proposed by Serge Doubrovsky (who

survived the war in hiding near Paris, with his parents) in the late 1970s, in response to Philippe Lejeune's classification in *Le pacte autobiographique*. For Lejeune, the main criterion dividing autobiography from fiction is that in fiction, the name of the narrator and/or the protagonist is different from the name of the author. Doubrovsky, using his own writing as an example, proposed to call "autofiction" a novel whose narrator/protoganist had the same name as the author, and whose content was all "true," yet was transformed by writing into something other than purely referential. It is a fairly confused notion allowing for enormous slippages between fact and invention. For an overview (and many different views) of this genre, see Doubrovsky, Lecarme, and Lejeune, eds., *Autofictions & Cie*.

39. There exists no authoritative biography of Federman, and his own versions of his life, as he never tires of repeating, are as much invented as recalled. What appears to be the least fanciful autobiographical account of his early years is the long essay he wrote for the reference book *Contemporary Authors*, "A Version of My Life—The Early Years" (volume 208, pp. 118–136). There he gives his age as fourteen when he was left on his own, whereas in his novels and even in some interviews, the "boy in the closet" is said to be twelve or thirteen years old. When I questioned him about the reasons for this, Federman responded in an e-mail that he thought "it would be more dramatic to have the boy of the story be 13." Besides, he added, "when I came out of the closet/womb, mentally, physically, emotionally, I was 13 or less. I was so unprepared. So dumb, so shy." (August 2, 2004). Although Federman's family was totally irreligious and he had no *bar mitzvah*, the fact that in Judaism age thirteen marks a boy's passage into manhood may also be relevant here.

40. "Surfiction—Four Propositions in Form of an Introduction," p. 11. Compare the last sentence to Jean Ricardou's declaration in an essay devoted to a novel by Alain Robbe-Grillet: "the fiction is an immense metaphor of its narration," in Ricardou, *Pour une théorie du nouveau roman*, p. 221.

41. Federman, "A Version of My Life—The Early Years," p. 121.

42. Hutcheon, *Poetics of Postmodernism*, p. 52.

43. One American critic who has written about Federman as both a postmodernist and a writer engaged with history is Marcel Cornis-Pope; he argues, à propos of Federman, that "innovative fiction proposes alternative narrations meant to correct the distortions perpetrated by traditional history" (*Narrative Innovation and Cultural Rewriting in the Cold War and After*, p. 24).

44. Federman, "A Version of My Life—The Early Years," p. 118.

45. McCaffery, "An Interview with Raymond Federman," pp. 299–300.

46. Robbe-Grillet, *Le miroir qui revient*, pp. 10–11.

47. The "recyclopedic" volume *Federman from A to X-X-X-X* lists no fewer than eleven entries under "List," including "List of Influential Writers" (itself subdivided into four different categories, from Beckett to Yeats, from Blake to Sterne, etc.), "List of Plagiarists," and "List of Lists!" (pp. 180–188).

48. McCaffery, Hartl, and Rice, *Federman from A to X-X-X-X*, p. 378.

49. McCaffery, "An interview with Raymond Federman," p. 293.

50. In what follows, I will quote and reproduce pages from the original 1971 edition. The current, 3rd edition (Boulder, CO: Fiction Collective, 1998) is adapted from the original and differs slightly in layout on many pages.

51. In more recent works, Federman has evoked his family in some detail, but

always in fragments that one needs to piece together from novel to novel. The most concrete information about his parents and sisters, including photographs and the dates of their deportation to Auschwitz (they left on three different transports) is given in various entries in McCaffery, Hartl, and Rice, *Federman from A to X-X-X-X*. See "Chronology," "Convoi," and "Mutter," as well as alphabetical entries under "Federman:" Jacqueline, Marguerite, Sarah and Simon.

52. Federman, "A Version of My Life—The Early Years," p. 119.

53. Federman, "The Necessity and Impossibility of Being a Jewish Writer," http://www.federman.com/rfsrcr5.htm.

54. Federman, *Double or Nothing*, p. 168.

55. In Robin, *L'Immense fatigue des pierres*, p. 77. Works in which the change of name is linked to a crisis of identity, including religious identity, in a young child include Friedländer, *When Memory Comes*; Begley, *Wartime Lies*; Kofman, *Rue Ordener, Rue Labat*; Berthe Burko-Falcman, *L'enfant caché*; and many others. In Perec's case, his own name was already ambiguous, given its Breton resonance.

56. Lapierre, *Changer de nom*, Chapters 4 and 9; see also her brief essay, "Les changements de noms."

57. In an e-mail message, Federman said that he does not recall using a false name on the farm where he worked from 1942 to 1945. Raymond is, of course, an ordinary French name, but it is unlikely that he was known as "Federman" at the time. Perhaps he was never asked to show identification. "I must admit that I lived those years on the Farm in total oblivion to what was happening in the world," he wrote (August 2, 2004). This is one question for future biographers to investigate.

58. The general configuration of the page also appears in the 1998 edition (p. 58), but the hand-drawn parentheses are absent, as is the arbitrary line break in "always." Such ungrammatical line breaks are frequent in the original edition, no doubt required or facilitated by the typewriter but no longer allowed by the computer.

59. Barthes, "Le bruissement de la langue," in *Le bruissement de la langue*, pp. 99–102.

60. Barthes, "Le bruissement de la langue," p. 99.

61. Robin, *Le deuil de l'origine*, p. 253.

62. Appelfeld, *The Story of a Life*, p. 103.

63. Federman, *The Twofold Vibration*, p. 9.

64. Federman, *The Twofold Vibration*, p. 118.

65. Federman, *La fourrure de ma tante Rachel*, p. 162.

66. There is a brief account of the boy's jumping into a freight train and eating raw potatoes in Federman, *The Twofold Vibration*, pp. 105–106. Federman has given several versions, in essays and interviews, of his peregrinations after the closet until he landed on the farm. The fullest version of his time on the farm, in which he appears under his own name but which he still calls a novel, is in *The Farm* (forthcoming).

67. Federman, *La fourrure de ma tante Rachel*, p. 162 (ellipses in text).

68. Freud, "Splitting of the Ego," p. 276.

69. Luce Irigaray, "a tache aveugle d'un vieux rêve de symétrie," in *Speculum de l'autre femme*; Sarah Kofman, "Ça cloche."

70. Freud, "Fetishism," pp. 155–156.

71. Freud, "Fetishism," p. 155–156.
72. Freud, "Fetishism," p. 156.
73. Mannoni, *Clefs pour l'imaginarire ou l'Autre scène*, pp. 10–13.
74. Kofman, "Ça cloche," pp. 110–111. For Derrida too, this generalized fetishism is necessarily linked to "undecidability" (discussion after Kofman's paper, pp. 113–114). However, undecidability is not the same thing as simultaneous affirmation and denial. For an interesting speculation on female fetishism, see Naomi Schor, "Female Fetishism: The Case of George Sand."
75. Freud, "Splitting of the Ego," p. 277.
76. Blanchot, *The Writing of the Disaster*, p. 61, translation modified; *L'écriture du désastre*, p. 101.
77. Federman, "The Necessity and Impossibility of Being a Jewish Writer," p. 3. www.federman.com/rfsrcr5.htm.
78. Were this chapter not too long already, I would devote extensive space to Régine Robin's *L'immense fatigue des pierres*, a collection of seven interconnected stories Robin calls "biofictions." In addition to frequent metacommentary and the figure of suspension, which Robin uses repeatedly in this work, one finds an interesting solution to the problem of split or multiple identities: Robin imagines alternative life stories for the recurring character of the writer who is a child survivor of the Holocaust and whose extended family in Poland was murdered (the writer in many of the stories is a woman, and is sometimes clearly Robin herself, but not in all). Robin was born in 1939 to Polish immigrants in France; her father, who like Perec's father volunteered for the Army, was taken prisoner and spent the war in a stalag in Germany. Robin herself survived in hiding in Paris with her mother, as she recounts in one of the autobiographical stories in the book, "Gratok."
79. Federman, "Notes and Counter-Notes," p. 8. www.federman.com/rfsrcr6.htm.
80. Federman, "The Necessity and Impossibility of Being a Jewish Writer," p. 4. www.federman.com/rfsrcr6.htm

9. Amnesia and Amnesty: Reflections on Forgetting and Forgiving

1. Augé, *Les formes de l'oubli*, p. 21; the English translation is titled *Oblivion*. Here the translation is mine and page numbers refer to the French. Further page references will be given in parentheses.
2. Borges, "Funès the Memorious," in *Ficciones*, p. 115.
3. Mannheim, "The Problem of Generations," p. 294.
4. Renan, *Qu'est-ce qu'une nation?*, p. 15.
5. Ricoeur, *La mémoire, l'histoire, l'oubli*, p. 634. Links among memory, forgetting, and forgiving are explored in multiple perspectives in the recent collective volume, *Devoir de mémoire, droit à l'oubli?* eds. Ferenczi and Boltanski, as well as in Abel, *Le pardon: briser la dette et l'oubli*.
6. My main source for the technical aspects of amnesty in France is the detailed study by Stéphane Gacon, *L'amnistie: De la Commune à la guerre d'Algérie*; see pp. 42–43 for a discussion of libel suits against journalists and historians. By contrast, in Argentina, South Africa, Guatemala, and the United States, there is

no law against referring to an amnestied person's past activities. I thank Martha Minow for informing me about this point of law.

7. Ricoeur, *La mémoire, l'histoire, l'oubli*, p. 580.

8. Quoted in Gacon, *L'amnistie*, p. 125.

9. Gacon, *L'amnistie*, pp. 20–22.

10. Occasionally, amnesty has even been invoked in the settlement of international disputes, not just civil war. Harald Weinrich notes that the Treaty of Wesphalia, putting an end to the bloody Thirty Years' War (1648), stipulated "perpetual oblivion and amnesty" ["perpetua oblivio et amnestia"] among the signers of the treaty; Weinrich, *Lethe: The Art and Critique of Forgetting*, p. 172.

11. Loraux, *La cité divisee*, p. 154.

12. Gacon, *L'ammistie*, p. 387.

13. Huizinga, *Homo Ludens*, p. 89.

14. Gacon, *L'amnistie*, p. 358.

15. The classic study of the postwar "purge" in France is Peter Novick's 1968 book, *The Resistance versus Vichy*. For more recent work, see Rousso, *Vichy: L'événement, la mémoire, l'histoire*, Part II, and Baruch, ed., *Une poignée de misérables: L'épuration de la société française après la Seconde Guerre mondiale*. For purges in the judiciary, see Weisberg, *Vichy Law and the Holocaust in France*, Chapter 5.

16. Rousso, "Juger le passé?" in *Vichy: L'événement, la mémoire, l'histoire*, p. 694.

17. Rousso, "Jugerle passé?" pp. 643–653.

18. See Kaplan, *The Collaborator: The Trial and Execution of Robert Brasillach*, Chapter 8; and Sapiro, "L'épuration du monde des lettres," in Baruch, ed., *Une poignée de misérables*.

19. Kattan, *Penser le devoir de mémoire*, pp. 2–3.

20. Todorov, *Les abus de la mémoire*. Paris: Arléa, 1995.

21. *The Observer*, London, November 29, 1998; quoted in Kattan, *Penser le devoir de mémoire*, p. 102.

22. Jankélévitch, "Pardonner?" in *L'imprescriptible*, pp. 39 and 47. Jankélévitch first published these reflections on the statute of limitations and the problem of "forgiving and forgetting" in 1965, shortly after the 1964 law had been passed declaring crimes against humanity *imprescriptibles*.

23. Minow, *Between Vengeance and Forgiveness: Facing History after Genocide and Mass Violence*, p. 59.

24. Ibid., p. 58.

25. Ibid., p. 56.

26. At least, it is a novel idea in modern times. In her discussion of the Athenian amnesty of 403 B.C., Nicole Loraux alludes to the fact that even the Thirty Tyrants, technically excluded from the amnesty, could be included if they "rendered an account of their activities"; see Loraux, *La cité divisée*, p. 256.

27. Arendt, *The Human Condition*, p. 237.

28. Arendt, *The Human Condition*, p. 240–241.

29. Minow, *Between Vengeance and Forgiveness*, p. 9.

30. Arendt, *The Human Condition*, p. 241.

31. Arendt, *The Human Condition*, pp. 239 and 241.

32. Arendt, *Eichmann in Jerusalem*, p. 269.

33. Arendt, *The Human Condition*, p. 241.

34. Kristeva, "Forgiveness: An Interview."

35. Arendt, *The Human Condition*, p. 241.

36. Arendt, *The Human Condition*, p. 239.

37. Kristeva, "Forgiveness," p. 281.

38. Ibid., p. 283.

39. Weigel, "Secularization and Sacralization, Normalization and Rupture: Kristeva and Arendt on Forgiveness," p. 321.

40. Derida, "On Forgiveness," pp. 32–33, trans. modified; in French, "Le siècle et le pardon," p. 108.

41. Ibid., p. 39.

42. Ibid., p. 36.

43. Ibid., p. 45; translation modified.

44. Ibid., p. 51.

45. Ricoeur, *La mémoire, l'histoire, l'oubli*, p. 605.

46. Ibid., p. 642.

47. Ibid., pp. 589 and 634.

48. Ibid., p. 651.

49. Minow, *Between Vengeance and Forgiveness*, p. 5.

50. Ibid., p. 24.

Works Cited

Abel, Olivier, ed. *Le pardon. Briser la dette et l'oubli.* Paris: Autrement, 1996.

Adelman, Sid. "Sunshine's Story Based on Director's Life . . . Sort Of." *The Toronto Star*, December 3, 1999.

Adorno, Theodor W. "What Does 'Coming to Terms with the Past' Mean?" Trans. Timothy Bahti and Geoffrey Hartman. In *Bitburg in Moral and Political Perspective*, ed. Geoffrey Hartman. Bloomington: Indiana University Press, 1986. Orig. in *Erziehung Zur Mündigkeit. Vorträge u. Gesprache Mit Hellmut Becker [und G. Kadelbach] 1959–1969*, eds. Hellmut Becker and Gerd Kadelbach. Frankfurt a.M.: Suhrkamp, 1970.

Agamben, Giorgio. *Remnants of Auschwitz: The Witness and the Archive.* Trans. Daniel Heller-Roazen. New York: Zone Books, 1999.

Alfonsi, Laurence. "La réception du film *Lucie Aubrac.*" *Communications et Langages* 116 (1998): 39–57.

Alter, Nora. "Marcel Ophuls' November Days: German Reunification as 'Musical Comedy.' " *Film Quarterly* 51, no. 2 (1997–1998): 32–43.

Amouroux, Henri. "Entretien avec les Aubrac." *Le Figaro*, April 12, 1997.

Andrieu, Claire. *Pour l'amour de la République: Le club Jean Moulin, 1958–1970.* Paris: Fayard, 2002.

Andrieu, Claire and Diane de Bellescize. "Les Aubrac, jouets de l'histoire à l'estomac." *Le Monde*, July 17, 1997: 12.

Antelme, Robert. *L'espèce humaine.* Edition revue et corrigée. Paris: Gallimard, 1957.

Appelfeld, Aharon. *The Story of a Life.* Trans. Aloma Halter. New York: Schocken Books, 2004.

Arendt, Hannah. *Eichmann in Jerusalem: A Report on the Banality of Evil.* Rev. and enl. ed. New York: Viking Press, 1964.

———. *The Human Condition.* Chicago: University of Chicago Press, 1998.

261

Aubrac, Lucie. *Ils partiront dans l'ivresse: Lyon, mai 43-Londres, février 44.* Paris: Editions du Seuil, 1984; later edition, Paris: Collection "Points," 1986; *Outwitting the Gestapo.* Trans. Konrad Bieber. Lincoln: University of Nebraska Press, 1993.

———. *La Résistance, naissauce et organisation.* Paris: Robert Lang, 1945.

———. *La Résistance expliquée à mes petits-enfants.* Paris: Seuil, 2000.

Aubrac, Raymond. "Ce que cette table-ronde m'a appris." *Libération,* July 10, 1997: 30.

———. "Ma part de vérité." *L'Histoire,* June 1997: 79.

———. *Où la mémoire s'attarde.* Paris: Editions O. Jacob, 2000. [orig. ed. 1996.]

Augé, Marc. *Les formes de l'oubli.* Paris: Payot & Rivages, 1998.

Aussaresses, Paul. *Services spéciaux: Algérie, 1955–1957.* Paris: Perrin, 2001.

Azéma, Jean-Pierre. "Affaire Aubrac: Les faits sont têtus." *Libération,* August 28, 1997: 4.

———. "Il n'y a pas d'affaire Aubrac." *L'Histoire,* June 1997: 81–85.

———, ed. *Jean Moulin face à l'histoire.* Paris: Flammarion, 2000.

Azéma, Jean-Pierre, and Georges Kiejman. "L'histoire au tribunal." *Le Débat,* November–December 1998: 45–51.

Baecque, Antoine de. "Un héros, Malraux?" *Libération,* November 24, 2001: 30.

Bailly, Danielle, ed. *Traqués, cachés, vivants: Des enfants juifs en France (1940–1945).* Paris: Harmattan, 2004.

Bair, Deirdre. *Simone de Beauvoir: A Biography.* New York: Summit Books, 1990.

Bal, Claude, dir. *Que la vérité est amère.* 1988, France.

Barthes, Roland. *Le bruissement de la langue.* Paris: Seuil, "Points," 1984.

Bartošek, Karel. *Les aveux des archives: Prague-Paris-Prague, 1948–1968.* Paris: Seuil, 1996.

Baruch, Marc Olivier, ed. *Une poignée de misérables: L'épuration de la société française après la Seconde Guerre mondiale.* Paris: Fayard, 2003.

Bauman, Zygmunt. *Modernity and the Holocaust.* Ithaca, NY: Cornell University Press, 2000.

Becker, Annette. *Maurice Halbwachs, un intellectuel en guerres mondiales, 1914–1945.* Paris: Agnès Vienot, 2003.

Becker, Jean-Jacques, and Annette Wieviorka, eds. *Les Juifs de France: de la Révolution française à nos jours.* Paris: Liana Levi, 1998.

Begley, Louis. *Wartime Lies.* New York: Knopf, 1991.

Bellos, David. *Georges Perec: A Life in Words.* Boston: D. R. Godine, 1993.

Ben-Amos, Avner. *Funerals, Politics, and Memory in Modern France, 1789–1996.* Oxford: Oxford University Press, 2000.

Bergmann, Martin S., and Milton E. Jucovy. *Generations of the Holocaust.* New York: Basic Books, 1982.

Bernstein, Michael André. *Foregone Conclusions: Against Apocalyptic History.* Berkeley: University of California Press, 1994.

Blanchot, Maurice. *L'écriture du désastre.* Paris: Gallimard, 1980; *The Writing of the Disaster.* Trans. Ann Smock. Lincoln: University of Nebraska Press, 1986.

Bonnet, Jean-Claude. "Les morts illustres." In *Les lieux de mémoire,* ed. Pierre Nora. Quarto ed. vol. 2, pp. 1831–1854. Paris: Gallimard, 1997.

Borges, Jorge Luis. "Funes the Memorious." In *Ficciones,* ed. Anthony Kerrigan, pp. 107–115. New York: Grove Press, 1962.

Boschetti, Anna. *Sartre et "Les Temps Modernes". Une entreprise intellectuelle.* Paris: Editions de Minuit, 1985.

Boutin, Alex, dir. *Sur les pas de Jean Moulin, 1899–1943 [Videorecording]/SIRP.* 1 Videocassette. (VHS). Paris: SIRP/Musée Jean Moulin, February 1999.

Braham, Randolph L. *The Politics of Genocide: The Holocaust in Hungary.* Rev. and enl. ed. 2 vols. New York: Rosenthal Institute for Holocaust Studies/City University of New York, 1994.

Breton, André. *Nadja.* Rev ed. Paris: Gallimard, "Folio," 1964; *Nadja.* Trans. Richard Howard. New York: Grove Press, 1960.

Burgelin, Claude. *Georges Perec.* Paris: Seuil, 1988.

———. *Les parties de dominos chez Monsieur Lefèvre: Perec avec Freud, Perec contre Freud.* Strasbourg: Circé, 1996.

Burko-Falcman, Berthe. *L'enfant caché.* Paris: Seuil, 1997.

Burrin, Philippe. *La France à l'heure allemande: 1940–1944.* Paris: Seuil, 1995.

———. "Vichy." In *Les lieux de mémoire,* ed. Pierre Nora. Quarto ed., vol. 2, pp. 2467–2487. Paris: Gallimard, 1997.

Cantor, Jay. "Death and the Image." In *Beyond Document,* ed. Charles Warren, pp. 23–49.

Carjaval, Doreen. "Disputed Holocaust Memoir Withdrawn." *New York Times,* October 14, 1999, sec. B1.

Carr, Jay. "Film Review of *Sunshine,* by István Szabó." *Boston Globe,* June 23, 2000.

Caruth, Cathy, ed. *Trauma: Explorations in Memory.* Baltimore, MD: Johns Hopkins University Press, 1995.

Chalandon, Sorj, and Pascale Nivelle. *Crimes contre l'humanité: Barbie, Touvier, Bousquet, Papon.* Paris: Plon: Libération, 1998.

Chauvy, Gérard. *Aubrac: Lyon, 1943.* Paris: Albin Michel, 1997.

———. "Les trois mystères Aubrac." *Historia* 603 (1997): 42–50.

———. "Réponse à Gilles Perrault." *Le Monde,* June 22/23, 1997: 15.

Chodorow, Nancy. "Born into a World at War: Listening for Affect and Personal Meaning." *American Imago* 59, no. 3 (2002): 297–316.

Ciment, Michel. "Joy to the World: An Interview with Marcel Ophuls." *American Film* (1988): 38–43.

Ciment, Michel, interview with M. Ophuls. "Un cinéaste sur la piste de Klaus Barbie." *Le Point,* September 26, 1988: 159–162.

Clément, Catherine. "Auschwitz ou la disparition." *L'Arc* 76 (1979): 87–90.

Cohn, Dorrit. *The Distinction of Fiction.* Baltimore, MD: Johns Hopkins University Press, 1999.

Combat. "Un industriel américain déclare . . ." January 7–8, 1945: 1.

Conan, Eric. "Aubrac: le passé revisité." *L'Express,* February 27, 1997.

———. "Prague ou la mémoire blessée." *L'Express,* November 7, 1996: 150–151.

Conan, Eric, and Henry Rousso. *Vichy: Un passé qui ne passe pas.* Paris: Fayard, 1994.

Contat, Michel, and Michel Rybalka. *Les écrits de Sartre.* Paris: Gallimard, 1970.

Cordier, Daniel. "Entretien (sur les Aubrac)." *Libération,* April 8, 1997: 31.

———. *Jean Moulin: La république des catacombes.* Paris: Gallimard, 1999.

Cornis-Pope, Marcel. *Narrative Innovation and Cultural Rewriting in the Cold War and After.* New York: Palgrave, 2001.

Courtois, Stéphane, and Rémi Kauffer. *Le livre noir du communisme: Crimes, terreurs et répression.* Paris: R. Laffont, 1997.

Cyrulnik, Boris. *Un merveilleux malheur.* Paris: O. Jacob, 1999.

Czech, Danuta. *Auschwitz Chronicle, 1939–1945.* New York: H. Holt, 1990.

Darriulat, Jean. "Affaire Jean Moulin: l'amère vérité de René Hardy." *Le Matin,* May 5–6, 1984: 12.

———. "Barbie-Hardy: scénario pour une manipulation." *Le Matin,* May 7, 1985: 22–23.

Davis, Colin. "Reviewing Memory: Wiesel, Testimony and Self-Reading." In *European Memories of the Second World War,* eds. H. Peitsch, C. Burdett, and Claire Gorrara, pp. 122–130. New York: Berghahn Books, 1999.

———. "Understanding the Concentration Camps: Elie Wiesel's *La nuit* and Jorge Semprun's *Quel beau dimanche!*" *Australian Journal of French Studies* 28.3 (1991): 291–303.

Deák, István. "Strangers at Home." *New York Review of Books,* July 20, 2000: 30–32.

Delbo, Charlotte. *Aucun de nous ne reviendra.* Paris: Editions de Minuit, 1970.

Delpla, François. *Aubrac: Les faits et la calomnie.* Pantin: Temps des cerises, 1997.

De Gaulle, Charles. *Discours et messages, t. 1: Pendant la guerre, juin 1940–janvier 1946.* Paris: Plon, 1970.

De Marchi, Bruno. *István Szabó.* Firenze: La nuova Italia, 1977.

Derogy, Jacques. "Affaire Barbie: Les masques de Vergès." *L'Express,* November 25, 1983: 64–66.

Derrida, Jacques. "Le siècle et le pardon: Entretien avec Michel Wieviorka." In *Foi et savoir,* suivi de Le *siècle et le pardon,* pp. 101–133. Paris: Seuil, "Points-essais," 2000; "On Forgiveness." In *On Cosmopolitanism and Forgiveness.* Trans. Mark Dooley and Michael Hughes, pp. 25–60. London: Routledge, 2001.

Doubrovsky, Serge, Jacques Lecarme, and Philippe Lejeune, eds. *Autofictions & Cie.* Nanterre: Université Paris X-Nanterre, 1993.

Douzou, Laurent. "La Résistance française en quête d'un héros éponyme." In *La France démocratique: Mélanges offertes à Maurice Agulhon,* ed. C. Charle et al., pp. 431–440. Paris: Publications de la Sorbonne, 1998.

Dwork, Debórah. *Children with a Star: Jewish Youth in Nazi Europe.* New Haven, CT: Yale University Press, 1991.

Eakin, Paul John. *Fictions in Autobiography: Studies in the Art of Self-Invention.* Princeton, NJ: Princeton University Press, 1985.

Epstein, Helen. *Children of the Holocaust. Conversations with Sons and Daughters of Survivors.* New York: G.P. Putnam and Sons, 1979.

Eskin, Blake. *A Life in Pieces: The Making and Unmaking of Binjamin Wilkomirski.* New York: W. W. Norton, 2002.

Ezrahi, Sidra DeKoven. *By Words Alone: The Holocaust in Literature.* Chicago: University of Chicago Press, 1980.

———. "Representing Auschwitz." *History and Memory* 7, no. 2 (Fall 1996): 121–164.

Federman, Raymond. *Double or Nothing: A Real Fictitious Discourse.* 1st ed. Chicago: Swallow Press, 1971.

———. *Retour au fumier.* Paris: Al Dante, 2005.

———. *La fourrure de ma tante Rachel: Roman improvisé en fourire.* Saulxures,

France: Circé, 1996; *Aunt Rachel's Fur.* Trans. Raymond Federman and Patricia Privat-Standley. Tallahassee, FL: Fiction Collective Two, 2001.

———. "The Necessity and Impossibility of Being a Jewish Writer." 2004. Available at www.federman.com/rfsrcr5.htm

———. "Notes and Counter-Notes." 2004. Available at www.federman.com/rfsrcr6.htm

———. "Surfiction—Four Propositions in Form of an Introduction." In *Surfiction: Fiction Now and Tomorrow*, ed. Raymond Federman. Chicago: Swallow Press, 1975.

———. *Take It or Leave It: An Exaggerated Second-Hand Tale to Be Read Aloud either Standing or Sitting.* New York: Fiction Collective, 1976.

———. *The Twofold Vibration.* Bloomington: Indiana University Press, 1982.

———. "A Version of My Life—the Early Years." *Contemporary Authors.* Vol. 208, 2003: 118–136.

———. *The Voice in the Closet.* Buffalo, NY: Starcherone Books, 2001.

Fejtö, François, with Gyula Zeke. *Hongrois et Juifs: histoire millénaire d'un couple singulier (1000–1997): contribution à l'étude de l'intégration et du rejet.* Paris: Balland, 1997.

Felman, Shoshana, and Dori Laub. *Testimony: Crises of Witnessing in Literature, Psychoanalysis, and History.* New York: Routledge, 1992.

Ferenczi, Thomas, and Christian Boltanski, eds. *Devoir de mémoire, droit à l'oubli.* Bruxelles: Complexe, 2002.

Finkielkraut, Alain. *La mémoire vaine: Du crime contre l'humanité.* Paris: Gallimard, 1989; *Remembering in Vain: The Klaus Barbie Trial and Crimes against Humanity.* Trans. Roxane Lapidus and Sima Godfrey. New York: Columbia University Press, 1992.

Flacke, Monika, ed. *Mythen der Nationen: 1945—Arena der Erinnerungen.* Berlin: Deutsches Historisches Museum, 2004.

Földes, Anna. "Sors Út" ["The Way of Fate" or "Sors's Way"]. *Népszabadság*, February 19, 2000.

Francos, Ania. *Il était des femmes dans la Résistance.* Paris: Stock, 1978.

Frenay, Henri. *L'énigme Jean Moulin.* Paris: R. Laffont, 1977.

———. *La nuit finira.* Paris: R. Laffont, 1973.

French, Philip. "Film Review of *Sunshine*, by István Szabó." *The Observer*, April 30, 2000.

Fresco, Nadine. "La diaspora des cendres." *La Nouvelle Revue de Psychanalyse*, no. 24 (1981): 205–220; "Remembering the Unknown." *International Journal of Psychoanalysis* 65 (1984): 417–427.

Freud, Sigmund. *Beyond the Pleasure Principle.* Ed. James Strachey, New York: Norton, 1961.

———. "Fetishism." In *The Standard Edition of the Complete Psychological Works of Sigmund Freud*, ed. James Strachey. Vol. 21, pp. 152–157. London: Hogarth Press, 1953.

———. "Screen Memories." In *The Standard Edition of the Complete Works of Sigmund Freud*, ed. James Strachey. Vol. 3, pp. 301–322. London: Hogarth Press, 1953.

———. "Splitting of the Ego in the Defensive Process." In *The Standard Edition of the Complete Psychological Works of Sigmund Freud*, ed. James Strachey. Vol. 23, pp. 271–278. London: Hogarth Press, 1953.

Friang, Brigitte. *Regarde-toi qui meurs.* Paris: Ed. du Félin, 1997 (orig. ed. 1970).
———. *Un autre Malraux.* Paris: Plon, 1977.
Friedländer, Saul. *Quand vient le souvenir.* Paris: Seuil, 1978; *When Memory Comes.* Trans. Helen R. Lane. New York: Farrar, Straus, and Giroux, 1979.
Friedman, Carl. *Nightfather.* Trans. Arnold and Erica Pomerans. New York: Persea Books, 1994.
Friedman, John S. " 'Hotel Terminus': Le point de vue d'un producteur." *Images documentaires,* no. 18–19 (1994): 39.
Frodon, Jean-Michel, and Laurent Greilshamer. "Film Review of *Lucie Aubrac.*" *Le Monde,* February 27, 1997: 16 and 28.
Frydman, Marcel. *Le traumatisme de l'enfant caché: Répercussions psychologiques à court et à long termes.* Gerpinnes: Quorum, 1999.
Gacon, Stéphane. *L'amnistie: De la Commune à la guerre d'Algérie.* Paris: Seuil, 2002.
Galster, Ingrid. *Le théâtre de Jean-Paul Sartre devant ses premiers critiques.* Paris: Jean-Michel Place, 1986.
Ganzfried, Bruno. "Bruchstücke Und Scherbenhaufen." *Weltwoche,* September 24, 1998.
———. "Die Geliehene Holocaust-Biographie." *Weltwoche,* August 27, 1998.
———. "Fakten Gegen Erinnerung." *Weltwoche,* September 3, 1998.
Gates, Henry Louis, Jr. " 'Authenticity,' or the Lesson of Little Tree." *New York Times Book Review,* November 14, 1991.
Gedi, Noa, and Yigal Elam. "Collective Memory—What Is It?" *History and Memory* 8, no. 1 (1996): 30–50.
Gener, Randy. "Fiennes, Ehle, Harris Play across Generations in Sunshine Film." www.theatre.com/news/public/newsbrief.asp?newsid=7710. (Accessed June 8 2000.)
George, Emery Edward. "Introduction." In Miklós Radnóti, *The Complete Poetry,* ed. and trans. Emery Edward George. Ann Arbor, MI: Ardis, 1980.
Gerassi, John. *Jean-Paul Sartre: Hated Conscience of His Century.* Chicago: University of Chicago Press, 1989.
Gilbert, Martin. *The Boys: The Untold Story of 732 Young Concentration Camp Survivors.* New York: Henry Holt and Company, 1997.
———. *The Holocaust: A History of the Jews of Europe During the Second World War.* New York: Holt, Rinehart and Winston, 1985.
Godard, Jean-Luc, dir. *Eloge de l'amour.* 2001, France.
———. *Eloge de l'amour: Phrases, sorties d'un film.* Paris: Pol, 2001.
Golsan, Richard J., ed. *The Papon Affair: Memory and Justice on Trial.* New York and London: Routledge, 2000.
———. *Vichy's Afterlife: History and Counterhistory in Postwar France.* Lincoln: University of Nebraska Press, 2000.
Gourevitch, Philip. "The Memory Thief." *New Yorker,* June 14, 1999: 48–68.
———. *We Wish to Inform You that Tomorrow We Will Be Killed with Our Families: Stories from Rwanda.* New York: Farrar, Straus, and Giroux, 1998.
Grassin, Sophie. "Review of *Lucie Aubrac,*" *L'Express,* February 27, 1997.
Guillebaud, Serge. "Calomnie d'outre-tombe." *Le Nouvel Observateur,* October 24–30, 1991: 57
Gyöngyyössi, Imre, and Barna Kabay, dirs. *The Revolt of Job* [*Job Lázadása*]. 1983, Hungary.

György, Péter. "Sorsválasztók" ("Those Who Chose Their Fate" or "Those Who Chose Sors"). *Élet és Irodalom*, February 11, 2000.

Halbwachs, Maurice. *Les cadres sociaux de la mémoire*. Paris: Mouton, 1976.

Hampl, Patricia. "Memory's Movies." In *Beyond Document*, ed. Charles Warren, pp. 51–77.

Hanks, Robert. "Review of Wilkomirski, *Fragments*." *Independent*, December 8, 1996: 31.

Haraszti, Miklós. "Hívasson esztétát! ["Call an Art Critic!"]." *Élet és Irodalom*, February 25, 2000.

Hardy, René. *Derniers mots: Mémoires*. Paris: Fayard, 1984.

Hartman, Geoffrey H. *The Longest Shadow: In the Aftermath of the Holocaust*. Bloomington: Indiana University Press, 1996.

Herf, Jeffrey. *Divided Memory: The Nazi Past in the Two Germanys*. Cambridge, MA: Harvard University Press, 1997.

Heschel, Susannah. "Review of Wilkomirski, *Fragments*." *Tikkun*, March 13, 1997: 73.

Hewitt, Leah D. "Identity Wars in 'L'affaire (Lucie) Aubrac': History, Fiction, Film." *Contemporary French Civilization* 22.2 (1998): 264–284.

Hirsch, Joshua. "István Szabó: Problems in the Narration of Holocaust Memory." *Journal of Film and Video* 51:1 (Spring 1999): 3–21.

Hirsch, Marianne. *Family Frames: Photography, Narrative, and Postmemory*. Cambridge, MA: Harvard University Press, 1997.

———. "Marked by Memory: Feminist Reflections on Trauma and Transmission." In *Extremities: Trauma, Testimony, Community*, eds. Jason Tougaw and Nancy K. Miller, pp. 71–91. Urbana: University of Illinois Press, 2002.

———. "Surviving Images: Holocaust Photographs and the Work of Postmemory." *Yale Journal of Criticism* 14, no. 1 (2001): 5–38.

Hirsch, Marianne, and Irene Kacandes, eds. *Teaching the Representation of the Holocaust*. New York: Modern Languages Association, 2004.

Hochschild, Adam. *King Leopold's Ghost: A Story of Greed, Terror, and Heroism in Colonial Africa*. New York: Houghton Mifflin Company, 1998.

Hoyos, Ladislas de. *Barbie*. Paris: R. Laffont, 1984.

Huizinga, Johan. *Homo Ludens: A Study of the Play-Element in Culture*. Trans. R. F. C. Hull. London: Routledge and K. Paul, 1949.

Hutcheon, Linda. *A Poetics of Postmodernism: History, Theory, Fiction*. New York: Routledge, 1988.

Huyssen, Andreas. *Present Pasts: Urban Palimpsests and the Politics of Memory*. Stanford, CA: Stanford University Press, 2003.

Igounet, Valérie. *Histoire du négationnisme en France*. Paris: Seuil, 2000.

Irigaray, Luce. *Speculum de l'autre femme*. Paris: Editions de Minuit, 1974.

Jackson, Julian. *France: The Dark Years, 1940–1944*. Oxford: Oxford University Press, 2001.

Jankélévitch, Vladimir, *L'imprescriptible: Pardonner? Dans l'honneur et la dignité*. Paris: Seuil, "Points Essais," 1986.

Jean Moulin 1899–1943. Exhibition booklet. Paris: Editions des musées de la ville de Paris, 1999.

Jeancolas, Jean-Pierre. "Entretien avec Marcel Ophuls sur *Hotel Terminus*." *Positif* 331, no. 29 (1988): 23–30.

Joseph, Gilbert. *Une si douce Occupation: Simone de Beauvoir, Jean-Paul Sartre, 1940–1944.* Paris: A. Michel, 1991.

Judt, Tony. *Past Imperfect: French Intellectuals, 1944–1956.* Berkeley: University of California Press, 1992.

———. "The Past Is Another Country: Myth and Memory in Postwar Europe." In *The Politics of Retribution in Europe*, eds. István Deák, Jan T. Gross, and Tony Judt, pp. 293–323. Princeton, NJ: Princeton University Press, 2000.

Kaplan, Alice Yaeger. *The Collaborator: The Trial and Execution of Robert Brasillach.* Chicago: University of Chicago Press, 2000.

———. *Reproductions of Banality: Fascism, Literature, and French Intellectual Life.* Minneapolis: University of Minnesota Press, 1986.

Karády, Viktor. "Some Social Aspects of Jewish Assimilation in Socialist Hungary, 1945–1956." In *The Tragedy of Hungarian Jewry*, ed. Randolph Braham, pp. 73–132. Boulder, CO: Social Science Monographs, 1986:

Kattan, Emmanuel. *Penser le devoir de mémoire.* Paris: Presses Universitaires de France, 2002.

Kaufman, Jonathan. *A Hole in the Heart of the World: Being Jewish in Eastern Europe after World War II.* New York: Viking, 1997.

Keilson, Hans. *Sequential Traumatization in Children: A Clinical and Statistical Follow-up Study on the Fate of the Jewish War Orphans in the Netherlands.* Trans. H. Coleman Y. Bearne, and D. Winter. Jerusalem: Magnes Press, 1992.

Kertész, Imre. *Sorstalanság.* Budapest: Szépirodalmi Könyvkiadó, 1975. *Fatelessness.* Trans. Tim Wilkinson. New York: Random House, 2004.

Kestenberg, Judith S., and Ira Brenner. *The Last Witness: The Child Survivor of the Holocaust.* Washington, DC: American Psychiatric Press, 1996.

Kestenberg, Judith S., and Charlotte Kahn. *Children Surviving Persecution: An International Study of Trauma and Healing.* Westport, CT: Praeger, 1998.

Klarsfeld, Serge. *Le mémorial de la déportation des Juifs de France.* Paris: Klarsfeld, 1978.

———. *Les enfants d'Izieu: Une tragédie juive.* Paris: Beate Klarsfeld Foundation, 1984.

———. "A Propos de Raymond Aubrac." *Le Monde*, July 25, 1997.

Klein, Kerwin Lee. "On the Emergence of *Memory* in Historical Discourse." *Representations* 69 (2000): 127–150.

Kofman, Sarah. "Ça Cloche." In *Les fins de l'homme*, eds. P. Lacoue-Labarthe and J.-L. Nancy, pp. 89–116. Paris: Galilée, 1981.

———. *Rue Ordener, Rue Labat.* Paris: Galilée, 1994; *Rue Ordener, Rue Labat.* Trans. Ann Smock. Lincoln: University of Nebraska Press, 1996.

Kosinski, Jerzy. *The Painted Bird.* New York: Modern Library, 1965.

Kovács, András. "Jewish Groups and Identity Strategies in Post-Communist Hungary." In *New Jewish Identities: Contemporary Europe and Beyond*, eds. Zvi Gitelman, Berry Kosmin, András Kovács, pp. 211–242. Budapest and New York: Central European University Press, 2002.

———. "Jews and Politics in Hungary." In *Values, Interests and Identity: Jews and Politics in a Changing World*, ed. Peter Y. Medding, pp. 50–63. New York: Oxford University Press, 1995.

Kozol, Jonathan. "Children of the Camps" (review of Wilkomirski, *Fragments*). *Nation*, October 28, 1996: 24–28.

Kristeva, Julia. "Forgiveness: An Interview (with Alison Rice)." *PMLA* 17.2 (2002): 281–295.

LaCapra, Dominick. *History and Memory after Auschwitz*. Ithaca, NY: Cornell University Press, 1998.

———. "Trauma, Absence, Loss." *Critical Inquiry* 25, no. 4 (1999): 696–727.

"La Marche du siècle." Television program. France 3, January 22, 1997. Inathèque de France: DL: DLT 199701 22FR3 008.001/002.

Langer, Lawrence L. "Fictional Facts and Factual Fictions: History in Holocaust Literature." In *Reflections of the Holocaust in Art and Literature*, ed. Randolph L. Braham, pp. 117–129. New York: Columbia University Press, 1990.

———.*The Holocaust and the Literary Imagination*. New Haven, CT: Yale University Press, 1975.

———. *Holocaust Testimonies: The Ruins of Memory*. New Haven, CT: Yale University Press, 1991.

Lanzmann, Claude. "Hier Ist Kein Warum." In *Au sujet de Shoah: Le film de Claude Lanzmann*, ed. Bernard Cuau, p. 279. Paris: Belin, 1990.

———. "The Obscenity of Understanding: An Evening with Claude Lanzmann." In *Trauma: Explorations in Memory*, ed. Cathy Caruth, pp. 200–220.

———. "Représenter l'irreprésentable," *Le Nouvel Observateur*, special issue: "La mémoire de la Shoah." December 2003/January 2004: 6–9.

———. dir. *Shoah*, 1985, France.

Lapierre, Nicole. *Changer de nom*. Paris: Stock, 1995.

———. "Les changements de noms." In *Les Juifs de France: de la Révolution à nos jours*, ed. Becker and Wieviorka, pp. 265–266.

Lappin, Elena. "The Man with Two Heads." *Granta* 66 (1999): 9–65.

Laub, Dori. "Bearing Witness, or the Vicissitudes of Listening." In Felman and Laub, *Testimony*, pp. 57–74.

Lefort, Gérard, and Oliver Séguret. "Les Mystères Aubrac." *Libération*, February 26, 1997: 28.

Lejeune, Philippe. "Introduction." In Perec, *Je suis né*, pp. 7–8.

———. *La mémoire et l'oblique: Georges Perec autobiographe*. Paris: P.O.L, 1991.

———. *Le pacte autobiographique*. Paris: Seuil, 1975; *On Autobiography*. Trans. Katherine Leary. Minneapolis: University of Minnesota Press, 1989.

Le Monde. "L'Assemblée déclare imprescriptibles les crimes contre l'humanité." December 18, 1964, p. 8.

———. "Le projet d'amnistie est approuvé par 269 députés." December 19, 1964, p. 2.

Le Monde. "Publication judiciaire." February 23, 1990, 12.

Le Monde. "Suite aux accusations de Klaus Barbie: M. Raymond Aubrac demande la création d'une commission d'historiens sur 'L'affaire de Caluire.' " October 10, 1991: 12.

Lesèvre, Lise. *Face à Barbie: Souvenirs-cauchemars de Montluc à Ravensbrück*. Paris: Nouvelles Editions du Pavillon, 1987.

Levy, Daniel, and Sznaider, Natan. "Memory Unbound: The Holocaust and the Formation of Cosmopolitan Memory." *European Journal of Social Theory* 5.1 (2002): 87–106.

Libération, special supplement: "Les Aubrac et les historiens." July 9, 1997.

Leys, Ruth. *Trauma: A Genealogy*. Chicago: University of Chicago Press, 2000.

Liebling, A. J., ed. *The Republic of Silence*. New York: Harcourt, Brace and Co., 1947.

Liebling, A. J., and Eugene Jay Sheffer. *La République du Silence: The Story of the French Resistance*. New York: Harcourt, Brace and Co., 1946.

Linklater, Magnus, Isabel Hilton, and Neal Ascherson. *The Nazi Legacy: Klaus Barbie and the International Fascist Connection*. London: Hodder and Stoughton, 1984.

Loftus, Elizabeth F. *Eyewitness Testimony*. Cambridge, MA: Harvard University Press, 1996.

Loraux, Nicole. *La cité divisée: L'oubli dans la mémoire d'Athènes*. Paris: Payot, 1997.

Maechler, Stefan. *The Wilkomirski Affair: A Study in Biographical Truth*. Trans. John E. Woods. New York: Schocken Books, 2001.

Magné, Bernard. "Les sutures dans *W ou le souvenir d'enfance*." *Textuel: Cahiers Georges Perec* 21 (1988): 39–55.

Maier, Charles S. "A Surfeit of Memory? Reflections on History, Melancholy, and Denial." *History and Memory* 5, no. 2 (Winter 1993): 136–152.

Malraux, André. *Antimémoires*. (1967). In Malraux, *Le miroir des limbes*. Paris: Gallimard, Pléiade ed., 1976, pp. 3–510.

———. *La politique, la culture: Discours, articles, entretiens (1925–1975)*, ed. Janine Mossuz-Lavau. Paris: Gallimard, 1996.

Mannheim, Karl. "The Problem of Generations." In Mannheim, *Essays on the Sociology of Knowledge*, ed. Paul Kecskemeti, pp. 276–322. New York: Oxford University Press, 1952.

Mannoni, Octave. *Clefs pout l'imaginaire ou l'Autre scène*. Paris: Seuil, 1969.

Margalit, Avishai. *The Ethics of Memory*. Cambridge, MA: Harvard University Press, 2003.

Marks, Jane. *The Hidden Children: The Secret Survivors of the Holocaust*. New York: Ballantine Books, 1993.

Maspero, François. *Les abeilles & la guêpe*. Paris: Seuil, 2002.

McCafferey, L., T. Hartl, and D. Rice, eds. *Federman from A to X-X-X-X*. San Diego, CA: San Diego State University Press, 1998.

McCafferey, Larry. "An Interview with Raymond Federman." *Contemporary Literature* 24, no. 3 (1983): 285–306.

McCourt, Frank. *Angela's Ashes: A Memoir*. New York: Scribner, 1996.

McNally, Richard J. *Remembering Trauma*. Cambridge, MA: Harvard University Press, 2004.

Minow, Martha. *Between Vengeance and Forgiveness: Facing History after Genocide and Mass Violence*. Boston: Beacon Press, 1998.

Modiano, Patrick. *Dora Bruder*. Paris: Gallimard, 1997.

Motte, Warren. "Georges Perec and the Broken Book." In *Auschwitz and After: Race, Culture, and "the Jewish Question" in France*, ed. Lawrence D. Kritzman, pp. 235–249. New York: Routledge, 1995.

Muratori-Philippe, Anne. "Affaire Aubrac: Les ombres d'une légende." *Le Figaro*, February 28, 1997: 28B.

New York Times. "Publisher Drops Holocaust Book." November 3, 1999: B2.

Nichols, Bill. *Representing Reality: Issues and Concepts in Documentary*. Bloomington: Indiana University Press, 1991.

Nietzsche, Friedrich Wilhelm. *The Use and Abuse of History.* 2nd rev. ed. Indian-apolis, IN: Bobbs-Merrill Educational Pub., 1957.

Noguères, Henri. *La vérité aura le dernier mot.* Paris: Seuil, 1985.

Nora, Pierre. *Les lieux de mémoire.* Quarto ed., Vols. 1, 2, 3. Paris: Gallimard, 1997.

Novick, Peter. *The Holocaust in American Life.* Boston: Houghton Mifflin, 1999.

———. *The Resistance versus Vichy.* New York: Columbia University Press, 1968.

Ophuls, Marcel. "Faut-il fusiller Speer au lieu de le filmer?" ["Should we shoot Speer instead of filming him?"]. *Positif* 200 (December 1977–January 1978): 111–115.

———. *Hotel Terminus: The Life and Times of Klaus Barbie [Videorecording]/MGM Home Entertainment.* 2 Videocassettes (VHS) (238 min.) Santa Monica, CA: MGM Home Entertainment, 1988.

———. *Le chagrin et la pitié: chronique d'une ville française sous l'Occupation/Milestone Film and Video.* 2 Videocassettes (VHS) (260 min.) Harrington Park, NJ: Milestone Film and Video, sold exclusively by New Yorker Video, 2000.

———. "The Sorrow and the Laughter." *Premier.* November 1988, pp. 112 and 115.

———. *The Sorrow and the Pity; a film* (Screenplay). New York: Outerbridge & Lazard, 1972.

Ozouf, Mona. "L'École normale des morts." In *Les lieux de mémoire,* ed. P. Nora. Quarto ed., Vol. 1, pp. 155–178. Paris: Gallimard, 1997.

Paretsky, Sara. *Total Recall.* New York: Random House, 2001.

Paris, Erna. *Unhealed Wounds: France and the Klaus Barbie Affair.* Toronto, ON: Methuen, 1985.

Patai, Raphael. *The Jews of Hungary: History, Culture, Psychology.* Detroit, MI: Wayne State University Press, 1996.

Paul, David. "Szabó." In *Five Filmmakers,* ed. David Goulding. Bloomington: Indiana University Press, 1994.

Pautrot, Jean-Louis. "Music and Memory: Listening to *Lacombe Lucien, Night and Fog,* and *Night Rounds.*" *Dalhousie French Studies* 55 (Summer 2001): 168–182.

Paxton, Robert O. *Vichy France: Old Guard and New Order, 1940–1944.* New York: Knopf, 1972.

Péan, Pierre. *Une jeunesse française: François Mitterrand, 1934–1947.* Paris: Fayard, 1994.

Perec, Georges. *Je suis né.* Paris: Editions du Seuil, 1990.

———. *La disparition.* Paris: les Lettres nouvelles, 1969; *A Void.* Trans. Gilbert Adair. London: Harvill, 1994.

———. *La vie mode d'emploi.* Paris: Hachette littérature, 1978; *Life, a user's manual.* Trans. David Bellos. Boston: D. R. Godine, 1987.

———. *Les revenentes.* Paris: Julliard, 1994.

———. *Penser, classer.* Paris: Hachette, 1986.

———. *W ou le souvenir d'enfance.* Paris: Denoël, 1975; *W or the Memory of Child-hood.* Trans. David Bellos. Boston: D. R. Godine, 1988.

Perrault, Gilles. "Barbie, son Tartuffe, et les Aubrac." *Le Monde,* May 23, 1997: 16.

Porter, Melinda Camber. *Through Parisian Eyes: Reflections on Contemporary French Arts and Culture.* New York: Oxford University Press, 1986.

Porton, Richard, and Lee Ellickson. "The Troubles He's Seen: An Interview with Marcel Ophuls." *Cineaste* 21, no. 3 (1995): 11.

Postone, Moishe. "After the Holocaust: History and Identity in West Germany." In *Coping with the Past: Germany and Austria after 1945*, eds. Lutz R. Reuter, Kathy Harms, and Volker Durr, pp. 233–251. Madison: University of Wisconsin Press, 1990.

Prost, Antoine. "Les historiens et les Aubrac: une question de trop. *Le Monde*, July 12, 1997:13

Proust, Marcel. *A la recherche du temps perdu*. 4 vols. Paris: Gallimard, Pléiade, 1989.

Quindlen, Anna. "How Dark? How Stormy? I Can't Recall." *New York Times Book Review*, May 11, 1997: 35.

Quinio, Paul. " 'Lucie Aubrac' hébergée dans les écoles." *Libération*, February 26, 1997: 29.

Rabinbach, Anson. "Beyond Bitburg: The Place of the 'Jewish Question' in Germany History after 1945." In *Coping with the Past: Germany and Austria after 1945*, ed. Lutz R. Reuter, Kathy Harms, and Volker Durr, pp. 187–218. Madison: University of Wisconsin Press, 1990.

Raczymow, Henri. *Contes d'exil et d'oubli*. Paris: Gallimard, 1979.

———. "Memory Shot through with Holes." Trans. Alan Astro. *Yale French Studies* 85 (1986): 98–105.

———. *Un cri sans voix*. Paris: Gallimard, 1985; *Writing the Book of Esther*. Trans. Dori Katz. New York: Holmes and Meier, 1994.

Renan, Ernest. *Qu'est-ce qu'une nation?* Paris: Editions Mille et une nuits, 1997.

Rév, István. *Retroactive Justice: Pre-History of Post-Communism*. Standord, CA: Stanford University Press, 2005.

Ricardou, Jean. *Pour une théorie du nouveau roman*. Paris: Seuil, 1971.

Ricks, Christopher. "Literature and the Matter of Fact." University Lecture, Boston University. Boston: The Trustees of Boston University, 1990.

Ricoeur, Paul. *La mémoire, l'histoire, l'oubli*. Paris: Seuil, 2000.

———. *Temps et récit*. 3 vols. Paris: Seuil, 1983.

Rioux, Jean-Pierre. "Review of *Où la mémoire s'attarde*." *Le Monde*, September 6, 1996, sec. Le Monde des Livres: XI.

Robbe-Grillet, Alain. *Angélique: Ou, l'enchantement*. Paris: Editions de Minuit, 1987.

———. *Le miroir qui revient*. Paris: Editions de Minuit, 1984.

———. *Les derniers jours de Corinthe*. Paris: Editions de Minuit, 1994.

Robin, Régine. "La honte nationale comme malédiction: autour de l'affaire 'Walser-Bubis.' " *Revue Internationale et Stratégique* 33 (Spring 1999): 45–69.

———. *La mémoire saturée*. Paris: Stock, 2003.

———. *Le deuil de l'origine: Une langue en trop, la langue en moins*. Saint-Denis, France: Presses Universitaires de Vincennes, 1992.

———. *L'immense fatigue des pierres*. Montréal, QC: XYZ éditeurs, 1996.

Rousso, Henry. *La hantise du passé. Entretien avec Philippe Petit*. Paris: Editions Textuel, 1998.

———. *Le syndrome de Vichy, de 1944 à nos jours*. 2nd ed. Paris: Seuil, 1990.

———. *Vichy: L'événement, la mémoire, l'histoire*. Paris: Gallimard, Folio, 2001.

Sanders, Ivan. "The Holocaust in Contemporary Hungarian Literature."

In *The Holocaust in Hungary Forty Years Later*, ed. R. Braham and B. Vago, Chapter 14. New York: Social Science Monographs, 1985.

Sapiro, Gisèle. *La guerre des écrivains: 1940–1953*. Paris: Fayard, 1999.

———. "L'épuration du monde des lettres." In *Une poignée de misérables*, ed. Marc Olivier Baruch, pp. 243–285.

Sartre, Jean Paul. "La colère d'une ville." *Combat*, August 30, 1944; reprint *Le Monde*, August 23, 1984.

———. "La délivrance est à nos portes." *Combat*, September 2, 1944; reprint *Le Monde*, August 26–27, 1984.

———. "La république du silence." *Les Lettres françaises*, September 9, 1944; reprint *Situations III*, pp. 11–14; "Paris Alive: The Republic of Silence." Trans. Lincoln Kirstein. *Atlantic Monthly*, December 1944: 39–40.

———. "Naissance d'une insurrection." *Combat*, August 29, 1944; reprint *Le Monde*, August 22, 1984.

———. "New Writing in France." *Vogue*, July 1945: 84–85.

———. "Paris sous l'occupation." *La France Libre*, December 1944: 9–18; reprint *Situations III*, pp. 15–42.

———. *Qu'est-ce que la littérature?* Paris: Gallimard, 1948; *"What Is Literature?" and Other Essays*. Trans. Bernard Frechtman et al. Cambridge, MA: Harvard University Press, 1988.

———. "Qu'est-ce qu'un collaborateur? I: Aspect social de la collaboration." *La République Française*, August 1945: 5–6; "Qu'est-ce qu'un collaborateur? II: Aspect psychologique du collaborationisme." *La république française*, September 1945: 14–17; reprint *Situations III*, pp. 43–61.

———. *Réflexions sur la question juive*. Paris: Nagel, 1946; *Anti-Semite and Jew*. Trans. George J. Becker. New York: Schocker Books, 1948.

———. *Situations III*. Paris: Gallimard, 1949.

———. *Sartre par lui-même*. [Videorecording]/ Dir. Alexandre Astruc and Michel Contat. New York: Interama Video Classics, 1989.

———. (Unsigned). "Drieu La Rochelle ou la haine de soi." *Les Lettres Françaises*, April 1943.

———. "Victoire du Gaullisme." *Le Figaro*, January 2, 1945: 2.

Schacter, Daniel L. *The Seven Sins of Memory: How the Mind Forgets and Remembers*. Boston: Houghton Mifflin, 2001.

Schöpflin, George. "Review of the Movie *Sunshine*, by István Szabó." Web site of the Center for the Study of Democracy, University College London. Available at www.ucl.ac.uk/cds/gsbr1.htm

Schor, Naomi. "Female Fetishism: The Case of George Sand." In *The Female Body in Western Culture*, ed. Susan R. Suleiman, pp. 363–372. Cambridge, MA: Harvard University Press, 1986.

Schumann, Maurice. "L'antidestin qui franchit le seuil du Panthéon." Funeral oration for André Malraux. *La Croix*, November 26, 1996.

Scott, A. O. "Film Review of *Sunshine*, by István Szabó." *The New York Times*, June 9, 2000.

Sebald, W. G. *Austerlitz*. Trans. Anthea Bell. New York: Random House, 2001.

———. *The Emigrants*. Trans. Michael Hulse. New York: New Directions, 1996.

Seidman, Naomi. "Elie Wiesel and the Scandal of Jewish Rage." *Jewish Social Studies*, 3, no. 1 (Fall 1996): 1–19.

Semprun, Jorge. *Adieu, vive clarté*. Paris: Gallimard, 1998.

———. *L'écriture ou la vie*. Paris: Gallimard, 1994; *Literature or Life*. Trans. Linda Coverdale. New York: Viking, 1997.

———. *Le grand voyage*. Paris: Gallimard, 1963; *The Long Voyage*. Trans. Richard Seaver. New York: Grove Press, 1964.

———. *Le mort qu'il faut*. Paris: Gallimard, 2001.

———. *Quel beau dimanche!* Paris: B. Grasset, 1980; *What a Beautiful Sunday!* Trans. Alan Sheridan. New York: Harcourt Brace Jovanovich, 1982.

———. "Rencontre avec Jorge Semprun: Propos recueillis par Lise Breuil, Catherine Sueur, Gille Mentre." 1995. Available at www.polytechnique.fr/eleves/binets/xpassion/numeros/xpnumero20/xpnum20pdfsi/semprun20.pdf

Semprun, Jorge, and Elie Wiesel. *Se taire est impossible*. Paris: Editions Mille et une nuits, 1995.

Simonin, Anne. *Les Editions de Minuit, 1942–1955: Le devoir d'insoumission*. Paris: IMEC Editions, 1994.

Sliwowska, Wiktoria, ed. *The Last Eyewitnesses: Children of the Holocaust Speak*. Evanston, IL: Northwestern University Press, 1998.

Sloan, James Park. *Jerzy Kosinski: A Biography*. New York: Penguin/Plume, 1997.

Sontag, Susan. *Regarding the Pain of Others*. New York: Farrar, Straus, and Giroux, 2003.

Soros, George. "Foreword." In Tivadar Soros, *Maskerado: Dancing around Death in Nazi-Occupied Hungary*, ed. and trans. Humphrey Tonkin, pp. ix–xi. Edinburgh: Canongate, 2000.

Spiegelman, Art. *Maus: A Survivor's Tale*. I: *My Father Bleeds History*. New York: Pantheon, 1986.

———. *Maus: A Survivor's Tale*. II: *And Here My Troubles Began*. New York: Pantheon, 1991.

Spitzer, Alan. "The Historical Problem of Generations." *The American Historical Review* 78 (1973): 1353–1385.

Stein, Gertrude. *Wars I Have Seen*. New York: Random House, 1945.

Sternberg, Meir. *The Poetics of Biblical Narrative: Ideological Literature and the Drama of Reading*. Bloomington: Indiana University Press, 1985.

Sudefeld, Peter, ed. *Light from the Ashes: Social Science Careers of Young Holocaust Refugees and Survivors*. Ann Arbor: University of Michigan Press, 2001.

Suleiman, Susan Rubin. "The 1.5 Generation: Thinking About Child Survivors and the Holocaust." *American Imago* 59, no. 3 (2002): 277–95.

———. "The 1.5 Generation. Georges Perec's *W or the Memory of Childhood*." In Hirsch and Kacandes, eds., *Teaching the Representation of the Holocaust*, pp. 372–385.

———. *Budapest Diary: In Search of the Motherbook*. Lincoln: University of Nebraska Press, 1996.

———. "Charlatan or Madman? What a Study of a Literary Hoax Can't Decide." *The Forward*, June 8, 2001: 10, 14.

———. "Discours de Charles de Gaulle du 25 Août 1944." CD-Rom. *La Résistance en Ile-de-France*. Paris: Association pour des Etudes sur la Résistance Intérieure, 2004.

————. "The Jew In Sartre's *Réflexions sur la question juive:* An Exercise in Historical Reading." In *The Jew in the Text: Modernity and the Construction of Identity,* ed. Linda Nochlin and Tamar Garb, pp. 201–218. London: Thames and Hudson, 1995.

————. "Malraux's Women: A Revision." In *Witnessing André Malraux: Visions and Revisions,* ed. Brian Thompson and Carl Viggiani, pp. 140–158. Middletown, CT: Wesleyan University Press, 1984.

————. "Monuments in a Foreign Tongue: On Reading Holocaust Memoirs by Emigrants." In *Exile and Creativity: Signposts, Travelers, Outsiders, Backward Glances,* ed. Susan Rubin Suleiman, pp. 397–417. Durham, NC: Duke University Press, 1998.

————. "Reflections on Memory at the Millennium." Presidential Address of the American Comparative Literary Association. *Comparative Literature* 51:3 (1999): v–xviii.

————. "Rereading Rereading: Further Reflections on Sartre's *Réflexions.*" *October* 87 (Winter 1999): 129–138.

————. *Risking Who One Is: Encounters with Contemporary Art and Literature.* Cambridge, MA: Harvard University Press, 1994.

Suleiman, Susan Rubin, and Éva Forgács, eds. *Contemporary Jewish Writing in Hungary: An Anthology.* Lincoln and London: University of Nebraska Press, 2003.

Szabó, István. "Itt vigyázni kell" ["Here We Must Be Careful"]: Interview with Dora Mülner. *Népszabadság,* February 8, 2000.

————, dir. *Apa (Father).* 1966, Hungary.

————, dir. *Being Julia.* 2004, Canada/USA/Hungary/UK.

————, dir. *Colonel Redl.* 1984, Hungary/Austria/West Germany.

————, dir. *Hanussen.* 1988, Hungary/West Germany/Austria.

————, dir. *Mephisto.* 1981, West Germany/Hungary/Austria.

————, dir. *Sunshine.* 1999, Germany/Austria/Canada/Hungary.

————, dir. *Tüzoltó Utca 25 (25 Fireman's Street).* 1973, Hungary.

Szabó, Miklós. "A fogadott prókátor üzeni: A zsidók ne merjenek félni" ["A Message from the Official Spokesman: The Jews had better not be afraid"]. *Magyar Hírlap,* September 1, 1999.

Thakur, Manavendra. "*Hotel Terminus* Is Sidetracked by Director Ophuls's Pent-up Feelings." *The Tech (MIT student paper),* February 7, 1989: 16, 21. Web site accessed February 2001 archive@the-tech.mit.edu

Théolleyre, Jean-Marc. "La provocation de l'avocat de Klaus Barbie." *Le Monde,* November 15, 1983: 48.

Todd, Olivier. *André Malraux: une vie.* Paris: Gallimard, 2001.

Todorov, Tzvetan. *Les abus de la mémoire.* Paris: Arléa, 1995.

————. *Les morales de l'histoire.* Paris: B. Grasset, 1991.

Ungvári, Tamás. "Választott Sors?" ["Chosen Fate?" or "Did Sors Choose?" or "Chosen Sors?"] *Élet és Irodalom,* March 10, 2000.

Van Alphen, Ernst. *Caught by History: Holocaust Effects in Contemporary Art, Literature, and Theory.* Stanford, CA: Stanford University Press, 1997.

Van der Kolk, Bessel, and Otto Van den Hart. "The Intrusive Past: The Flexibility of Memory and the Engraving of Trauma." In *Trauma: Explorations in Memory,* ed. Cathy Caruth, pp. 158–182. Baltimore, MD: Johns Hopkins University Press, 1995.

Vegh, Claudine. *Je ne lui ai pas dit au revoir.* Paris: Gallimard, 1979; *I Didn't Say Goodbye.* Trans. Ros Schwartz. New York: E. P. Dutton, 1984.

Veillon, Dominique, and Eric Alary. "Caluire: Un objet d'histoire entre mythe et polémique." In *Jean Moulin face à l'histoire,* ed. Jean-Pierre Azéma, pp. 184–194.

Veillon, Dominique, and Jean-Pierre Azéma. "Le point sur Caluire." *Les Cahiers de l'IHTP,* 27 (1994): 127–144.

Vernant, J-P. "La mémoire et les historiens." In *Mémoire et histoire: La résistance,* eds. Jean-Marie Guillon and Pierre Laborie, pp. 341–345. Toulouse: Editions Privat, 1995.

Vidal-Naquet, Pierre. *Les assassins de la mémoire: Un Eichmann de papier et autres essais sur le révisionnisme.* Paris: Éditions de la Découverte, 1987; *Assassins of Memory: Essays on the Denial of the Holocaust.* Trans. Jeffrey Mehlman. New York: Columbia University Press, 1992.

———. *Le trait empoisonné: Réflexions sur l'affaire Jean Moulin.* Paris: La Découverte, 1993.

———. "Remembrances of a 1946 Reader." *October* 87 (Winter 1999): 7–23.

Viollet, Catherine. "Raymond Federman: la voix plurielle." In *Autofictions & Cie,* ed. Doubrovsky, Lecarme, and Lejeune, pp. 193–206.

Warren, Charles, ed. *Beyond Document: Essays on Non-Fiction Film.* Middletown, CT: Wesleyan University Press, 1996.

Weigel, Sigrid. "Secularization and Sacralization, Normalization and Rupture: Kristeva and Arendt on Forgiveness." *PMLA* 17.2 (2002): 321–323.

Weill, Nicolas. "L'historien Gérard Chauvy condamné pour diffamation envers les Aubrac." *Le Monde,* April 4, 1998: 9.

Weinrich, Harald. *Lethe: The Art and Critique of Forgetting.* Trans. Steven Rendall. Ithaca, NY: Cornell University Press, 2004.

Weisberg, Richard H. *Vichy Law and the Holocaust in France.* New York: New York University Press, 1996.

White, Hayden V. *Metahistory: The Historical Imagination in Nineteenth-Century Europe.* Baltimore, MD: Johns Hopkins University Press, 1973.

———. *Tropics of Discourse: Essays in Cultural Criticism.* Baltimore, MD: Johns Hopkins University Press, 1978.

Wiedmer, Caroline Alice. *The Claims of Memory: Representations of the Holocaust in Contemporary Germany and France.* Ithaca, NY: Cornell University Press, 1999.

Wiesel, Elie. *La nuit.* Paris: Editions de Minuit, 1958; *Night.* Trans. Stella Rodway. New York: Hill and Wang, 1960; *Night.* Trans. Stella Rodway. New York: Bantam, 1982.

———. *Tous les fleuves vont à la mer: Mémoires.* Paris: Editions du Seuil, 1994; *All Rivers Run to the Sea: Memoirs.* New York: Knopf, 1995.

Wieviorka, Annette. *L'ère du témoin.* Paris: Plon, 1998.

———. "Les secrets de l'affaire Jean Moulin." *Le Monde,* November 18, 1998: 30.

Wilkomirski, Benjamin. *Fragments: Memories of a Wartime Childhood.* Trans. Carol Brown Janeway. New York: Schocken Books, 1996. Reprinted in Maechler, *The Wilkomirski Affair,* pp. 375–496.

———. "Niemand Muss Mir Glauben Schenken." *Tages Anzeiger,* September 1, 1998.

Winter, Jay M., and Emmanuel Sivan, eds. *War and Remembrance in the Twentieth Century.* Cambridge: Cambridge University Press, 1999.

Winter, Jay. "The Generation of Memory: Reflections on the 'Memory Boom' in Contemporary Historical Studies." *Bulletin of the German Historical Institute* 27 (2000): 69–92.

Wolton, Thierry. *Le grand recrutement.* Paris: B. Grasset, 1993.

Young, James E. *At Memory's Edge: After-Images of the Holocaust in Contemporary Art and Architecture.* New Haven, CT: Yale University Press, 2000.

———. *Writing and Rewriting the Holocaust: Narrative and the Consequences of Interpretation.* Bloomington: Indiana University Press, 1988.

Zelizer, Barbie. *Remembering to Forget: Holocaust Memory through the Camera's Eye.* Chicago: University of Chicago Press, 1998.

Zhou, Min, and Carl L. Bankston III. *Growing Up American: How Vietnamese Children Adapt to Life in the United States.* New York: Russell Sage Foundation, 1998.

Index

279